Excel

ADVANCED SKILLS

MATHS

YEAR 3

AGES 8–9

ADVANCED MATHEMATICS

Get the Results You Want!

PASCAL PRESS

Allyn Jones

Written for the NSW Curriculum and the Australian Curriculum Version 9.0

ISBN 978 1 74125 656 7

Pascal Press
PO Box 250
Glebe NSW 2037
(02) 9198 1748
www.pascalpress.com.au

Publisher: Vivienne Joannou
Project editor: Rosemary Peers
Edited and proofread by Rosemary Peers
Answers checked by Melinda Amaral
Cover and page design by Sonia Woo
Typeset by Julianne Billington
Printed by Vivar Printing/Green Giant Press

The publisher thanks the Royal Australian Mint for granting permission to use Australian currency coin designs in this book.

Contents

Introduction

The aim of the ***Excel*** Advanced Skills: Advanced Mathematics series is to build on and extend students' skills in Mathematics. Each book in the series supports the requirements of the Australian Curriculum (Mathematics) at each year level.

The series consists of six books, one for each year level, from Year 1 to Year 6. The series is supported by other books in the ***Excel*** Mathematics range.

Structure of the book

Section 1

This section consists of twelve double-page units of teaching and learning activities. Each page provides questions on specific topics from the Number, Algebra, Measurement, Space, Statistics or Probability areas of the syllabus.

- **Unit A** provides skills practice.
- **Unit B** provides problem-solving practice of the skills covered in Unit A.

Section 2

This section consists of 30 carefully graded double-page units of teaching and learning activities. Each page provides questions from all areas of the syllabus: Number, Algebra, Measurement, Space, Statistics and Probability.

- **Unit A** provides extensive revision practice in skills-type questions.
- **Unit B** provides extensive practice in problem-solving questions.

Worked Solutions & Answers

Worked solutions are provided for every question to support students' learning. Answers are also provided in bold for quick reference.

How to use this book with the *Excel* Advanced Skills English series

For a complete weekly English and Mathematics program use this book in conjunction with the ***Excel* Advanced Skills English Year 3** book. This way a student will have work set for four days a week—two days for English and two days for Mathematics.

How to assess students' progress

The results of the work undertaken in each unit can be recorded on the marking grids. The marking grids on pages 7, 8 and 9 are easy-to-use diagnostic tools that indicate where students' strengths and weaknesses lie in relation to specific areas of Mathematics. (Please see the example on page 5.) These results can be used to gather extra information about students' progress and their further revision needs.

The *Excel* Basic and Advanced Skills series

If students are experiencing difficulty, require additional practice or need extension in any area of the course, further books are available to support them in the ***Excel*** Basic Skills and Advanced Skills series. (Please see the comprehensive list of ***Excel*** books on page 6.)

The *Excel* step-by-step improvement plan

Step 1

Read the introduction on page 4.

Step 2

The results of the work undertaken in each unit can be recorded on the marking grids.

These are easy-to-use diagnostic tools that indicate where each student's strengths and weaknesses are in relation to specific areas of Mathematics as well as their ability to work at different levels of difficulty.

These results can be used to gather extra information about each student's progress and their further revision needs.

When marking answers on the grid, simply mark incorrect answers with 'X' in the appropriate box. This will result in a graphical representation of areas needing further work.

Section 1 Marking grid

See the sample Section 1 marking grid below:

Questions	1	2	3	4	5	6
Unit 1A						
Unit 1B		X	X	X	X	
Unit 2A						
Unit 2B						
Unit 3A						
Unit 3B						
Unit 4A						
Unit 4B						

This grid indicates that the student needs extra help and practice with questions in Unit 1B (Whole numbers and place value).

Section 2 Marking grid

See the sample Section 2 marking grid below.

If a student is consistently getting more than one in five questions wrong in any topic, they need help in this area.

An example for the first five units is shown below. If a question has several parts, it should be counted as wrong if one or more mistakes are made.

	Whole numbers and place value	Mixed operations	Mixed operations	Mixed operations	Mixed operations
Questions	1	2	3	4	5
Unit 1A					
Unit 1B					X
Unit 2A					
Unit 2B					X
Unit 3A					
Unit 3B					X
Unit 4A					
Unit 4B					X
Unit 5A					
Unit 5B					X

This grid indicates that the student needs extra help and practice with questions on mixed operations.

Step 3

Refer to page 6: *Excel* books to help you *get the results you want*!

Under each topic there is a comprehensive list of books in our range to help students practise the topic they are having difficulty with.

Each ***Excel*** book has a comprehensive contents page that will identify the appropriate pages in the book to target the specific topic area that is causing problems.

Excel books to help you *get the results you want!*

NUMBER AND ALGEBRA

Whole numbers, place value and patterns

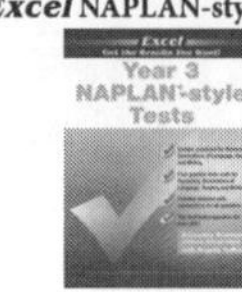

- ***Excel* Basic Skills**: 9781741251807, 9781741256185, 9781741257120
- ***Excel* Advanced Skills**: 9781741252583
- ***Excel* NAPLAN-style Tests**: 9781741252071, 9781741251722, 9781741253177

Addition and subtraction

- ***Excel* Basic Skills**: 9781864412864, 9781741251807, 9781741256185, 9781741257120
- ***Excel* Advanced Skills**: 9781741252583
- ***Excel* NAPLAN-style Tests**: 9781741252071, 9781741251722, 9781741253177

Multiplication and division

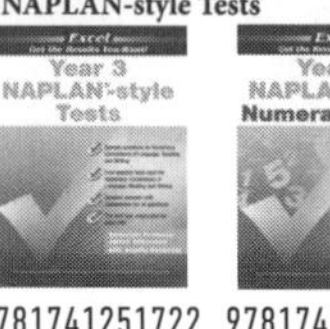

- ***Excel* Basic Skills**: 9781864412888, 9781740200301, 9781741251807, 9781741256185, 9781741257120
- ***Excel* Advanced Skills**: 9781741252583
- ***Excel* NAPLAN-style Tests**: 9781741252071, 9781741251722, 9781741253177

Fractions and money

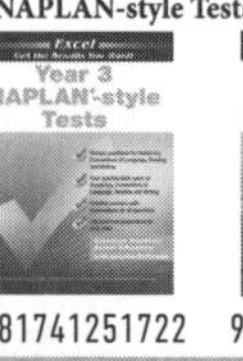

- ***Excel* Basic Skills**: 9781741255898, 9781741251807, 9781741256185, 9781741257120
- ***Excel* Advanced Skills**: 9781741252583
- ***Excel* NAPLAN-style Tests**: 9781741252071, 9781741251722, 9781741253177

MEASUREMENT AND SPACE

Length, area, volume, capacity, mass and time

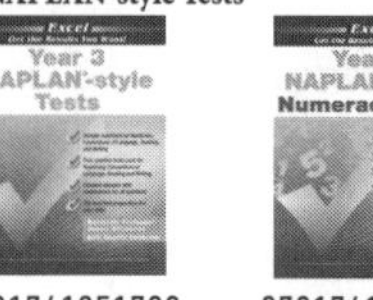

- ***Excel* Basic Skills**: 9781741251807, 9781741256185, 9781741257120
- ***Excel* Advanced Skills**: 9781741252583
- ***Excel* NAPLAN-style Tests**: 9781741252071, 9781741251722, 9781741253177

3D shapes, 2D shapes and angles

- ***Excel* Basic Skills**: 9781741251807, 9781741256185, 9781741257120
- ***Excel* Advanced Skills**: 9781741252583
- ***Excel* NAPLAN-style Tests**: 9781741252071, 9781741251722, 9781741253177

Symmetry and position

- ***Excel* Basic Skills**: 9781741251807, 9781741256185, 9781741257120
- ***Excel* Advanced Skills**: 9781741252583
- ***Excel* NAPLAN-style Tests**: 9781741252071, 9781741251722, 9781741253177

STATISTICS AND PROBABILITY

Chance and data

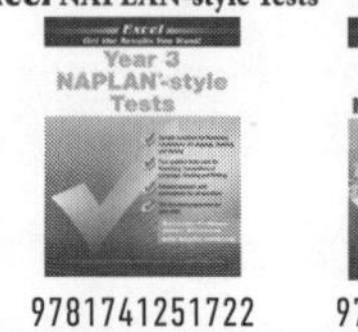

- ***Excel* Basic Skills**: 9781741251807, 9781741256185, 9781741257120
- ***Excel* Advanced Skills**: 9781741252583
- ***Excel* NAPLAN-style Tests**: 9781741252071, 9781741251722, 9781741253177

Section 1 Marking grid

Number and algebra
Units 1A & 1B: Whole numbers and place value
Units 2A & 2B: Addition and subtraction
Units 3A & 3B: Multiplication and division
Units 4A & 4B: Fractions
Units 5A & 5B: Money
Units 6A & 6B: Patterns

Measurement and space
Units 7A & 7B: Length and area
Units 8A & 8B: Volume, capacity, mass and time
Units 9A & 9B: 3D shapes
Units 10A & 10B: 2D shapes and angles
Units 11A & 11B: Symmetry and position

Statistics and probability
Units 12A & 12B: Data and chance

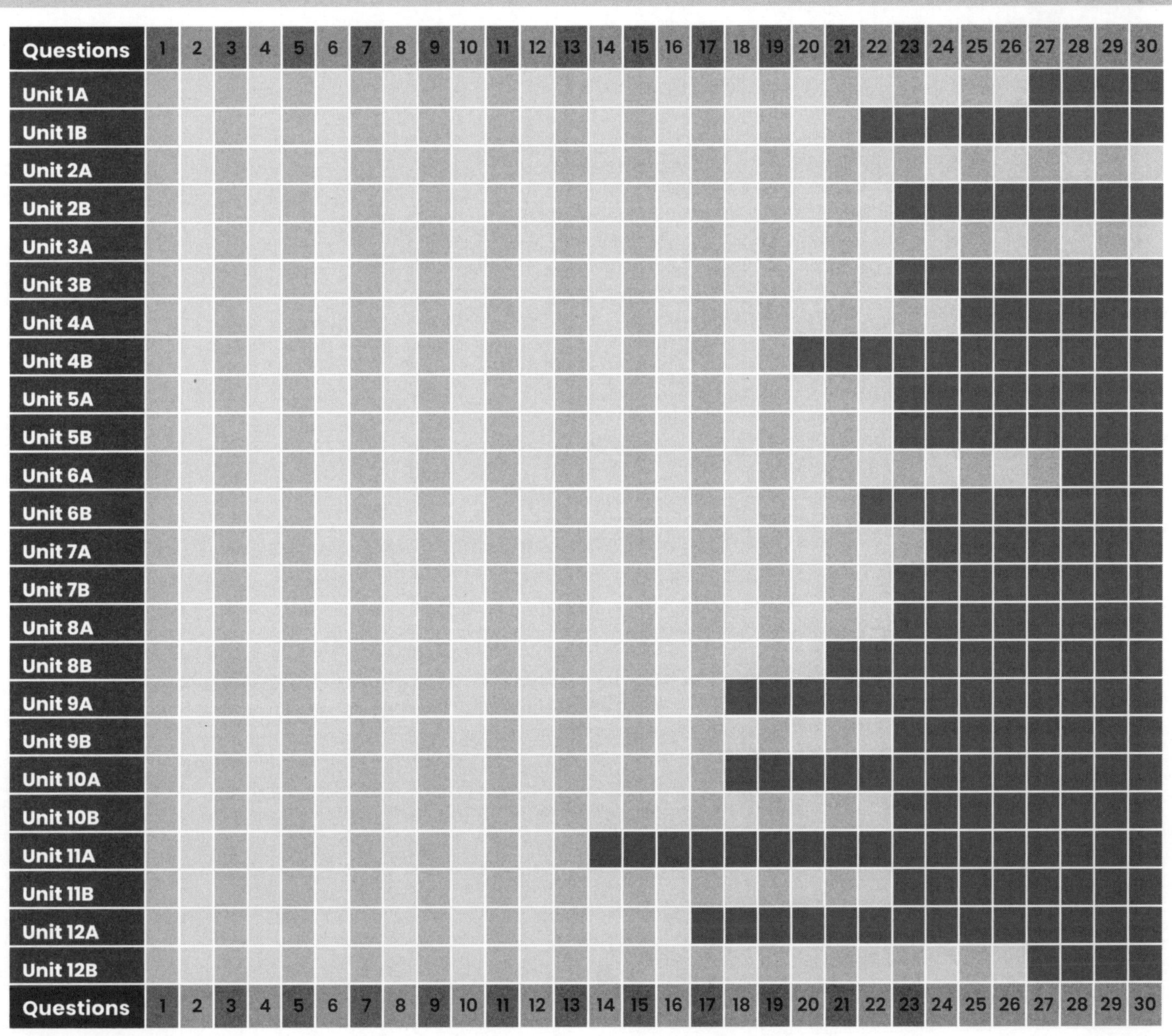

Questions	1	2	3	4	5	6	7	8	9	10	11	12	13	14	15	16	17	18	19	20	21	22	23	24	25	26	27	28	29	30
Unit 1A																														
Unit 1B																														
Unit 2A																														
Unit 2B																														
Unit 3A																														
Unit 3B																														
Unit 4A																														
Unit 4B																														
Unit 5A																														
Unit 5B																														
Unit 6A																														
Unit 6B																														
Unit 7A																														
Unit 7B																														
Unit 8A																														
Unit 8B																														
Unit 9A																														
Unit 9B																														
Unit 10A																														
Unit 10B																														
Unit 11A																														
Unit 11B																														
Unit 12A																														
Unit 12B																														
Questions	1	2	3	4	5	6	7	8	9	10	11	12	13	14	15	16	17	18	19	20	21	22	23	24	25	26	27	28	29	30

Section 2 Marking grid

	Number and algebra								Measurement and space								Statistics and probability	
	Whole numbers and place value	Mixed operations	Mixed operations	Mixed operations	Mixed operations	Fractions	Money	Patterns	Length and area	Volume and capacity	Mass	Time	3D shapes	2D shapes and symmetry	Angles	Position	Chance	Data
Questions	1	2	3	4	5	6	7	8	9	10	11	12	13	14	15	16	17	18
Unit 1A																		
Unit 1B																		
Unit 2A																		
Unit 2B																		
Unit 3A																		
Unit 3B																		
Unit 4A																		
Unit 4B																		
Unit 5A																		
Unit 5B																		
Unit 6A																		
Unit 6B																		
Unit 7A																		
Unit 7B																		
Unit 8A																		
Unit 8B																		
Unit 9A																		
Unit 9B																		
Unit 10A																		
Unit 10B																		
Unit 11A																		
Unit 11B																		
Unit 12A																		
Unit 12B																		
Unit 13A																		
Unit 13B																		
Unit 14A																		
Unit 14B																		
Unit 15A																		
Unit 15B																		
Questions	1	2	3	4	5	6	7	8	9	10	11	12	13	14	15	16	17	18

Section 2 Marking grid

	Number and algebra								Measurement and space								Statistics and probability	
	Whole numbers and place value	Mixed operations	Mixed operations	Mixed operations	Mixed operations	Fractions	Money	Patterns	Length and area	Volume and capacity	Mass	Time	3D shapes	2D shapes and symmetry	Angles	Position	Chance	Data
Questions	1	2	3	4	5	6	7	8	9	10	11	12	13	14	15	16	17	18
Unit 16A																		
Unit 16B																		
Unit 17A																		
Unit 17B																		
Unit 18A																		
Unit 18B																		
Unit 19A																		
Unit 19B																		
Unit 20A																		
Unit 20B																		
Unit 21A																		
Unit 21B																		
Unit 22A																		
Unit 22B																		
Unit 23A																		
Unit 23B																		
Unit 24A																		
Unit 24B																		
Unit 25A																		
Unit 25B																		
Unit 26A																		
Unit 26B																		
Unit 27A																		
Unit 27B																		
Unit 28A																		
Unit 28B																		
Unit 29A																		
Unit 29B																		
Unit 30A																		
Unit 30B																		
Questions	1	2	3	4	5	6	7	8	9	10	11	12	13	14	15	16	17	18

FOCUS ON WHOLE NUMBERS AND PLACE VALUE

1. Write the number for two thousand, eight hundred and forty-six.

2. Use the digits 7, 2, 6, 3 to make the largest possible number.

3. What is the missing number?
 ________, 7400, 7401, 7402

4. What is the number 1 more than 999?

5. What is the missing number?
 638, 648, 658, ________

6. Circle the smallest number.
 587 2003 921 87

7. Underline the number which is closest to 300.
 30 400 350 3000

8. How many of these numbers are less than 780?
 79 870 381 1780

9. True or false?
 538 < 640

10. What is the place value of 5 in the number 3592?

11. Complete the number sentence.
 9375 = 9000 + 300 + ________ + 5

12. What is 482 rounded to the nearest hundred?

13. Round 7089 to the nearest thousand.

14. Write the number with 5 thousands, 4 tens and 2 ones.

15. Circle the largest number.
 509 1984 4001 2999

16. Write the number 8503 in words.

17. Circle the largest number.
 four hundred and ninety-eight
 two thousand and sixty
 seven hundred and nine

18. Use the digits 3, 4 and 5 to make the largest possible even number.

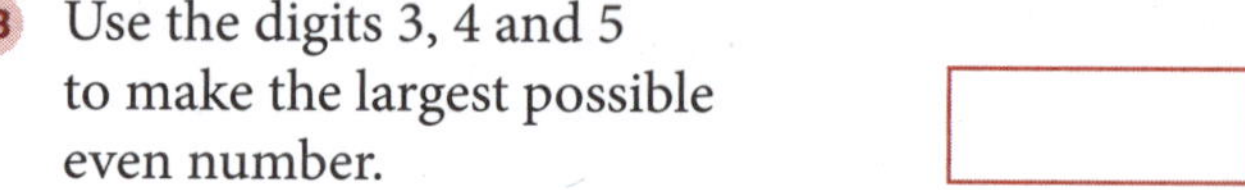

19. Circle the number which is closest to 500.
 400 599 471 50

20. Write the missing numbers.
 ______, 478, 488, 498, ______

21. Here is a number line.

 77 78 79 ? 81

 What is the missing number?

22. What is 3864 rounded to the nearest 10?

23. What is the smallest three-digit number?

24. What digit is in the hundreds place in the number 3872?

25. How many whole numbers are between 20 and 30?

26. What number is represented by these squares?

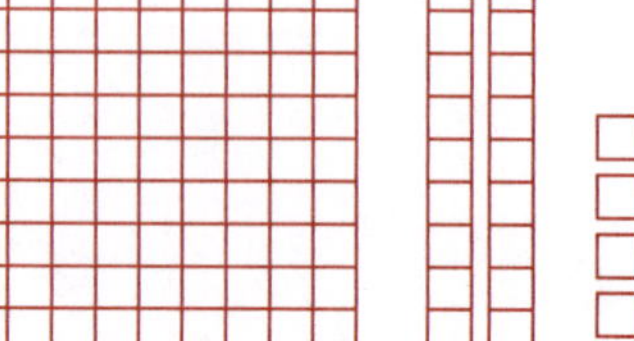

FOCUS ON WHOLE NUMBERS AND PLACE VALUE

1 Owen has these four numbered cards.

7 9 2 4

He uses the cards to make a four-digit odd number. The number is greater than 8000. The digit in the hundreds place is less than the digit in the tens place. What is Owen's number?

2 Frida buys a car which has travelled 9739 km. How far has the car travelled to the nearest 100 kilometres?

3 Ella has a coin collection. She looked at some coins issued in these years: 1982, 1966, 2001 and 1971. Which of these is the oldest coin?

4 Logan wrote a four-digit number using identical digits. If the sum of his digits is 24, what is Logan's number?

5 Ashley's grandmother is aged between 70 and 90 years old. Her age is an even number where the sum of the digits is 13. How old is her grandmother?

6 Romy thinks of a three-digit number. The digit in the hundreds place is twice the digit in the ones place. The digit in the tens place is three times the digit in the hundreds place. What is the number?

7 In one week a factory makes 10 620 beads. How many beads were made to the nearest thousand?

8 Ivy filled a jar with 1152 jelly beans. How many jelly beans are in the jar, to the nearest hundred?

9 Liam placed 10 coins in a line across his desk. How many coins are between the second coin and the second-last coin in the row?

10 Oliver collected four dozen eggs this morning. How many eggs did he collect, to the nearest ten?

11 Bella counted forwards by tens starting at 523. What will be Bella's fourth number?

12 The four-digit PIN on the card Elon uses to withdraw money from ATMs is made up of odd digits that add to 8. The first and last digit are identical. The middle two digits are identical. If the first digit is 2 more than the second digit, what is Elon's PIN?

13 There were 6729 spectators at a soccer match. A newspaper recorded the number of spectators to the nearest hundred. What was the number reported by the newspaper?

14 Lara used the digits 3, 7, 4 and 9 to make the largest possible four-digit number. What digit is in the tens place?

15 Hannah, Maria and Eli worked as a team to count to 100. Hannah called out 1, Maria 2, Eli 3, then Hannah 4, Maria 5, and so on. Which person called out the number 10?

16 Ava has these four numbered cards.

5 0 6 3

What is the largest four-digit number Ava can make using the cards?

17 Cameron and Levi looked at the number 672. Cameron rounded the number to the nearest hundred. Levi rounded the number to the nearest ten. What is the difference between their new numbers?

18 Here are five numbers: 1387 1822 1803 1378 1087. Thomas rearranged the numbers in descending order. What is Thomas's middle number?

19 Each morning Lincoln wants to increase the number of push-ups he completes. On Sunday he completed 24 and on Monday 25. On what day of the week will Lincoln complete 30 push-ups?

20 Brian has about 1400 sheep on his property. Which of these could be the exact number of sheep? Circle your answer.

400 1380 14 000 141

21 Here are four numbers.

486 285 798 497

Which of these numbers is more than the smallest even number but less than the largest odd number? Circle your answer.

368 209 490

FOCUS ON ADDITION AND SUBTRACTION

1 4 + 7 + 3 + 6 =

2
```
   2
   9
   3
+  8
```

3 20 + 50 + 10 =

4 638 + 2 + 10 =

5 40 + 20 + 7 + 2 =

6 3 + 5 + 20 + 30 + 400 =

7 25 + 5 + 70 + 100 =

8 35 + 47 =

9 35 + 63 =

10 174 + 20 + 6 =

11 300 + 400 + 100 + 50 =

12 90 + 910 + 3000 =

13 2320 + 80 + 600 =

14 3780 + 20 + 200 =

15 10 – 4 – 2 =

16 39 – 4 – 4 =

17 100 – 53 =

18 1000 – 680 =

19 58 + ? = 64

20 264 + ? = 271

21 ? + 23 = 31

22 55 – ? = 46

23 100 – ? = 39

24 ? – 18 = 72

25 12 + 38 = ? – 10

26 15 – 8 + 3 + 8 =

27 100 – 70 + 20 – 40 =

28 2 + 4 + 8 + 16 – 15 =

29 5 + 2 + 8 + 4 + 5 + 6 =

30 60 – 10 + 20 =

FOCUS ON ADDITION AND SUBTRACTION

1 There are 26 students in 3P and 25 students in 3T. What is the total number of students in both classes?

2 On Saturday Cyril picked 16 tomatoes. He picked 21 on Monday and 28 on Thursday. What was the total number of tomatoes picked?

3 Jensen has 12 blue blocks, 16 red blocks and 13 green blocks. What is the total number of blocks?

4 Helena visited a pet shop. There were 23 fish in one tank and twice as many in another. What was the total number of fish in the two tanks?

5 Charley sold 23 muffins before midday and 28 muffins after midday. What was the total number sold?

6 A bag contains red, green and blue counters. There are twice as many red counters in the bag as blue counters. There are 10 green counters and 12 blue counters. What is the total number of counters in the bag?

7 Dane has 42 marbles. James has 6 more marbles than Dane. How many marbles do the boys have altogether?

8 Grace counted the balloons she had bought for her party. There were 12 red, 16 pink and 24 white balloons. How many balloons did Grace buy?

9 What is the sum of 39 and 47, to the nearest ten?

10 Ariana thinks of a number. She adds 16 to her number and the answer is 40. What was Ariana's original number?

11 William plans to ride 80 km before lunch. If he has already ridden 37 km, how far has he yet to ride?

12 Abe has 35 toy cars, which is 19 more than his brother Ben. How many toy cars does Ben have?

13 Addison is 18 years old today. Her mother Kate is 43 years old. How old was Kate when Addison was born?

14 Halfway through lunch there are 47 students in the school's learning centre. After 10 minutes there are 28 students. Assuming no students have entered, how many have left the learning centre?

15 A car park has 81 parking spaces. If there are 24 available spaces, how many are occupied?

16 Florence baked 96 cookies for a market stall. She sold 58 cookies before lunchtime. How many cookies remained to be sold?

17 What is the difference between 8 hundreds and 24 tens?

18 Jalailah has these cards:

5 7

She uses the cards to make two different two-digit numbers. What is the difference between her numbers?

19 How many hundreds are in the number which is 320 less than 500?

20 A plane has a total of 180 seats. If there are 97 passengers, how many seats are vacant?

21 A driver delivered 430 packages in one day. If 160 packages were delivered by 10 am, how many were delivered after 10 am?

22 The sum of two numbers is 100. If the smaller number is 29, what is the difference between the two numbers?

FOCUS ON

MULTIPLICATION AND DIVISION

1 8 lots of 2 =

2 $5 \times 4 =$

3 $7 \times 3 =$

4 $9 \times 5 =$

5 4 groups of 6 =

6 Circle the multiples of 2.

12 21 26 45

7 Circle the numbers that are **not** multiples of 2.

9 21 26 30

8 What is the missing number?

$10 \times 6 = 6 \times$?

9 What is the missing number?

$5 \times 6 =$?

10 Double 30 =

11 Triple 8 =

12 Double 400 =

13 $75 \times 10 =$

14 $13 \times 2 \times 5 =$

15 What is 4×2 added to 6×2?

16 What is the missing number?

12×5 is the same as $6 \times$?.

17 What is the missing number?

$9 \times$? $= 45$

18 Is the answer for 11×4 odd or even?

19 $2 \times 4 \times 5 \times 0 \times 10 =$

20 Half of 24 =

21 $40 \div 4 =$

22 What number is divided by 10 to give an answer of 5?

23 $48 \div 2 =$

24 How many 5s can be subtracted from 20 to give 0?

25 What is one-third of 12?

26 What is 25 divided by 5?

27 How many 10s can be subtracted from 120 to give 0?

28 If $26 \times 10 = 260$, what is the missing number in

$260 \div$? $= 26$?

29 $13 \times 5 \div 5 =$

30 What is half of 48×20?

FOCUS ON MULTIPLICATION AND DIVISION

1 A packet contains 9 biscuits. How many biscuits are in 3 packets?

2 Jake washes 8 pairs of socks. He uses a peg for each sock he hangs on his clothesline. How many pegs does Jake use?

3 Myles drew 5 squares. What is the total number of sides on his squares?

4 Every night Frida reads 10 pages of her book. How many pages does she read in 6 nights?

5 Charlotte placed 5 cookies on each of 8 plates. What is the total number of cookies?

6 A supermarket sells bags of 5 lemons. How many lemons are in 7 bags?

7 Mrs Jacobs has 20 students in her class and gives each student 2 sheets of cardboard. How many sheets of cardboard have been handed out?

8 There are 4 swimmers in a relay team. If 5 lanes of a swimming pool are used for a race, how many swimmers compete?

9 A restaurant has 10 tables. Each table has 6 chairs. How many customers can be seated in the restaurant?

10 Medium-sized pizzas are cut into 8 slices. How many slices are in 3 pizzas?

11 Amelia has 9 stuffed animal toys. Matilda has three times as many as Amelia. How many stuffed animal toys has Matilda?

12 Mia arranged one-dollar coins in rows of 6. If she made 5 rows, how many coins did Mia use?

13 Archer has some blocks. He can arrange all his blocks into groups of 2, 3 or 5. What is the smallest possible number of blocks?

14 Agnes has a bag containing 24 lollies. She gives 3 lollies to each of her friends. How many of her friends receive lollies?

15 Stephanie arranged 36 oranges into 3 equal groups. How many oranges were in each group?

16 A group of 15 students needs to be transported to the town hall by car. If each car can transport 3 students, how many cars are required?

17 James arranged some stickers into 5 groups of 6. He then picked up all his stickers and placed them into 3 boxes. If each box had the same number, how many stickers were in each box?

18 Pencils are packed into boxes of 10. Students are to be given 2 pencils each. If there are 20 students in a class, how many boxes are needed?

19 Oliver arranged the chairs in the school hall into 6 rows of 10 chairs. Jack then rearranged the chairs into rows of 5. How many rows are in Jack's arrangement?

20 Two numbers are multiplied to give an answer of 12. One of the numbers is 4. Thomas halved the larger number and doubled the smaller number. What was his answer when he multiplied his two numbers?

21 Jasper wrote a number on a card. He multiplied the number by 3 and his answer was 18. What answer would he get if he had divided the number on the card by 3?

22 Ms Turnbull has 24 students in her class. She arranged her students into groups of 3. How many more groups would she have if she had arranged her students in pairs?

FOCUS ON FRACTIONS

1 Shade $\frac{3}{4}$ of the circles.

2 How many eighths are in one whole?

3 Shade $\frac{3}{5}$ of the shape.

4 Shade $\frac{1}{2}$ of the shape.

5 Shade $\frac{2}{3}$ of the circles.

6 What fraction of the shape is shaded?

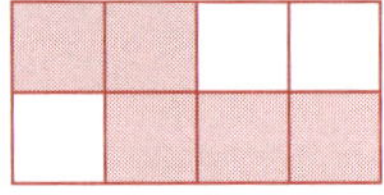

7 True or false? $\frac{1}{3} < \frac{1}{6}$

8 What fraction of the shape is shaded?

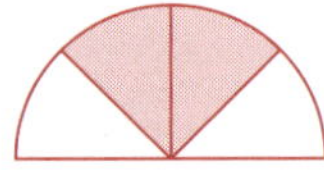

9 What fraction of the shape is **not** shaded?

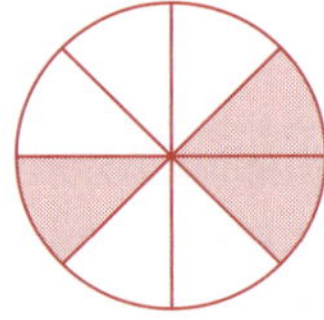

10 Shade $\frac{1}{4}$ of the shape.

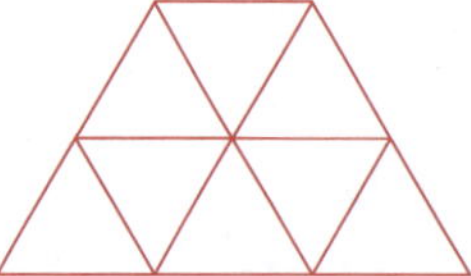

11 What is the missing fraction on the number line?

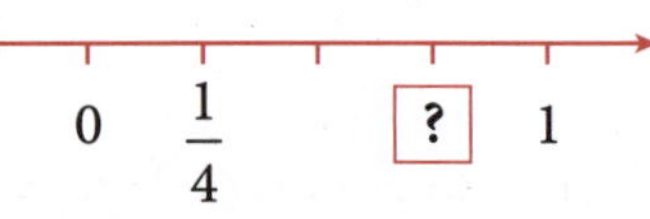

12 Circle the biggest fraction.

$\frac{3}{5}$ $\frac{4}{5}$ $\frac{1}{5}$ $\frac{2}{5}$

13 Circle the smallest fraction.

$\frac{2}{5}$ $\frac{2}{3}$ $\frac{2}{8}$ $\frac{2}{4}$

14 If $\frac{3}{?} = 1$, what is the missing number?

15 What is the missing fraction on the number line?

$\frac{2}{5}$ $\frac{3}{5}$? 1

16 Write the fraction with denominator 8 and numerator 7.

17 Here is a sequence of fractions:

$\frac{1}{5}, \frac{2}{5}, \frac{3}{5}, \frac{4}{5}, 1,$?

What is the next number?

18 Here is a collection of circles.

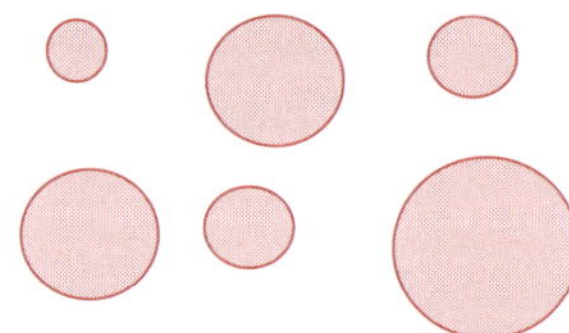

Draw a box around $\frac{1}{3}$ of the circles.

19 Using a dot, locate $\frac{7}{8}$ on the number line below.

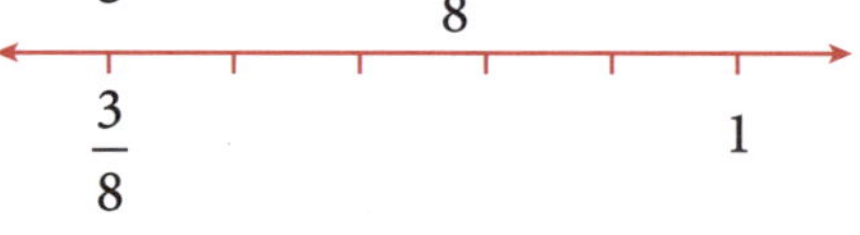

20 What is $\frac{1}{2}$ of 12?

21 What is $\frac{1}{3}$ of 15?

22 What is the missing fraction on the number line?

23 Arrange these fractions from smallest to largest.

$\frac{4}{3}$ $\frac{4}{4}$ $\frac{4}{8}$ $\frac{4}{2}$

24 True or false? $2 > 1\frac{4}{5}$

FOCUS ON FRACTIONS

1. A shape is formed using eight identical squares. Eleni shades seven of the eight squares. What fraction of the shape is shaded?

2. Six cookies are placed on a plate. Half of the cookies are chocolate. How many chocolate cookies are on the plate?

3. 

Here are eight apples. A quarter of the apples are removed. How many apples remain?

4. There are eight balls in a bag. Half of the balls are red and there are two green balls. The remaining balls are blue. How many balls in the bag are blue?

5. Here is a shape made from five identical squares.

Mia and Theo shade two squares each. What fraction of the shape is unshaded?

6. Aria bought a dozen eggs. She used six eggs to make some omelettes. What fraction of the eggs were used?

7. 

Here are some coloured pencils. Asher used one-third of the pencils to colour a picture. How many pencils did he use?

8. Anne cuts some apples in half. Here are the pieces of apple. How many apples did Anne start with?

9. Noah has 10 balls. He gives $\frac{5}{10}$ of the balls to Felix and $\frac{2}{10}$ of the balls to Levi. What fraction of the balls has Noah kept?

10. For her birthday Alice received five books. A month after her birthday she had read three of the books. What fraction of her books had she read?

11. Lydia, Chloe, Caleb and Miles shared a box of chocolates equally. What fraction of the chocolates was eaten by Caleb?

12. A group of eight students were surveyed about the way they had travelled to school that morning. Three students had caught a bus, two students were driven in cars and the remaining students walked. What fraction of the students walked?

13. Kai started with two pizzas. He sliced each pizza. If each slice was $\frac{1}{8}$ of a pizza, how many slices were there?

14. Rory drew 10 circles. She coloured in three of the circles. What fraction of the circles were **not** coloured in?

15. Blake has eight cushions on her bed. Every night she keeps a quarter of them on her bed and throws the rest of the cushions on the floor. How many cushions does she keep on her bed?

16. There were six bananas in Emma's fruit bowl. After a few days she had eaten half of the bananas. How many bananas remained?

17. At a party Andrew ate half a pizza, Elias ate a quarter of a pizza and Astrid ate a third of a pizza. Who ate the smallest amount of pizza?

18. Here is a shape made of identical squares.

Ivy shaded $\frac{1}{2}$ of the shape.

Audrey shaded $\frac{1}{2}$ of the remaining unshaded squares. How many squares remain unshaded?

19. A bag contains four different-coloured jelly beans. There are 10 jelly beans in the bag. There are three red jelly beans and five black jelly beans. There is an equal number of green and white jelly beans. What fraction of the jelly beans in the bag are white?

FOCUS ON MONEY

1 Here are four prices:

$12.60 $1.40 650 cents $10

Circle the lowest price.

2 A box of tissues costs $2.45.
A can of soup costs a dollar more.
What is the cost of the soup?

3 Round off $2.31 to the nearest 5 cents.

4 Round off $11.56 to the nearest 5 cents.

5 How many 5-cent coins make $1?

6 What is the total value of the money?

7 How much change from $5 would you get if you spent $4.20?

8 Add $5, $2 and 5 cents.

9 How much money is eight 20-cent coins?

10 What is the total of $1.40 and $3.55?

11 What is the total value of the money?

12 What is $5 – $2.30?

13 How many $2 coins make a total of $20?

14

What is the total of the money shown?

15 Add $7.50 and $2.50.

16 How many 5-cent coins make a total of $0.30?

17 How many 20-cent coins equal the total amount shown below?

18

How many $2 coins equal the total amount shown above?

19

How many $5 notes equal the total amount shown above?

20

What is the total amount of money shown?

21

What is the total amount of money shown?

22 What is the smallest number of coins that add to 80 cents?

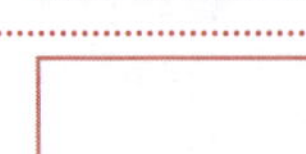

FOCUS ON MONEY

1 Maryam has these six coins.

?

If the total value is $4.75, what is the missing coin?

2 Stella bought three cans of dog food for $12.

What was the cost of each can?

3 Josiah bought a pair of jeans for $65. He used a $100 gift card to pay for the items.

How much money remains on the gift card?

4 Skylar is paid $6 for each dog she walks. How much will she be paid if she walks four dogs?

5 Isaac bought a birthday card for $9 and wrapping paper for $3.20.

How much in total did he spend?

6 For her birthday, Stella was given money. She received $50 from her parents, $20 from her uncle and $10 from her grandmother.

What was the total amount she received?

7 Brielle makes silver jewellery. At a market she sells two bangles for $80 each. What is the total amount she received?

8 Hannah bought a set of highlighters for $3.00 and a ruler for 75 cents.

How much change did she receive from a $5 note?

9 Henry bought a magazine for $9.20 and a newspaper for $2.80. How much in total did he spend?

10 Ethan bought six apples at 40 cents each. He paid for the apples with two $2 coins. What change did Ethan receive?

11 A supermarket charges $12 to deliver groceries. What is the total cost of $130 worth of groceries home delivered?

12 Zoey bought two bunches of flowers. If each bunch cost $45, how much change did she receive from $100?

13 Liam bought milk from a supermarket and paid the exact amount of $3.65 in coins. What is the smallest number of coins he could have used to pay for the milk?

14 A cinema charges $18.50 for adult tickets and $11.50 for child tickets. What is the total cost of two child tickets?

15 Mason bought three pens at $1.99 each. How much money did he spend?

16

Kiara is given $100 for her birthday. This is the money she had left after her trip to the shopping centre.

How much money did she spend?

17 Sebastian bought a tube of toothpaste priced at $3.42. He paid with a $5 note. How much change did he receive?

18 $240 is to be shared between four people. How much will each person receive?

19 Layla has $10. Mia has $3.60 less than Layla. How much do the girls have in total?

20 Benjamin has saved $42. Levi has saved $10 more than Benjamin. What is the total amount saved?

21 A grocer is selling apples for 90c each, bananas for 60c and mandarins for 50c. Lyla buys two of each fruit. How much did Lyla spend?

22 Noah has three stacks of coins. He has a stack of ten $2 coins, five 10c coins and four 5c coins. What is the total amount of money?

FOCUS ON PATTERNS

1 What is the missing number?
4, 8, 12, 16, ________

2 What is the missing number?
15, 20, 25, 30, ________

3 Write the missing numbers in this pattern of numbers.

12	15	18			27

4 What is the missing number?
________, 6, 9, 12, 15

5 What is the missing number?
27, 36, 45, ________, 63

6 Write the missing numbers in this pattern of numbers.

55	49	43	37		

7 What is the missing number?
30, 27, ________, 21, 18

8 Circle the odd numbers.
136 483 350 67

9 What is the largest two-digit even number?

10 Here is a pattern of numbers: 16, 19, 22, 25 …
What is the sixth number in the pattern?

11 Write the missing numbers in this pattern of numbers.

40	49	58			85

12 Here is a pattern of numbers: 100, 96, 92, 88 …
What is the seventh number in the pattern?

13 Here is a pattern of numbers: 170, 150, 130, 110 …
What is the next number in the pattern?

14 A pattern of numbers is written using the rule 'Start with 6 and add 5'. Write the first four numbers.

________, ________, ________, ________

15 Here is a pattern of numbers: 12, 18, 24, 30.
Complete the rule.
Start with 12 and add ________.

16 Here is a pattern of numbers: 90, 81, 72, 63.
Complete the rule.
Start with 90 and subtract ________.

17 How many odd numbers are between 20 and 40?

18 A rule is used to complete the numbers in the bottom row of the table.

Top row	1	3	5	7	9
Bottom row	5	15	25	35	?

What is the missing number?

19 What is the next number in this pattern? 266, 466, 666, 866, ________

20 What is the third odd number after 70?

21 A rule is used to complete the numbers in the table.

Top row	4	6		10	12
Bottom row	8	12	16	20	

What are the two missing numbers?

22 Here is a pattern of numbers: 109, 106, 103 …
What is the largest two-digit number in the pattern?

23 Write the missing numbers in this pattern of numbers.

	54		66	72	78

24 Here is a pattern of numbers:
676, 777, 878, 979, ________
What is the missing number?

25 What will be the seventh number in the pattern 6, 8, 10, 12 …?

26 The rule 'adding 7' is used to list this pattern.
________ 288, 295, ________
What are the two missing numbers?

27 Here is a pattern of numbers: 540, 430, 320 …
What is the fifth number in the pattern?

FOCUS ON PATTERNS

1 Charlotte uses the rule 'start with 7 and add 6' to write a list of numbers. Which of these is on Charlotte's list?

14 19 21 27

2 Lincoln uses the rule 'start with 43 and subtract 9' to write a list of numbers. Which of these is **not** on Lincoln's list?

34 26 25 16

3 Hudson rode 2 km on Monday, 4 km on Tuesday, 6 km on Wednesday, and so on, increasing the distance by 2 km each day. On what day did he ride 12 km?

4 William thinks of a number. It is odd. Harper's number is 4 more than William's number. They add their numbers. Is the total an even or odd number?

5 The smallest three-digit odd number and the largest two-digit even number are subtracted. What is the answer?

6 Olivia is trying to sell her car for $5400. Every week the car does not sell she reduces the price by $200. What is the price of the car if it has **not** sold after 3 weeks?

7 Scarlett wrote this pattern: 15, 20, 25, 30 … If Scarlett continues the pattern, what would be the sixth number?

8 Students are arranged into different-sized groups. There are six students in Group 1, nine students in Group 2, 12 students in Group 3, and so on. How many students are in Group 6?

9 Adrian used the rule 'start with 28 and subtract 4'. What is the fourth number in the pattern?

10 Zoey wrote this pattern: 440, 320, 200, 80 … Complete the rule Zoey used. Start with 440 and subtract ______.

11 Ryan used the rule 'start at 100 and subtract 10' to write a pattern of numbers. What is the fourth number in Ryan's pattern?

12 Maya wrote a number pattern using the rule 'start with 20 and add 5'. What is the difference between the first and the fourth numbers in the pattern?

13 Here is a pattern of symbols.

○□△▭○□△▭○□ …

What shape is the 16th symbol?

14 The height of a tomato plant is measured every week. When it is planted it is 12 cm high. The plant grows 8 cm each week. How tall is the tomato plant 3 weeks after it is planted?

15 In turn Isla, Willow and Lucy count from 1. Isla counts 1, 3, 5, and so on. Willow counts 1, 4, 7, and so on. Lucy counts 1, 5, 9, and so on. How many numbers less than 20 are not counted by any of them?

16 A supermarket display of tissue boxes has 12 boxes on the bottom row, 10 on the second bottom row, eight on the third bottom row and so on. If there are four boxes on the top row, how many rows of boxes are in the display?

17 Layla used a rule to write this pattern.

______, 8, 12, 16, 20, ______

What is the total of Layla's two missing numbers?

18 Eliana wrote a pattern of numbers where she subtracted 4 from the previous number. The third number in her pattern was 20. What was the first number in her pattern?

19 Gianna charges $12 to babysit for the first hour. She charges $10 for the second hour, $8 for the third hour, and so on. How much will she charge to babysit for 4 hours?

20 Emma, Ava and Amelia take turns lighting a row of candles. Emma lights the first candle, Ava the second and Amelia the third. Emma lights the fourth, Ava the fifth, Amelia the sixth, and so on. What is the smallest possible number of candles in the row if Ava lights four candles?

21 Dylan wrote a list of numbers using the rule start at 4 and add 5. Miles wrote a list of numbers using the rule 'start at 30 and subtract 6'. What number is on both lists?

FOCUS ON LENGTH AND AREA

1 Circle the best estimate of the length of a pencil.

20 mm   13 cm   3 cm   45 mm

2 Use the ruler to measure the length of the rectangle, in centimetres.

cm 0 1 2 3 4 5 6 7 8 9 10 11 12 13 14 15 16 17 18

3 A rectangle is drawn on a centimetre grid.

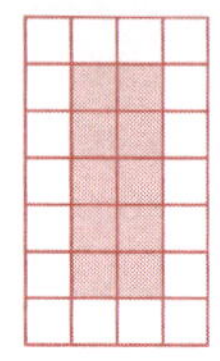

What is the width of the rectangle?

4 Circle the best estimate for the length of your handspan.

13 cm   13 mm   13 m   1 m 3 cm

5 Use the ruler to measure the length of the pencil, to the nearest centimetre.

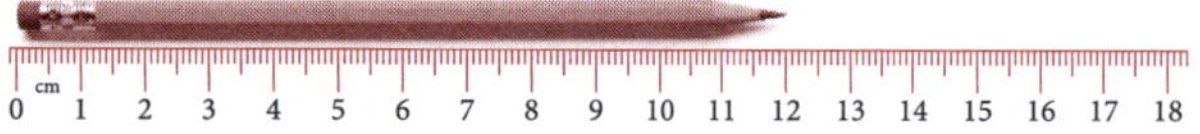

cm 0 1 2 3 4 5 6 7 8 9 10 11 12 13 14 15 16 17 18

6 Circle the best estimate for the height of the ceiling.

3 m   30 cm   3 cm   3 mm

7 Here are four lengths.

12 cm   1 m   56 mm   4 cm

Circle the shortest length.

8 How many centimetres are in 2 m?

9 Circle the longest distance.

1 m 25 cm   120 cm   26 mm

10 Here are four lengths.

60 mm   5 cm   10 cm   55 mm

Circle the longest length.

11 5 cm 3 mm = ☐ mm

12 A rectangle is drawn on a centimetre grid.

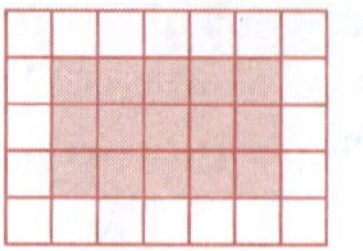

What is the length of the rectangle?

13 How many millimetres are in the length 4 cm 2 mm?

14 Two lengths of wire are 50 cm and 23 cm. What is the difference between the lengths?

15 Add 3 cm and 12 mm, writing your answer in millimetres.

16 How many millimetres are in 10 cm?

17 Circle the best estimate for the length of a car.

2 m   5 m   60 cm   1000 mm

18 What is 52 mm rounded to the nearest centimetre?

19 Circle the best estimate of the width of this page.

20 mm   100 mm   200 mm   2 m

20 2 m 3 mm = ☐ mm

21 Insert < or > to make a true statement.

1 m 6 cm ☐ 150 cm

22 A rectangle is drawn on a centimetre grid.

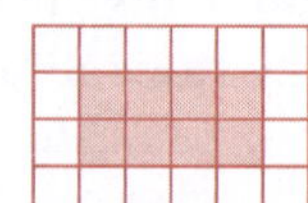

What is the area of the rectangle?

23 A shape is drawn on a centimetre grid.

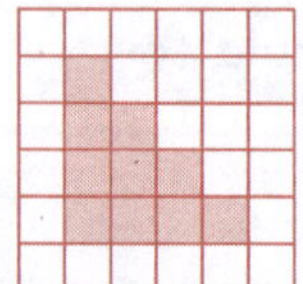

What is the area of the shape?

FOCUS ON LENGTH AND AREA

1. Jo is 1 m 45 cm tall. Her father is 35 cm taller than her. What is the height of Jo's father?

2. Each side of a square is 5 cm long. What is the distance around the outside of the square?

3. Each morning Jack leaves home and drives 15 km to work. He drives the same route home in the evening. What is the total distance?

4. A rectangle is three times longer than it is wide. If it is 15 cm long, find its width.

5. The distance around the outside of a square is 28 cm. What is the length of each side?

6. Levi drew a line 25 mm long. Jack drew a line twice the length of Levi's line. What is the length of Jack's line, in centimetres?

7. Anastacia is knitting a scarf. Last Sunday the scarf was 12 cm long. Today the length is 19 cm.
How much longer is the scarf now compared to last Sunday?

8. On the first tee Ely hit his golf ball 155 m. Symon hit his ball 30 m further. How far did Symon hit his golf ball?

9. What is the difference between the lengths of the USB and the pen?

10. Scott walked 4 km every morning for a week. What was the total distance Scott walked?

11. On her second birthday, Sophia's dad measures her height as 90 cm. If she expects to double her height when fully grown, what will be Sophia's eventual height?

12. 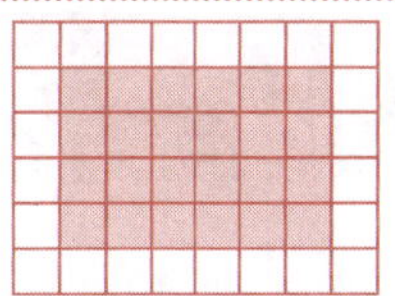
A rectangle is drawn on a centimetre grid.
How much longer is the rectangle than it is wide?

13. A piece of timber is 1 metre in length. It is cut into two smaller lengths. If the shorter length is 45 cm, what is the longer length?

14. Mr Johnson used chalk to draw a square on the school's playground. Each side of the square was 5 m. What is the total length of the chalk drawn?

15. Chloe and Grace are twins. Grace is 3 cm taller than Chloe. If Chloe's height is 139 cm, what is the height of Grace?

16. Alice's backyard pool is 8 m long. What is her total distance if she swims 20 laps of the pool?

17. Athena's fingernails grow about 2 mm each month. How long will it take for her nails to grow 2 cm?

18. Sebastian has a set of coloured pencils. Each pencil is exactly 20 cm in length. He lays all his pencils end to end. The line of pencils is 2 m. How many pencils has Sebastian used?

19. The distance around a rectangle is 20 cm. If the length of the rectangle is 8 cm, what is the width?

20. Mateo walks 240 m from his home to school each morning. He takes the same route home in the afternoon. How far does he walk each day?

21. Allison bought a 1-m roll of ribbon. How many lengths of 20-cm ribbon can she cut from the roll?

22. Here is a centimetre grid.

Lucas wants to use the grid to draw a rectangle with an area of 15 cm^2.
He has started to draw the rectangle.
What will be the width of Lucas's rectangle?

FOCUS ON VOLUME, CAPACITY, MASS AND TIME

1 How many cubic-centimetre cubes are in this solid?

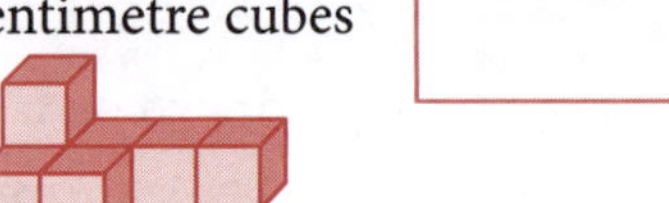

2 Circle the shape with a capacity of less than one litre.

kitchen sink bottle of hand sanitiser

bucket swimming pool

3 A shape has two layers of eight cubic-centimetre blocks. What is the total volume in cubic centimetres?

4 How many centimetre cubes are in this shape?

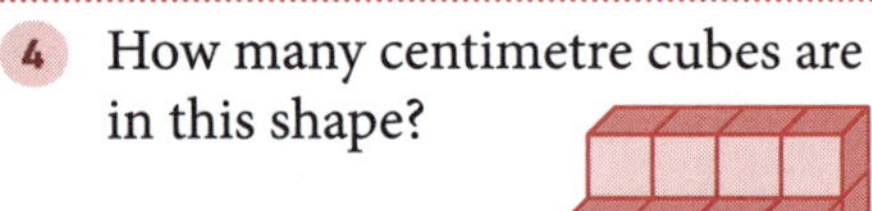

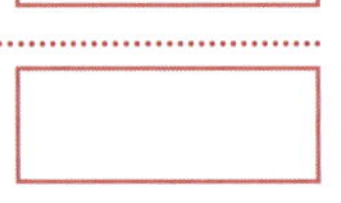

5 Circle the shape with the smallest volume.

6 Here is a jug containing juice. How much juice is in the jug?

7 A bucket is filled with water. Circle the best estimate for the capacity of the bucket.

100 mL 10 L 100 L 1000 L

8 This container holds 1 L when full. Circle the best estimate for the amount of liquid in the container.

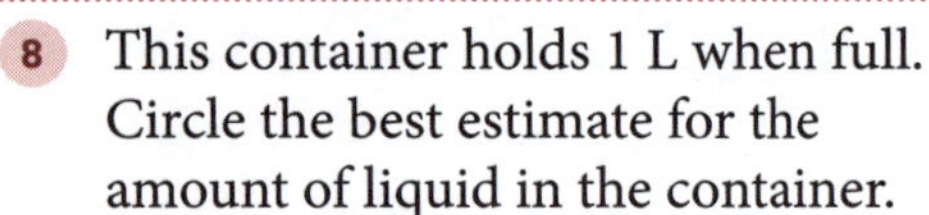

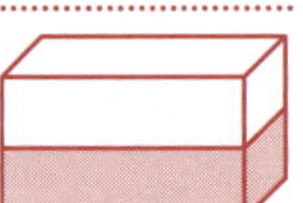

$\frac{3}{4}$ L $\frac{1}{10}$ L $\frac{1}{4}$ L $\frac{1}{2}$ L

9 A jug of water can fill four glasses. How many glasses can be filled using three jugs of water?

10 A jug containing water is shown. Circle the fraction of the jug that is filled with water.

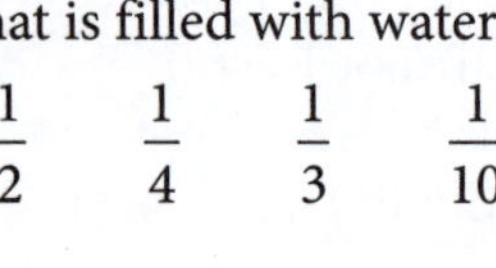

$\frac{1}{2}$ $\frac{1}{4}$ $\frac{1}{3}$ $\frac{1}{10}$

11 Cereal is sold in a box with a mass of 480 g. If Erica buys two boxes, what is the total mass of cereal?

12 Using the pan balance, what is the mass of each ball?

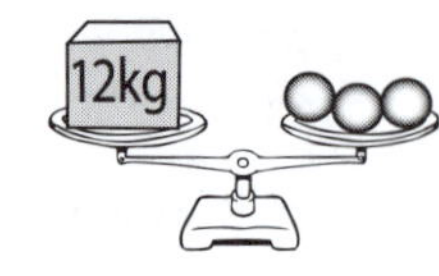

13 $\frac{1}{2}$ kg + $\frac{1}{2}$ kg = ☐ kg

14 Discs have a mass of 2 kg each. How many discs are in a total mass of 12 kg?

15 What is the total mass of these four solids?

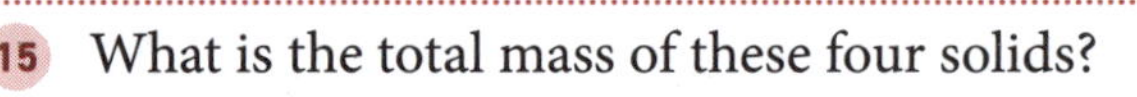

16 Circle the **four** masses that total 19 kg.

17 A cylinder has the same mass as four identical blocks.

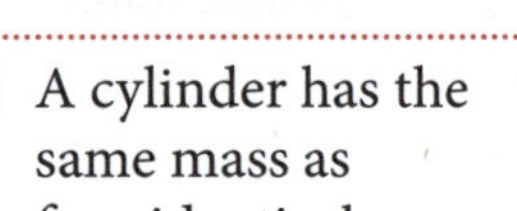

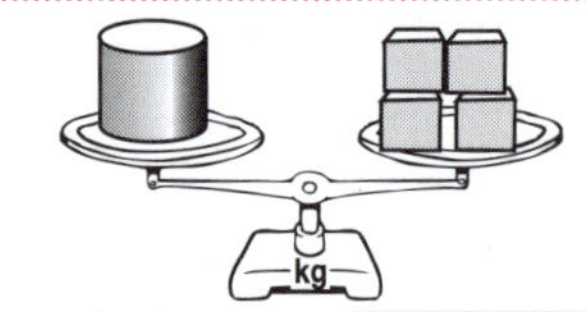

If each block has a mass of 3 kg, what is the mass of the cylinder?

18 The mass of three identical balls is measured.

What is the mass of each ball?

19 Insert < or > to make a true statement.

$1\frac{1}{2}$ kg ☐ $2\frac{1}{4}$ kg

20 What is the time written in digital form?

21 Write this time in words.

☐ minutes to ☐

22 Use the clock face to record the time of 3:42.

FOCUS ON VOLUME, CAPACITY, MASS AND TIME

1 A solid is made from identical cubes. The volume of the solid is 45 cm³. What is the volume of each cube?

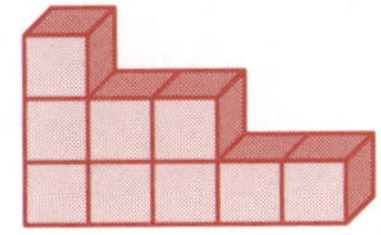

2 Khloe fills a large container using 12 buckets of water. How many buckets would half-fill the container?

3 A backyard water tank presently contains 950 L. During a storm another 600 L of water is added. How much water is now in the tank?

4 Cameron has four identical buckets each with a capacity of 10 L. He uses two full buckets and another half-full bucket to water his plants. How much water has Cameron used?

5 A restaurant purchased six bottles of olive oil. Four of the bottles contained 3 L each and the others contained 2 L each. What was the total quantity of olive oil?

6 Monty has a large container with a capacity of 48 L and a small container with a capacity of 8 L. Both containers are empty. How many small containers of water will be needed to half-fill the large container?

7 Mo has two cylinders. Cylinder A contains 6 L of water and Cylinder B is empty. Cylinder B is completely filled with water and emptied into Cylinder A. This is repeated. Cylinder A now contains 26 L of water. What is the capacity of Cylinder B?

Cylinder A Cylinder B

8 Teagan's car has 24 L of petrol in its tank. The capacity of the tank is 50 L. If Teagan fills the tank, how much petrol does she buy?

9 Taylor bought 3 kg of potatoes, 2 kg of onions and a kilogram of celery. What is the total mass of the vegetables?

10 A supermarket manager orders two cartons of boxes of washing powder. Each carton contains six boxes. Each box has a mass of 2 kg. What is the total mass of the washing powder?

11 Mark made this solid using identical cubes, each with a mass of 6 kg. What is the total mass of the solid?

12 The mass of a bag of potting mix is 15 kg. What is the mass of four bags?

13 The total mass of three boxes is 24 kg. If two of the boxes each have a mass of 7 kg, what is the mass of the other box?

14 The total mass of two identical balls is 6 kg. The mass of one of the balls and a cube is 5 kg. What is the mass of the cube?

15 Ahmad bought six bags of salt for his pool. If each bag had a mass of 20 kg, what was the total mass of salt?

16 The diagram shows two identical cylinders and five identical blocks.

If a cylinder has a mass of 10 kg, what is the mass of three blocks?

17 Nadia has a mass of 47 kg. Her father has a mass 5 kg less than twice her mass. What is the mass of Nadia's father?

18 A bus is due at the time shown on the clock. The bus is late and does not arrive until half past 9. How many minutes is the bus late?

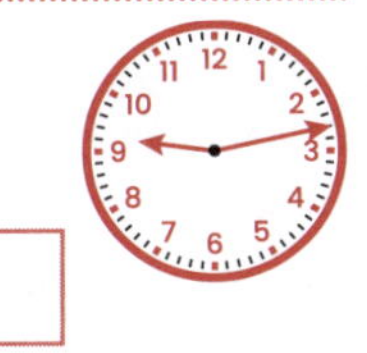

19 Here are the start and finish times for a NAPLAN practice test.

Start time

Finish time

How much time was allowed for the test?

20 Xavier's dental appointment commenced at a quarter to 11 and finished at 20 past 11. How long was the appointment?

FOCUS ON 3D SHAPES

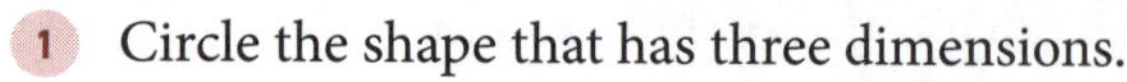

1 Circle the shape that has three dimensions.

square   cone   parallelogram

2 Circle the shape that is **not** three-dimensional.

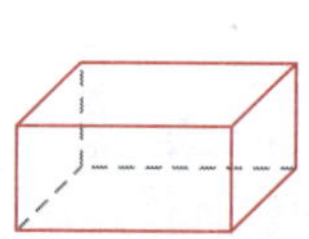 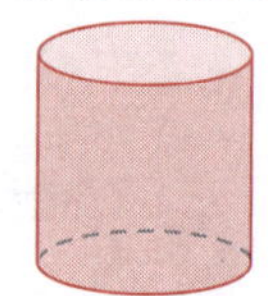 

3 In the space, draw a cone.

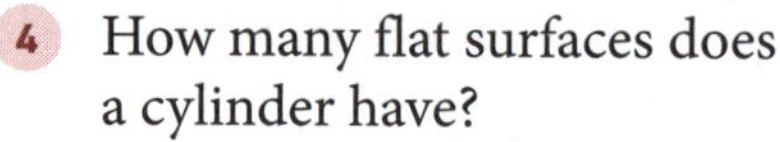

4 How many flat surfaces does a cylinder have?

5 How many curved surfaces does a cone have?

6 Circle the pyramid.

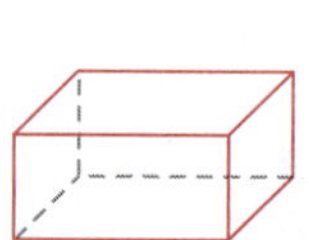 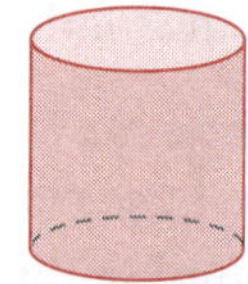 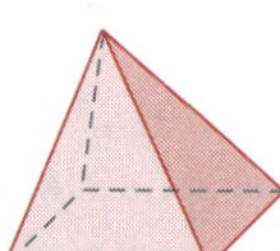

7 Circle the object that is a sphere.

ball   box   can

8 How many faces does a triangular prism have?

9 What 3D shape is formed using this net?

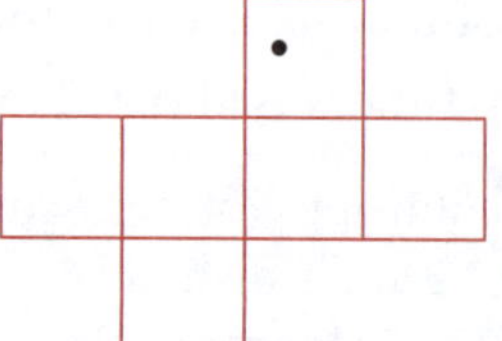

10 Circle a shape that can be seen in the net of a cone.

rectangle   square   circle   ellipse

11 How many faces does a hexagonal prism have?

12 What 3D shape is formed using this net?

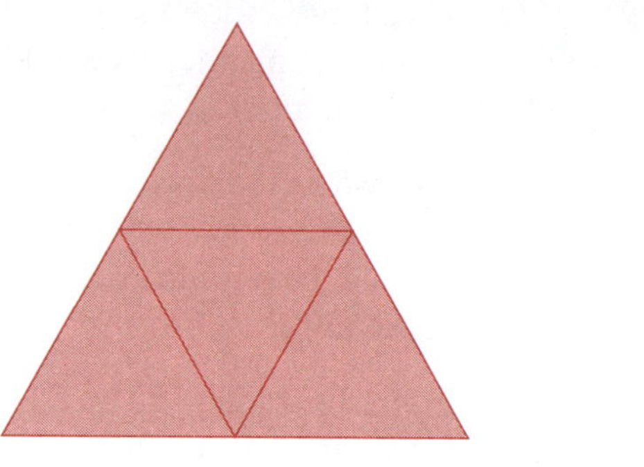

13 Circle the shape that is **not** the net of a cube.

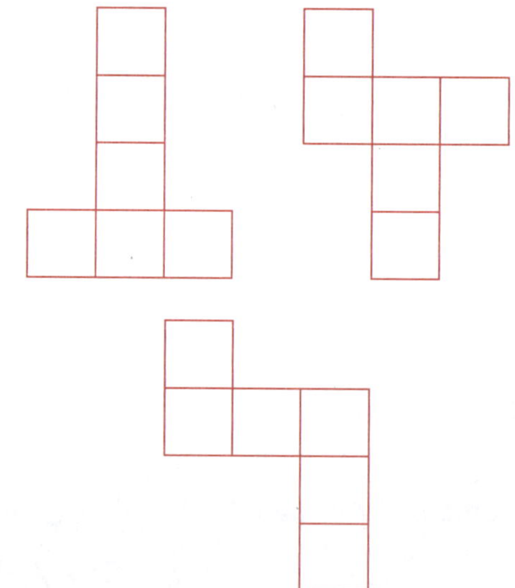

14 What shape is the base of a cylinder?

15 How many edges has a rectangular prism?

16 The opposite sides of a dice add to 7. What number is on the opposite face to 5?

17 How many triangles has the net of a hexagonal pyramid?

FOCUS ON 3D SHAPES

1 Emma placed a cube on the floor and looked at it from above. What shape is the top of the cube?

2 Paul picked up a can of tomatoes. He rolled the can across the kitchen floor. When it stopped rolling, he looked down on the can. What 2D shape did he see?

3 Ms Reynolds pretends to be a shape. She gives these clues:

- I have three dimensions.
- I have one curved surface.
- I have no flat surfaces.

What shape is she pretending to be?

4 James removed the label from a tin of beans. What shape is the label?

5 Lucas looked at a pyramid. One of the faces is a square. How many triangular faces does the pyramid have?

6 Camilla used a piece of paper to make a rectangular prism. She numbered each face with consecutive numbers starting at 1. What is the highest number used?

7 Alec painted this 3D shape. How many faces did Alec paint?

8 Layla looked at a 3D shape. From all directions she saw a circle. What is the name of the shape?

9 Ilena drew a net of a cube where opposite faces add to the same number. What is the missing number marked with *?

1		
2	3	
	4	*

10 The area of the circular face on the top of a cylinder is 40 cm^2. What is the area of the circle on the bottom of the cylinder?

11 This net is used to form a 3D shape. How many edges does the 3D shape have?

12 Angie uses clay to make a rectangular prism. She then cuts off one of the corners. How many faces does the new shape have?

13 How many more faces has a square prism than a square pyramid?

14 Mingli made a cube. The area of the top face is 5 cm^2. What is the total area of all the faces?

15 Alissa has 12 sticks. She uses the sticks to make a prism. Four of the sticks are 6 cm long, four sticks are 5 cm long and the others are 4 cm long. What shape is the base of the prism?

Here is a net on centimetre grid paper. Use it to answer questions 16, 17, 18 and 19.

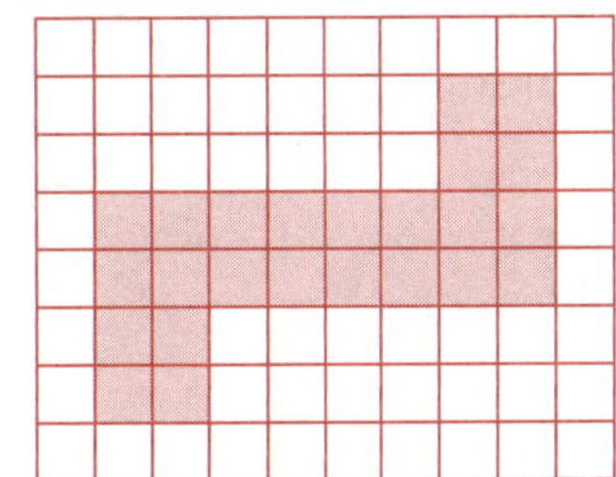

16 What is the area of the net?

17 What 3D shape is formed using the net?

18 When the net forms a 3D shape, what is the area of each face?

19 What is the total length of the edges of the 3D shape?

20 Ben subtracted the number of faces on a hexagonal prism from the number of faces on an octagonal pyramid. What was Ben's answer?

21 Isa drew the net of a square pyramid. The area of the square is 12 cm^2 and the area of each triangle is 8 cm^2. What is the total area of the faces of the pyramid?

22 Ajit noted that a triangle has 3 sides and a triangular prism has 5 faces. He also observed that a square has 4 sides and a square prism has 6 faces. The same pattern applies to a decagon and a decagonal prism. How many faces does a decagonal prism have?

FOCUS ON 2D SHAPES AND ANGLES

1 Circle the shapes that are quadrilaterals.

   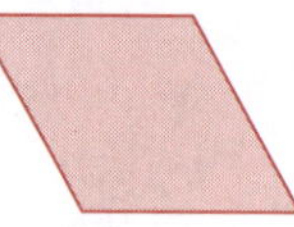

2 How many of these shapes are two-dimensional?

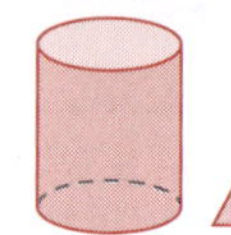  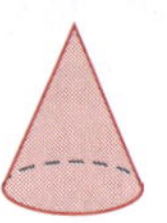 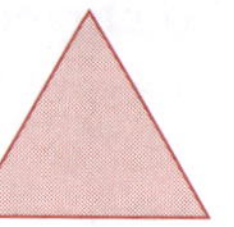

3 How many pairs of parallel sides are in a trapezium?

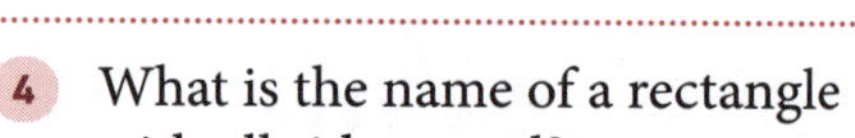

4 What is the name of a rectangle with all sides equal?

5 True or false?
All rhombuses are parallelograms.

6 Circle the name of the regular quadrilateral.

rectangle trapezium hexagon square

7 Which of these shapes has exactly eight sides?

quadrilateral octagon pentagon decagon

8 How many angles are inside a pentagon?

9 The angles inside a regular shape

are ________.

10 Circle the shape that contains a right angle.

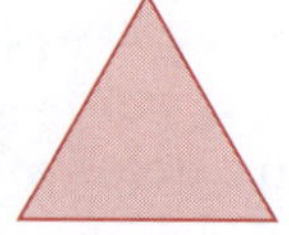 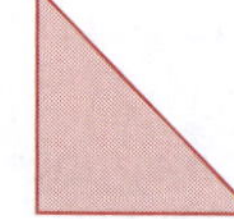 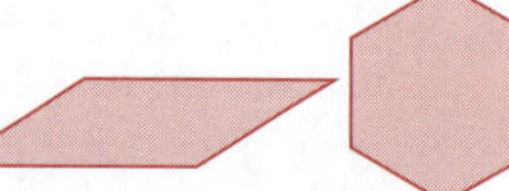

11 Which angle (A, B or C) is the largest?

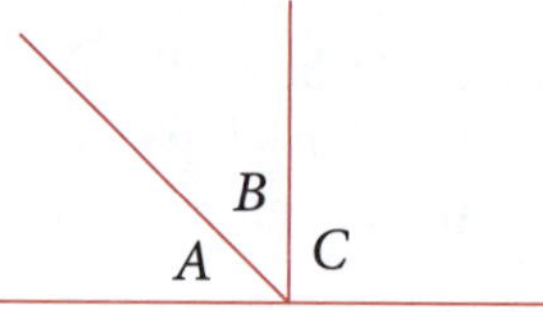

12 The diagram shows perpendicular lines.

How many right angles can be seen?

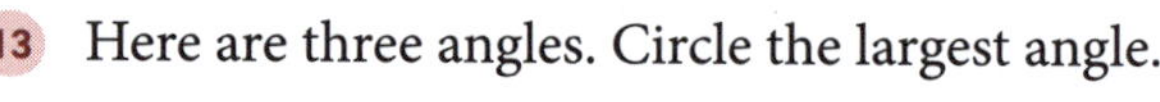

13 Here are three angles. Circle the largest angle.

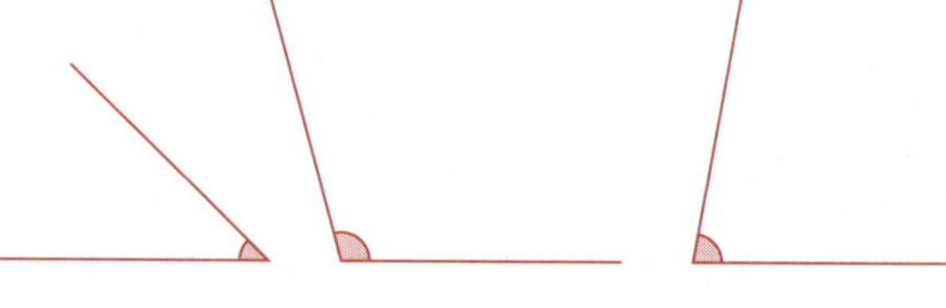

14 How many of these letters have perpendicular lines?

T O L W H

15 How many of these letters have parallel lines?

K H M A I

16 How many of these shapes have at least one pair of parallel sides?

square regular pentagon
trapezium triangle

17 Here are three lines. The two parallel lines are perpendicular to the third line.
How many right angles can be seen?

FOCUS ON 2D SHAPES AND ANGLES

1 Use a straight line to cut the rectangle into a triangle and a trapezium.

2 Use a straight line to cut the hexagon into two pentagons.

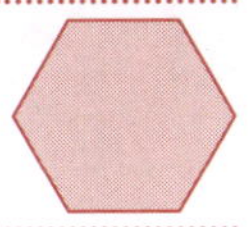

3 Draw a pentagon with two right angles.

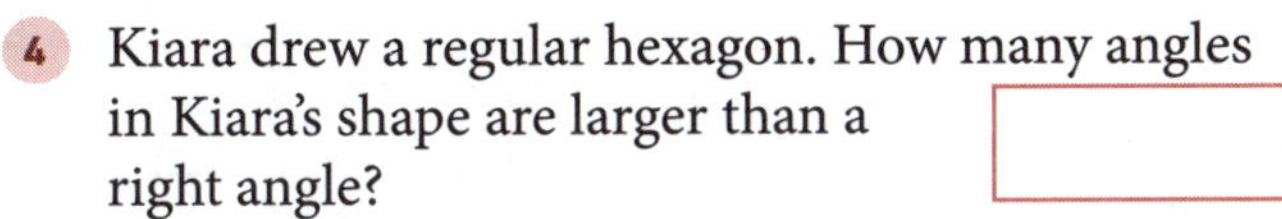

4 Kiara drew a regular hexagon. How many angles in Kiara's shape are larger than a right angle?

Tayla uses a centimetre grid to draw a rectangle. Use it to answer questions 5, 6 and 7.

5 Complete Tayla's rectangle.

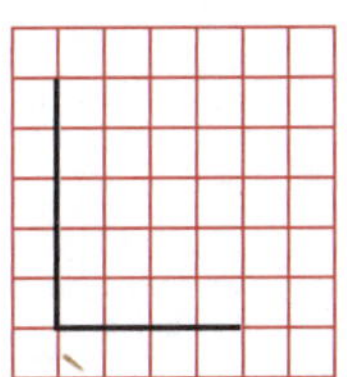
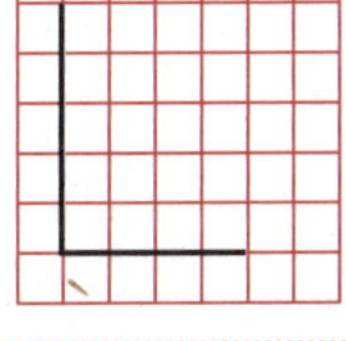

6 What is the area of Tayla's rectangle?

7 What is the distance around the outside of Tayla's rectangle?

Oscar uses a centimetre grid to draw a rhombus, which is used to answer questions 8 and 9.

8 Complete Oscar's rhombus.

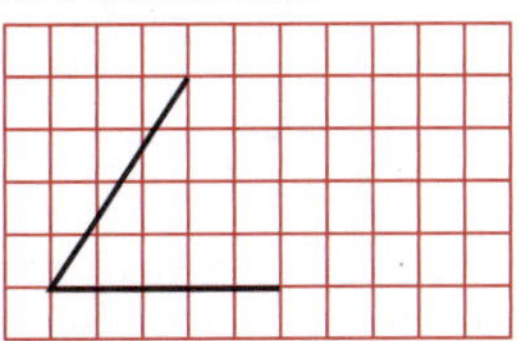

9 What is the distance around the outside of Oscar's rhombus?

10 Callie drew a sequence of shapes.

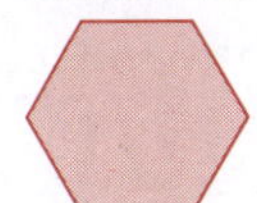

?

What is the next shape?

Sienna uses a centimetre grid to draw an irregular hexagon. Use it to answer questions 11 to 14.

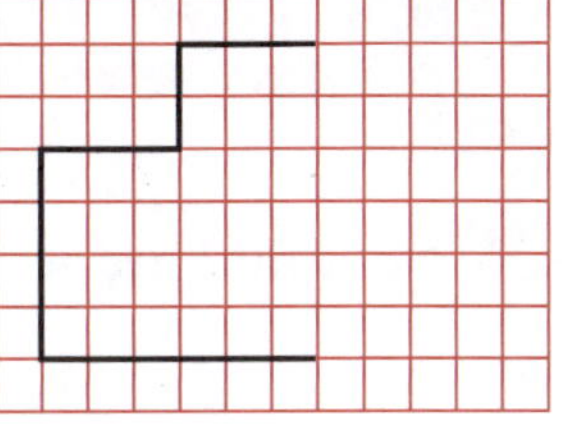

11 Complete Sienna's hexagon.

12 What is the area of Sienna's hexagon?

13 What is the distance around the outside of Sienna's hexagon?

14 How many right angles are inside the completed hexagon?

15 Rhiannon drew a pentagon. What is the highest possible number of right angles inside the shape?

16 The hands on an analog clock make angles. What size is the angle between the hands at 9:00?

17 Thomas drew a regular octagon. How many pairs of parallel sides are on his shape?

18 The time on an analog clock is 7 o'clock. The hour hand moves through a right angle. What is the new time?

19 Angus used a protractor to prove that a right angle measures exactly 90°. Angus drew a rectangle. What is the total of the angles in a rectangle?

20 Kristie drew a quadrilateral which has a pair of opposite sides equal and parallel. What does she notice about the other two sides?

21 Draw a quadrilateral which has exactly three angles that are less than a right angle.

22 The time showing on an analog clock is 10 past 7. If the minute hand moves through an angle of 90°, what is the new time, in digital form?

FOCUS ON SYMMETRY AND POSITION

1 Draw the lines of symmetry on the rectangle.

2 How many lines of symmetry does a square have?

3 Circle the letter(s) which has/have exactly one line of symmetry.

A E I O U

4 Draw the line(s) of symmetry on the shape.

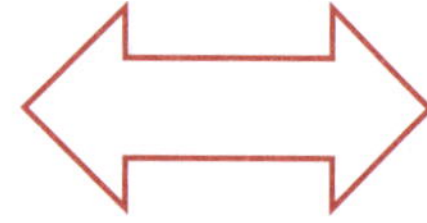

5 Circle the shape(s) with more than one line of symmetry.

6 Shade the squares so that the dotted line is a line of symmetry.

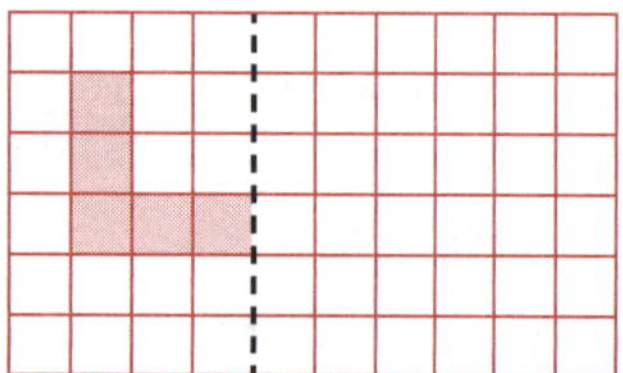

7 Draw the other half of the figure below using the vertical line of symmetry.

8 Complete the diagram if the dotted line is a line of symmetry.

The grid is used to answer questions 9 and 10.

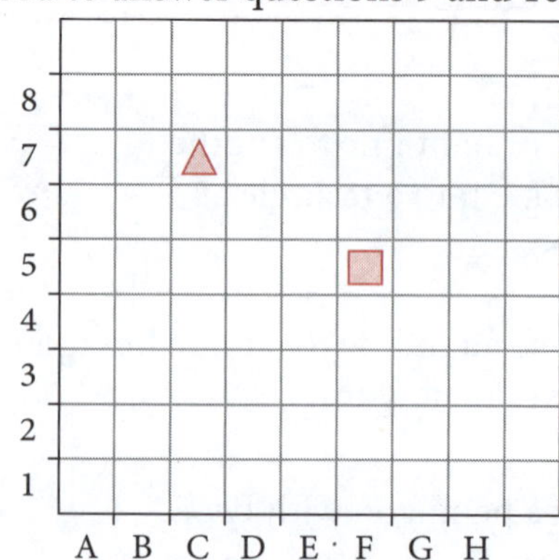

9 A triangle is located at C7. What is the location of the square?

10 Place a circle in H3.

11 From C2, move up 4 squares and then left 2 squares. What is the new location?

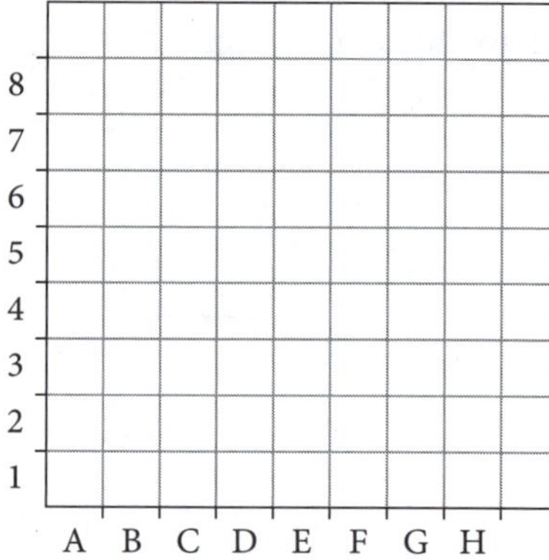

The grid below is used to answer questions 12 and 13.

12 Point *P* is located on the grid.

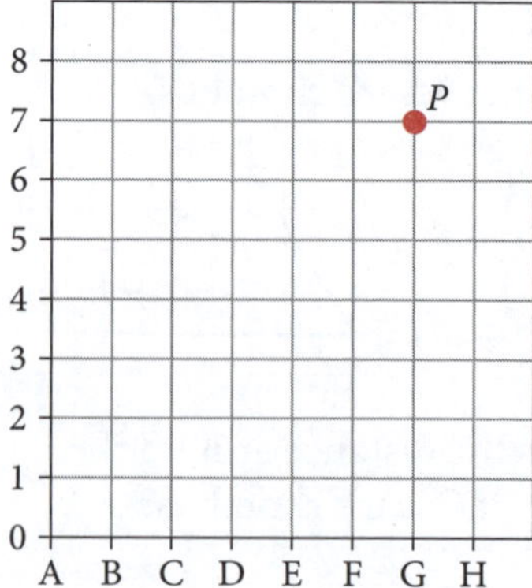

From *P*, move left 3 units, down 5 units and left 1 unit. What is the location of the destination?

13 What is the length of the line joining B3 and F3, in units?

FOCUS ON SYMMETRY AND POSITION

1. Cedric wrote his name using capital letters. How many letters had at least one line of symmetry?

2. Dimitri drew a regular hexagon. How many lines of symmetry does the shape have?

3. Joachim used the grid to draw a shape. Part of the shape is drawn.

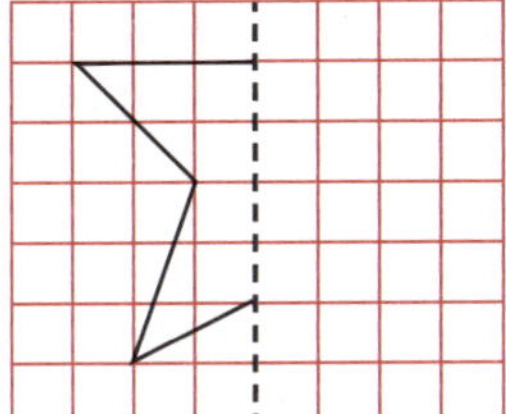

If the dotted line is a line of symmetry of the completed shape, how many sides does Joachim's shape have?

4. Elsie draws a regular triangle. How many lines of symmetry does Elsie's shape have?

5. Dorothy draws a quadrilateral with four equal sides. The shape has exactly two lines of symmetry. What shape did Dorothy draw?

6. Bianca uses a grid to shade squares.

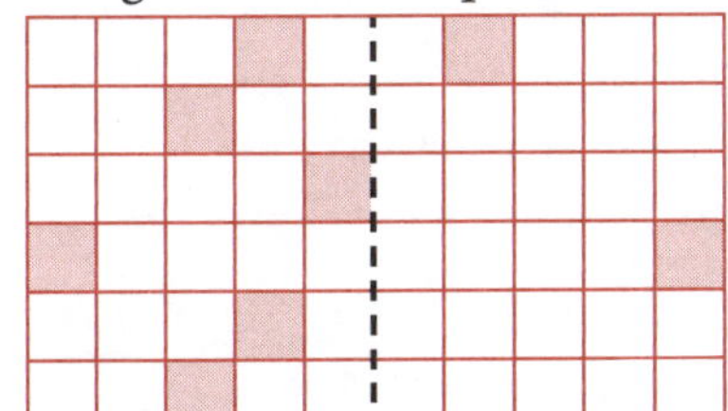

The dotted line is to be a line of symmetry. How many more squares should she shade?

7. John draws a logo in the shape of a rectangle inside a regular octagon, which is inside a circle.

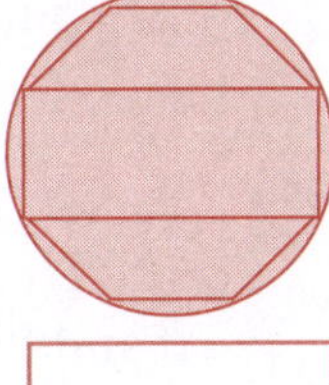

How many lines of symmetry does the logo have?

8. Freya has drawn a regular octagon. She has drawn three lines of symmetry on the shape. How many more lines of symmetry can be drawn on the shape?

9. Robert drew this shape on a grid. The horizontal line is to be a line of symmetry.

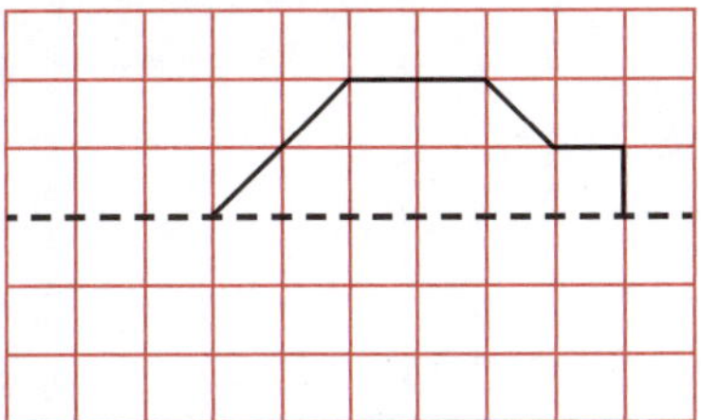

Complete the shape.

10. Larry has started to shade some squares on the diagram. He wants the finished shape to have four lines of symmetry.

What is the smallest number of squares to be shaded?

11. Haydn drew a diagram with five circles. He can add circles to the right of the shape. What is the smallest number of circles he can draw so that the diagram has a vertical line of symmetry?

12. Damon starts to shade squares on this grid.

When finished there will be two lines of symmetry.

How many more squares does Damon shade?

13. The shape is translated 3 units to the left.

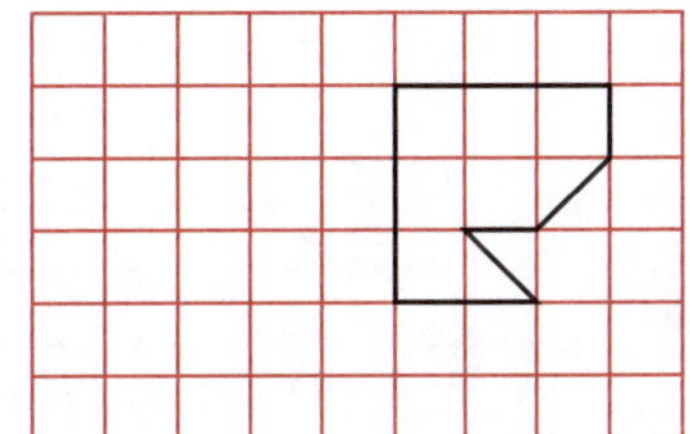

Draw the image of the new shape.

14 The arrow represents the location on a grid of Sharne's toy car.

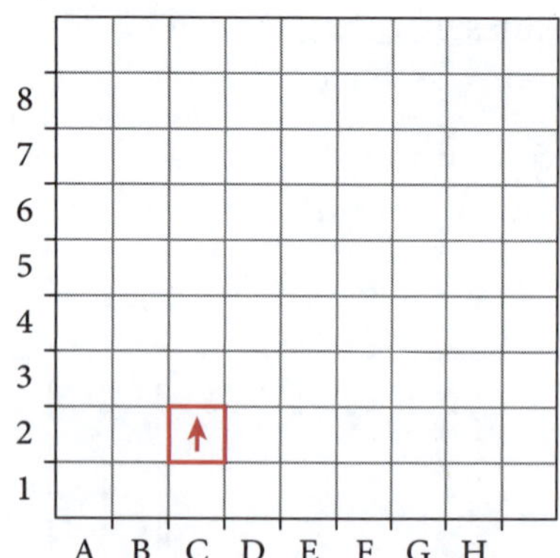

She moves the car forward 4 squares. She turns the car to the left and moves it 1 square. She then reverses the car 5 squares. What is the location of the car now?

15 Tom turns left out of school and takes the second street on his left. He walks to the end of the street and turns right. What does he see on his left?

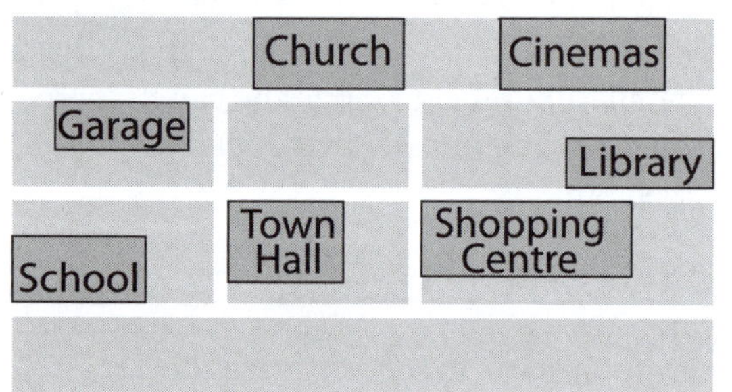

16 Denis locates 3 points on the grid.

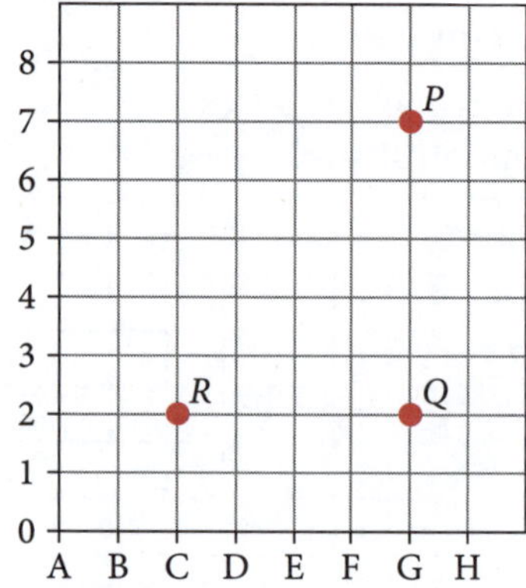

He locates the point S on the grid and the four dots form a rectangle. How many units is the point S from the point P?

17 The shape is to be reflected about the dotted line.

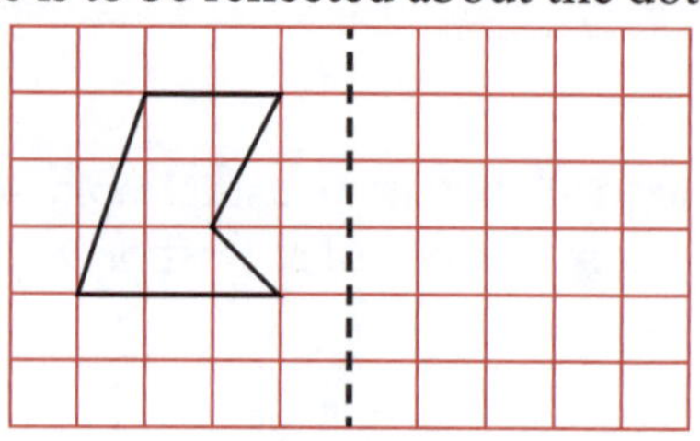

Draw the image of the shape.

18 In a class photo Toby is standing in the middle of the middle row. There are three students on his left. There are fewer than 30 students in the class and each of the rows has the same number of students. How many students are in the class photo?

The map is used to answer questions 19 to 22.

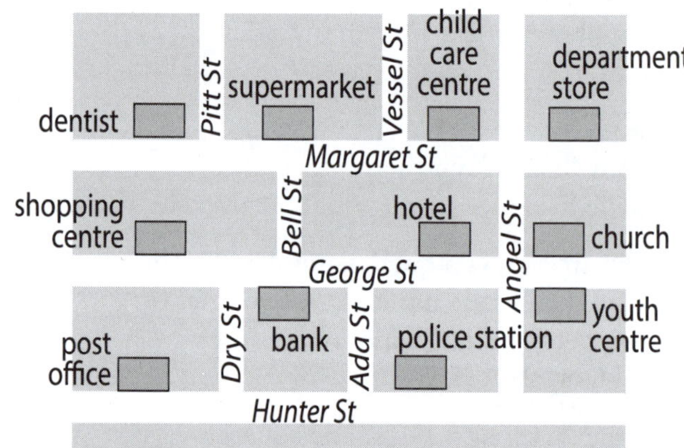

19 Bernard walked directly from the bank to the church. On what street did Bernard walk?

20 Aaron is walking in Dry Street then turns right into George Street. What is the second street he passes?

21 Chelsea left the department store and turned right. She then took the second street on her left. At the end of that street, she turned left. What is the first building she passed on her left?

22 Zane left the dentist, walked past the child care centre, turned right, then right again, left and then left. What is on his left?

FOCUS ON

DATA AND CHANCE

1 How many outcomes are possible when a coin is tossed?

2 When a normal dice is rolled, how many outcomes are less than 3?

This spinner is used to answer questions 3 and 4.

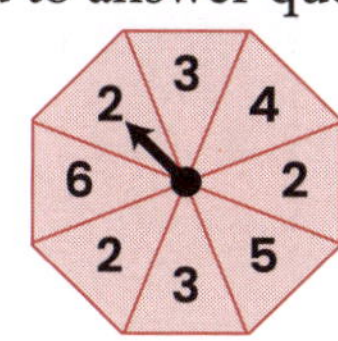

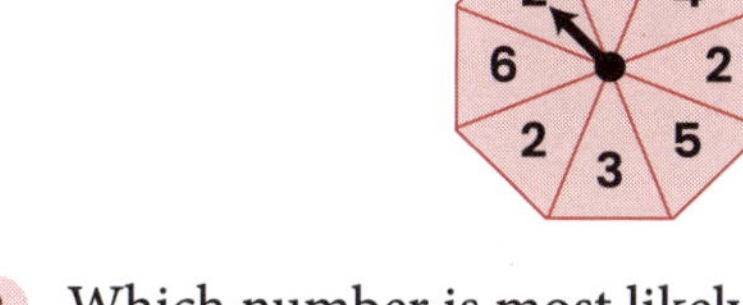

3 Which number is most likely to be spun?

4 Circle the numbers that would be impossible for the arrow to point to.

1 3 5 7

Students were asked about their favourite snacks and the results are shown in a table. This data is used to answer questions 5 to 7.

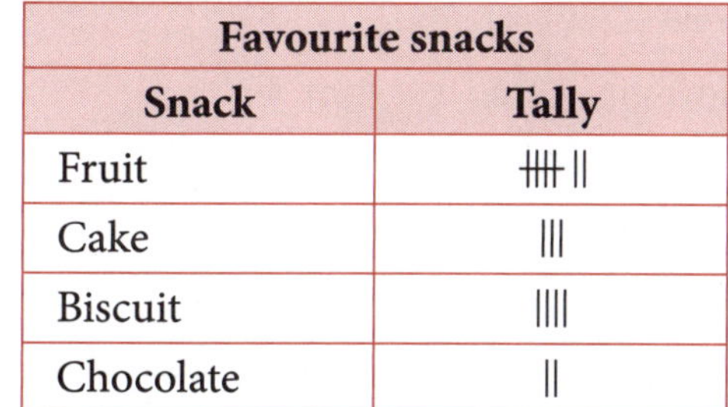

Favourite snacks	
Snack	**Tally**
Fruit	卌 ||
Cake	|||
Biscuit	||||
Chocolate	||

5 How many students said their favourite snack was chocolate?

6 What was the most popular snack?

7 What was the total number of students?

Students were asked about their favourite primary colour. The results are shown in the graph which is used to answer questions 8 to 10.

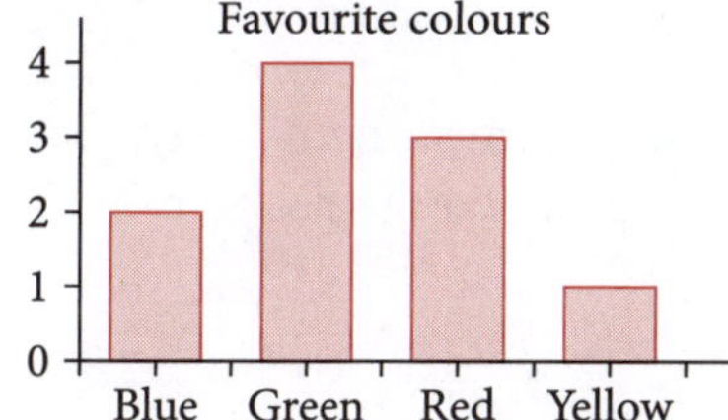

8 How many students said red?

9 What colour was favoured by two students?

10 What was the least favourite colour?

The graph shows the number of balls found in a school's storage cupboard. The graph is used to answer questions 11 to 13.

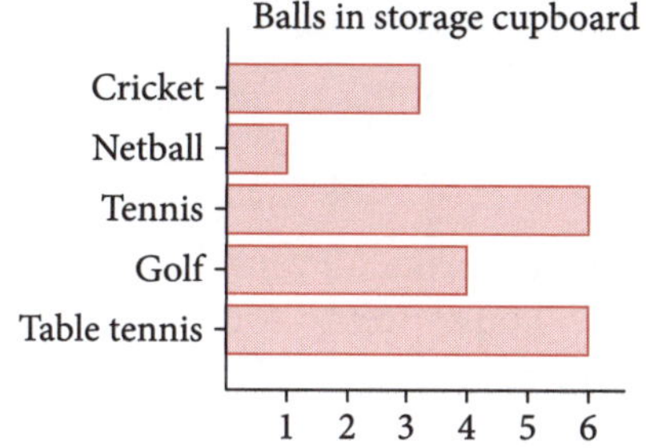

11 How many golf balls were in the cupboard?

12 The cupboard contained ______ tennis balls.

13 What was the total number of cricket balls and netballs?

The dot plot shows the number of cars sold on each day of the week. The graph is used to answer questions 14 to 16.

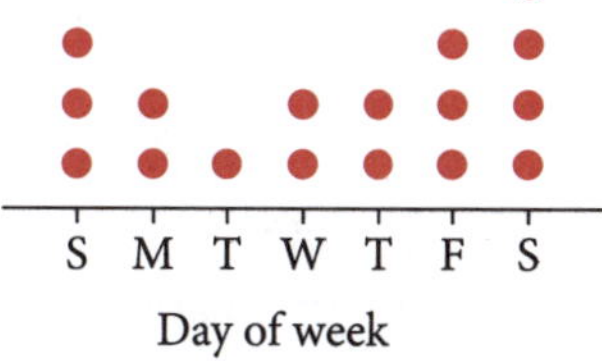

14 How many cars were sold on Friday?

15 On what day was the highest number of cars sold?

16 What was the total number of cars sold on Tuesday and Wednesday?

DATA AND CHANCE

A normal dice is numbered 1 to 6 and is used to answer questions 1 and 2.

1 Olivia rolls the dice once. Circle the outcome which is least likely.

rolling a number less than 3

rolling an even number

rolling a 5

2 John rolls the dice 30 times. About how many times will he expect to roll an odd number?

3 A box contains blue, green and white balls. A ball is chosen at random from the box. The chance that it is blue is twice the chance that it is green. It is equally likely that it is green as it is white. If there are four white balls in the box, what is the total number of balls?

4 A bag contains 12 balls coloured red, green and purple. There are six red balls and four green balls. A ball is taken at random from the bag. Which coloured ball is the least likely to be selected?

5

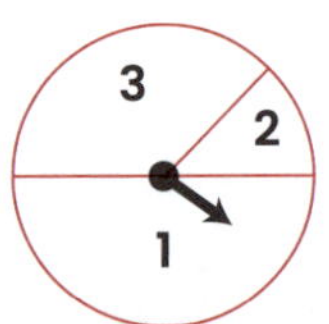

The arrow on this spinner is spun and stops on 1. The arrow is spun again and stops on 2. If the arrow is spun a third time, which number is the arrow most likely to stop on?

The diagram shows a box of balls which are coloured red (*R*), blue (*B*) or green (*G*) and is used to answer questions 6 and 7.

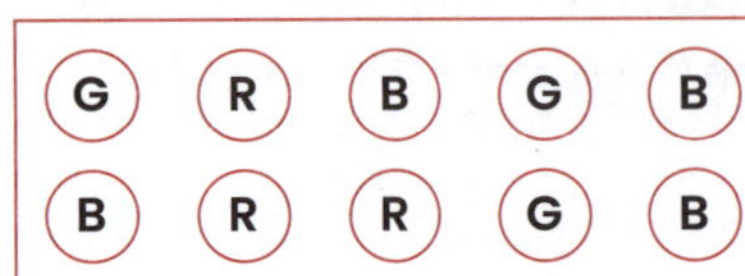

6 Which coloured ball is the most likely to be chosen?

7 Two blue balls and a green ball are removed from the box. Which coloured ball is now the most likely to be chosen?

A group of students were surveyed to find their favourite sport. The graph is used to answer questions 8 to 10.

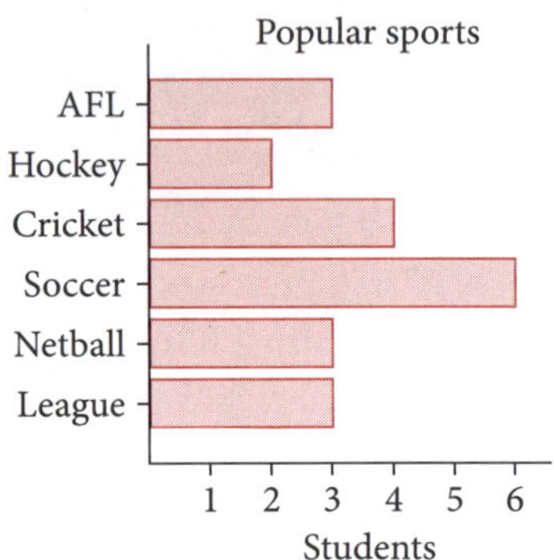

8 What was the second most popular sport?

9 How many more students liked soccer than hockey?

10 How many students were surveyed?

A group of Year 3 students were surveyed to find their favourite colour.

Favourite colours	
Colours	**Students**
pink	𝍸
purple	𝍸 |
red	||||
yellow	||
blue	|||

The results are shown in the table which is used to answer questions 11 to 13.

11 How many students were surveyed?

12 How many more students liked purple or pink, compared to red or blue?

13 Jake said 'More than half the students liked either pink or purple'. Is he correct?

The way students came to school on Tuesday is recorded on the graph. Use the graph to answer questions 14 to 17.

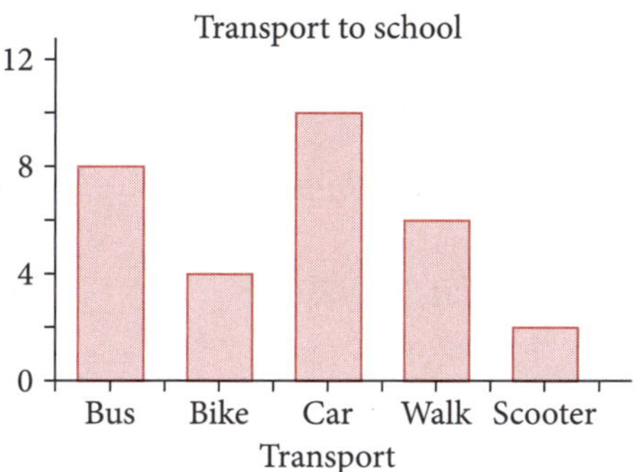

14 How many more students travelled by car than walked?

15 Which method of transport did 22 students **not** use to travel to school?

16 Three students who travelled by car on Tuesday caught the bus on Wednesday. How many students on Wednesday walked or travelled by car?

17 On Friday, half the students who travelled by bus on Tuesday and all the Tuesday bike riders walked to school. The students who walked on Tuesday also walked on Friday. What was the total number of students who walked to school on Friday?

The number of laps of a swimming pool swum by a group of students is recorded in the dot plot. Questions 18 to 21 use the data in the graph.

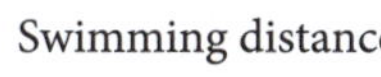

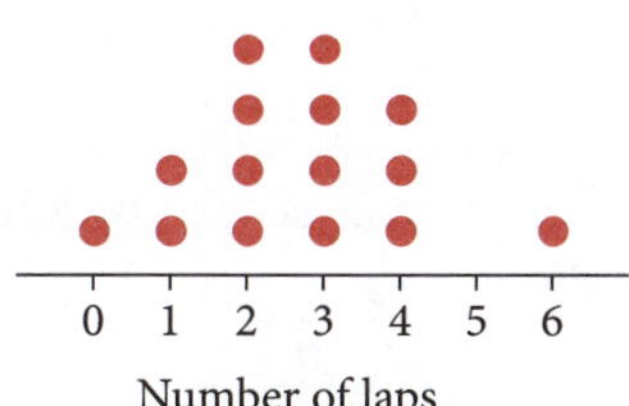

18 How many students are in the group?

19 How many students swam at least 2 laps?

20 Each lap of the pool is 50 metres. Jake swam the most laps of the group. What was the distrance swum by Jake?

21 What was the total number of laps swum?

The number of adults and children on a bus each morning is recorded in the graphs. Questions 22 to 26 use the data in the graphs.

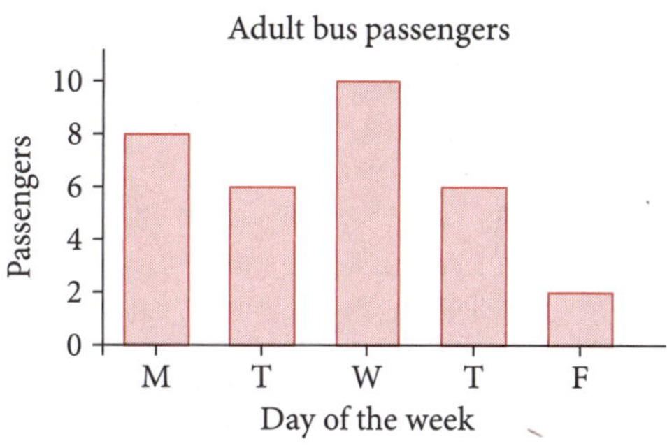

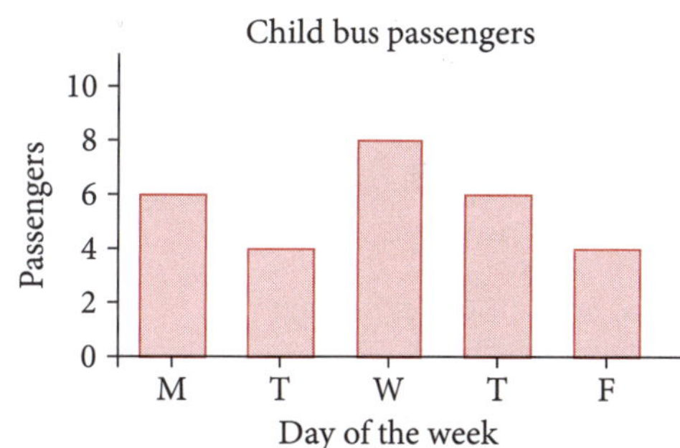

22 What was the total number of passengers on Wednesday?

23 On which day were there more children than adults?

24 On how many days were there more than four children on the bus?

25 What was the total number of adult passengers on the bus during the week?

26 On what day were there 12 passengers on the bus?

NUMBER AND ALGEBRA

1 Here are the ages of four cousins:

12 9 17 11

What is the age of the youngest cousin?

2 Lukas added 5, 3, 7 and 2. What was the total?

3 Kai is 12 years old. He is 4 years older than his brother Mo. How old is Mo?

4 On each of four plates, Lucy arranged three cakes. What was the total number of cakes?

5 Brianna has eight buttons. She arranges the buttons into two rows. How many buttons are in each row?

6 Shade two-thirds of the shape.

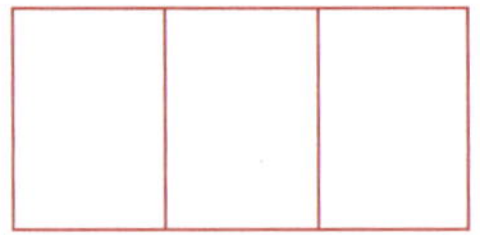

7 Matilda has three 20-cent coins and a 10-cent coin. What is the total amount of money?

8 What is the next number?

10, 14, 18, 22, 

MEASUREMENT AND SPACE

9 Ben used a ruler to measure the length of a pencil.

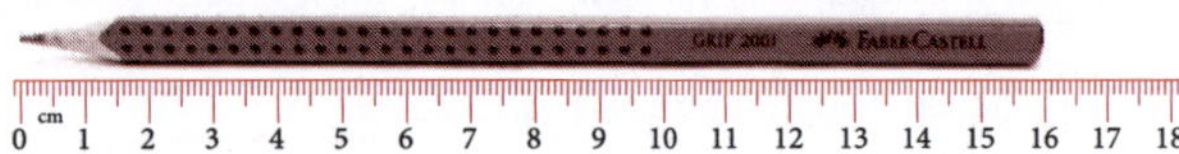

What is the length in centimetres?

10 A bucket can hold 10 L of water. Marin fills two buckets with water. What is the total amount of water?

11 Circle the three fruits with a mass less than 1 kg.

peach watermelon apple grape

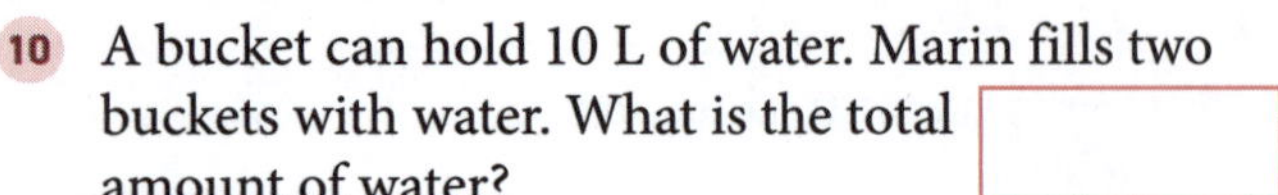

12 Complete the time.

 past 9

13 How many faces does a rectangular prism have?

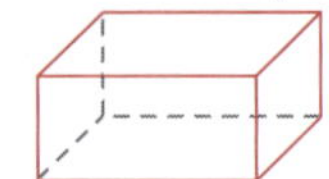

14 Circle the name of a four-sided polygon.

triangle quadrilateral hexagon

15 Circle the bigger angle.

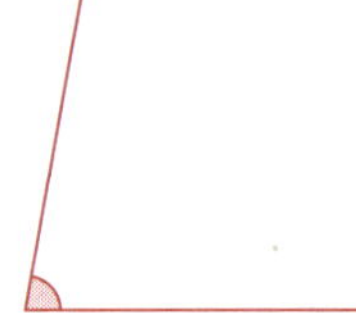

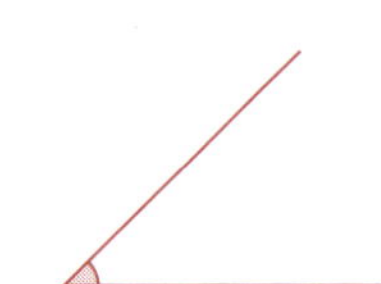

16 Shape A has been translated to the right to be named Shape B.

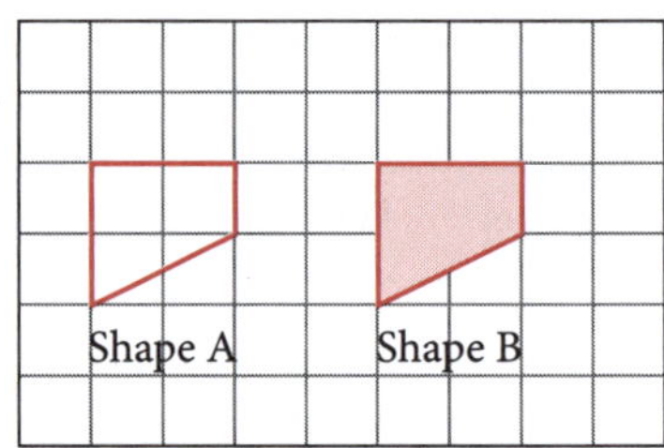

How many units has Shape A been translated?

STATISTICS AND PROBABILITY

17 Circle the event that is certain.

Tomorrow the sun will rise.

This weekend Macy's netball team will win.

18 The number of goals scored by a team in a soccer match is shown.

How many goals were scored

NUMBER AND ALGEBRA

1 Reeve wrote these four numbers.
Circle the largest number.

1067 1076 1760 1706

2 Carol has two stacks of cards. One stack has 12 cards and the other has 18. What is the total number of cards?

3 Zoe and Chloe used beads to make necklaces. Zoe used 22 beads and Chloe 38 beads. How many more beads did Chloe use?

4 Jenna added these numbers.

5 5 5 5

What was her total?

5 Georgia has 30 balls. She arranges them into three rows. How many balls are in each row?

6 Shade two-thirds of the shape.

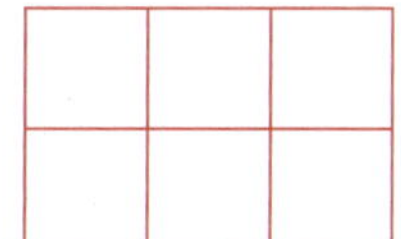

7 Hudson has $2.65. He wants to buy a $3 carton of chocolate milk. How much money does he need to borrow?

8 What is the missing number?

?, 10, 16, 22, 28

MEASUREMENT AND SPACE

9 Ben used a ruler to measure the length of a pen.

What is the length in centimetres?

10 A container holds 40 L of water. Silas pours enough water into the container so that it is half full. How many litres of water are in the container?

11 How many grams are in 2 kg?

12 How many minutes are there until 10 o'clock?

13 How many faces does a hexagonal prism have?

14 Isaac drew a triangle, a quadrilateral, a hexagon and an octagon. What was the total number of sides drawn?

15 Here is a statement: 'These angles are the same size'. Is the statement true or false?

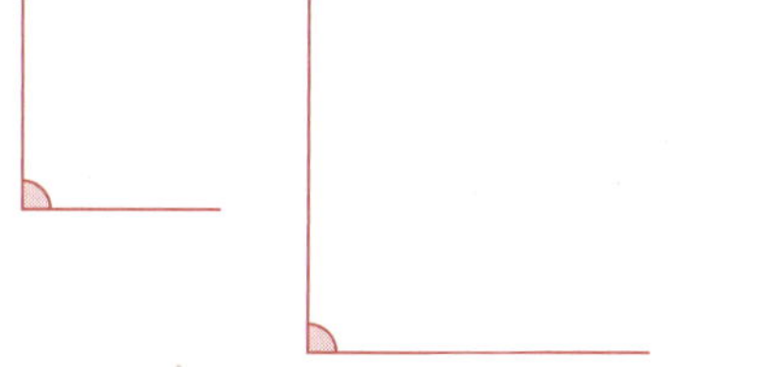

16 The unshaded shape is translated to the right. The image has been shaded.

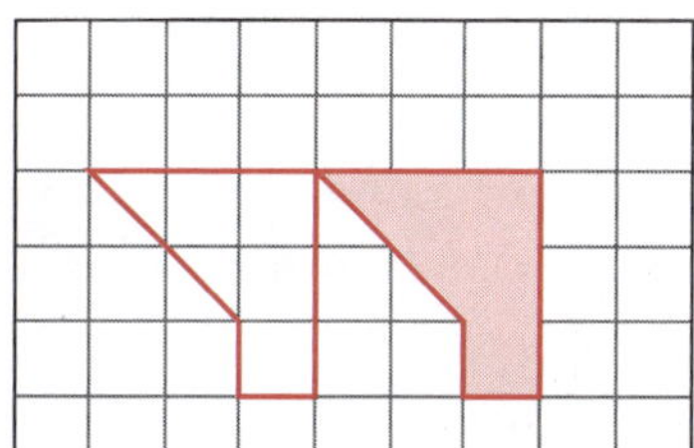

How many units has the unshaded shape been translated?

STATISTICS AND PROBABILITY

17 Circle the event that is **not** certain.

The traffic light will be green.

Lachie will get wet when he jumps in his swimming pool.

18 The number of goals scored by a team in a netball match is shown.

𝍸 𝍸 𝍸 𝍸 ||||

How many goals were scored?

NUMBER AND ALGEBRA

1 Edie wrote the number 6729. What digit is in the hundreds place?

2 There are 11 adults and 13 children on a bus. What is the total number of passengers?

3 There are 23 students enrolled in a class. Today four students are absent from class. How many students are present in class?

4 Every morning Liz walks 4 km. How far has she walked in 6 days?

5 Fifteen cows are divided evenly into three paddocks. How many cows are in each paddock?

6 What fraction of the circles are shaded?

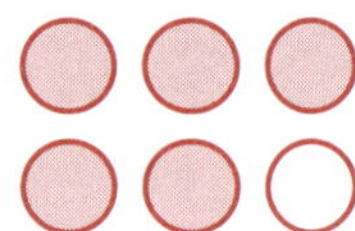

7 Liam has six 10-cent coins. What is the total value of money?

8 What is the next number?

4, 12, 20, 28, ?

MEASUREMENT AND SPACE

9 Mila drew this line on a centimetre grid.

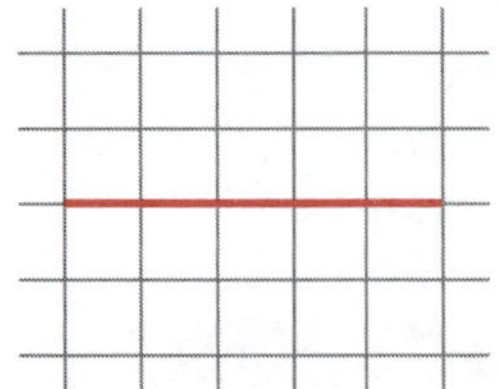

What is the length of the line in centimetres?

10 Circle the container with a capacity of about 200 mL.

drinking glass kitchen sink medicine cup

11 Rice is sold in 1-kg bags. What is the mass of four bags of rice?

12 Complete the time.

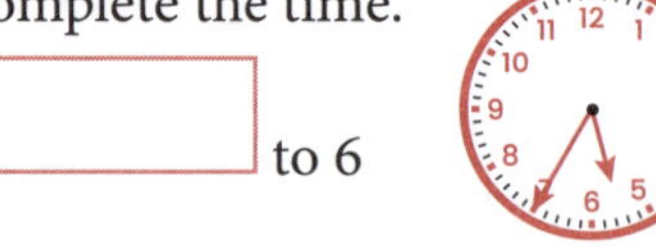

____ to 6

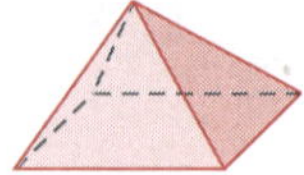

13 How many faces does this pyramid have?

14 Circle the shape(s) with two pairs of parallel opposite sides.

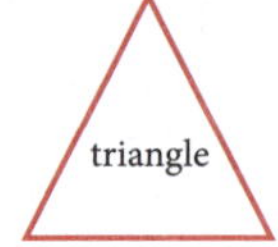

rectangle square triangle

15 Circle the angles that are more than a right angle.

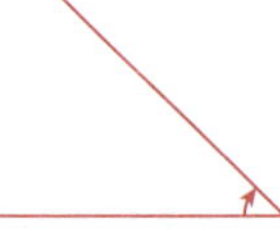

16 A triangle is located at B4.

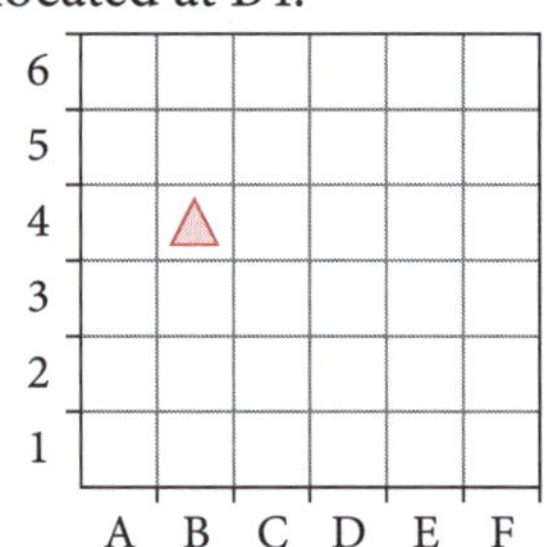

Draw a circle at E6.

STATISTICS AND PROBABILITY

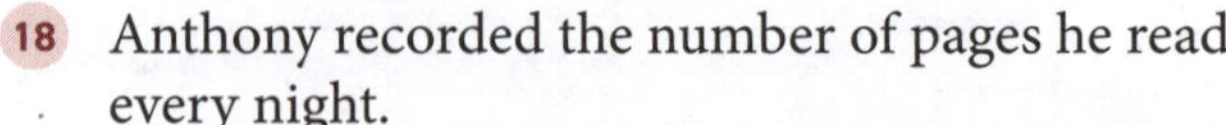

17 Ned tosses a fair coin. What are the two possible outcomes?

18 Anthony recorded the number of pages he read every night.

Pages read each day		
Day	**Tally**	**Number**
Monday	|||	3
Tuesday	||	
Wednesday	~~||||~~	

Finish the table by writing the numbers for the other two days.

NUMBER AND ALGEBRA

1 Callum formed a number with a 6 in the tens place. There was a 9 in the thousands place and 0 in the hundreds place. Which of these could be Callum's number?

960 6902 9063 9601

2 William ran 6 km on Monday and Wednesday mornings. He ran 8 km on Friday and Saturday afternoons. On the other days he rested. How far did he run in the week?

3 There are 28 apartments in a new building. If 16 apartments are already sold, how many are yet to sell?

4 Bailey gave five balls to each of four friends. How many balls did he give away?

5 James has 16 shoes in his closet. He arranges the shoes in pairs. How many pairs of shoes does James have?

6 What fraction of the circles are **not** shaded?

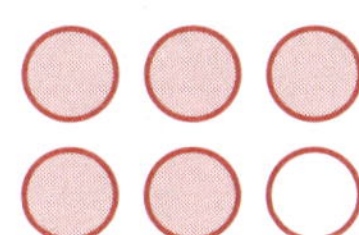

7 How many 10-cent coins total $1.30?

8 What is the missing number?

?, 36, 45, 54, 63

MEASUREMENT AND SPACE

9 Grandpa's index finger is 80 mm long. His little finger is 65 mm long. How much longer is his index finger than his little finger?

10 Ezra buys three containers of milk. Each container holds 2 L. What is the total amount of milk?

11 On New Year's Eve, Chris bought eight bags of ice from the service station. If the mass of each bag was 5 kg, what was the total mass of ice?

12 How many minutes are there since 5 o'clock?

13 Jackson made a pyramid with a square base. How many triangular faces does the pyramid have?

14 Circle the regular shape(s).

rhombus rectangle square

15 Circle the angles that are more than a right angle.

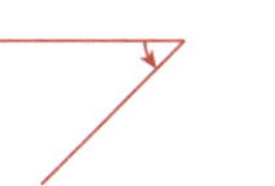

16 A cross is located at B2.

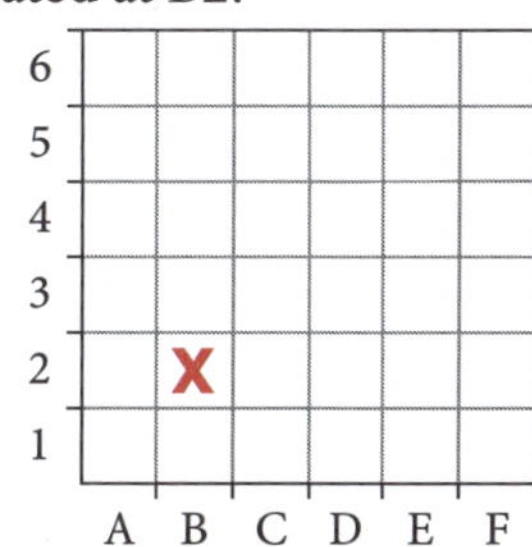

From X move up 3 units, to the right 2 units and down a unit. Place a Y on the destination.

STATISTICS AND PROBABILITY

17 Sophia tosses a fair coin and it lands on heads. She tosses it again and it lands on heads. What are the two possible outcomes if she tosses the coin a third time?

18 Brianna recorded the number of pages she read every night.

Pages read each day		
Day	**Tally**	**Number**
Monday		3
Tuesday	||	2
Wednesday		5
Thursday	||	2
Friday	||||	

Finish the table by writing the missing tallies and numbers.

NUMBER AND ALGEBRA

1 William wrote the number that was one more than three thousand six hundred. Write his number in digits.

2 Peta has two coffees on Monday and Tuesday, three on Wednesday and one each on Thursday and Friday. How many coffees did she drink in the five days?

3 Otis has two pieces of wire. One piece is 78 cm long and is 10 cm longer than the other piece. What is the length of the shorter piece?

4 Chelsea swims three laps of her backyard pool. Each lap is 8 metres. How far did Chelsea swim?

5 Bruce caught 12 fish. He shared the fish between three friends. How many fish did each friend receive?

6 This shape is formed using four identical rectangles. What fraction of the shape is shaded?

7 A half dozen donuts costs $6. What is the cost of each donut?

8 What is the next number?

10, 13, 16, 19, ?

MEASUREMENT AND SPACE

9 A rectangle is drawn on a centimetre grid.

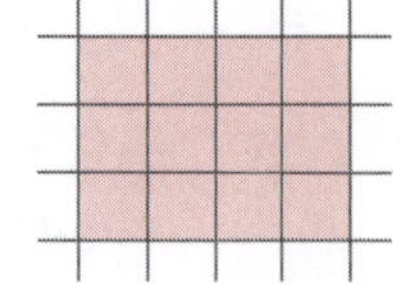

What is the length of the rectangle?

10 This shape is made using cubic-centimetre blocks.

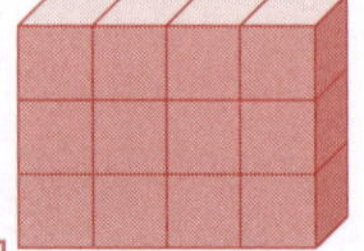

How many layers are in the shape?

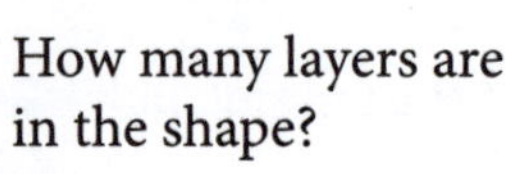

11 A block has the same mass as two balls.

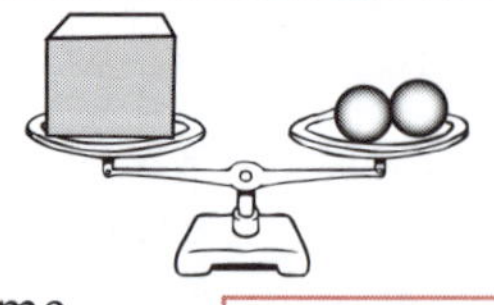

How many balls have the same mass as three blocks?

12 Gavin left home at 20 past 7. Draw this time on the clockface.

13 How many flat surfaces does a cylinder have?

14 Draw a 2D four-sided shape with sides of different lengths.

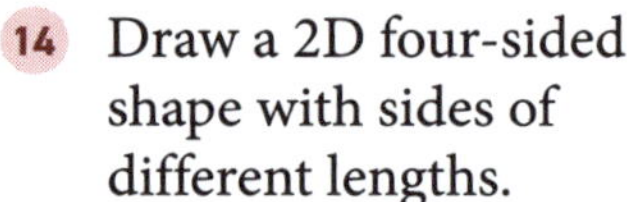

15 Draw a right angle.

16 A rectangle is located at E4.

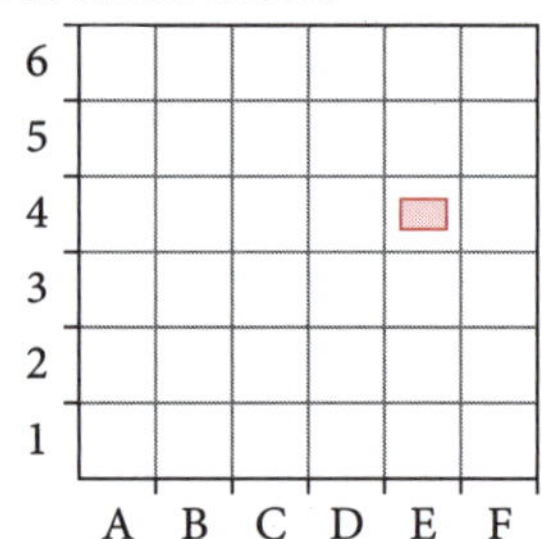

Draw a triangle three squares to the left of the rectangle.

STATISTICS AND PROBABILITY

17 Circle the spinner that has a chance the arrow will land on yellow.

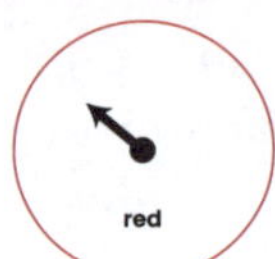

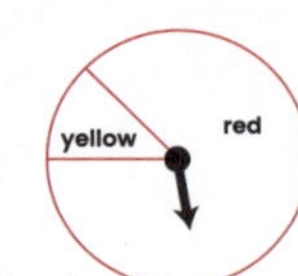

18 Bella's parents use a star chart at home. Here is the star chart for two weeks.

Week 1	☆ ☆ ☆ ☆
Week 2	☆ ☆ ☆ ☆ ☆ ☆

How many stars was Bella given in week 2?

NUMBER AND ALGEBRA

1 Peter wrote the number twenty-six thousand and nine in digits. What is the number which is twenty more than Peter's number?

2 A basketball team scored 86 in the first round of a competition and 72 in the second. How many points were scored in total?

3 For party decorations, 40 balloons are to be blown up. Jude has already blown up 26 balloons. How many balloons remain **not** blown up?

4 Each school desk has four legs. How many legs are on 10 desks?

5 A teacher opens a box of 20 pencils and gives four pencils to each of the students sitting in a group. There are none left over. How many students were in the group?

6 This shape is formed using four identical rectangles.

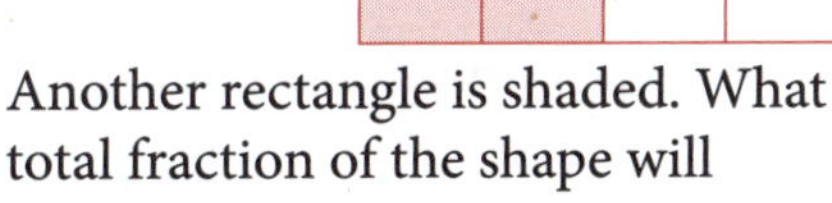

Another rectangle is shaded. What total fraction of the shape will be shaded?

7 How many 5-cent coins equal 50 cents?

8 How many odd numbers are between 100 and 110?

MEASUREMENT AND SPACE

9 A rectangle is drawn on a centimetre grid.

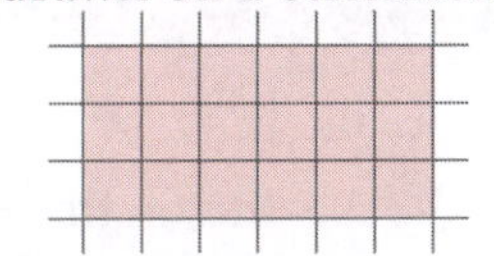

How much longer is the length than the width?

10 This shape is made using cubic-centimetre blocks.

What is the volume of the shape?

11 A block has the same mass as two balls.

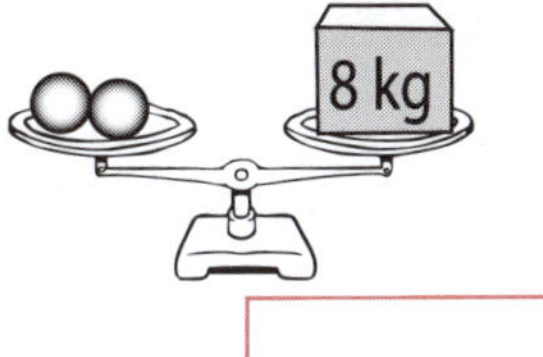

The mass of the block is 8 kg. What is the mass of each ball?

12 Alyson left home at 8 o'clock and arrived at work 25 minutes later.

Show the time of arrival on the clock face.

13 What is the shape of each of the flat surfaces on a cylinder?

14 Two sides of a parallelogram are 6 cm and 4 cm. What are the lengths of the other two sides?

15 In the space below, draw an angle larger than a right angle.

16 Draw circles at F6 and B3.

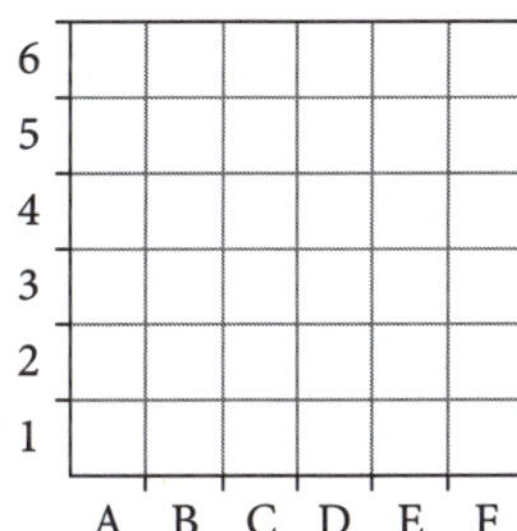

STATISTICS AND PROBABILITY

17 Circle the spinner that has the higher chance of the arrow landing on yellow.

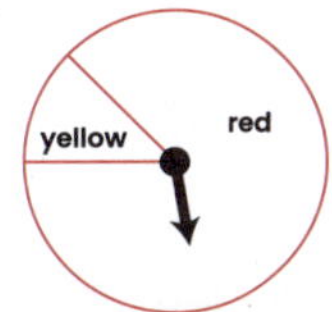

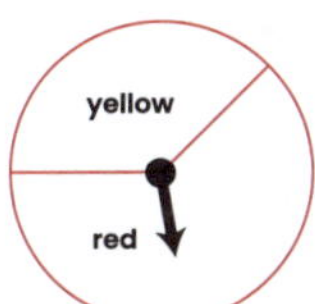

18 Bella's parents use a star chart at home. Here is the star chart for two weeks.

Week 1	☆ ☆ ☆ ☆
Week 2	☆ ☆ ☆ ☆ ☆ ☆

How many stars did Bella receive in total?

NUMBER AND ALGEBRA

1 Ava wrote these digits: 4 8 2 5. What is the smallest number she can write using all the digits?

2 Patrick has eight marbles in one bag, seven marbles in a second bag and five marbles in a third bag. How many marbles has Patrick in total?

3 Sienna is having dinner and counts 23 peas on her plate. She eats nine peas. How many peas remain?

4 What is double 25?

5 Each debating team has three students. If there are 18 students in a competition, how many teams have entered?

6 This shape is formed using five squares. Some of the squares are shaded.

Jack shades another square. What fraction of the shape is now shaded?

7 Heidi has these coins.

What is the total value of the money?

8 What is the missing number?

14, 18, ?, 26, 30

MEASUREMENT AND SPACE

9 A square is drawn on a centimetre grid.

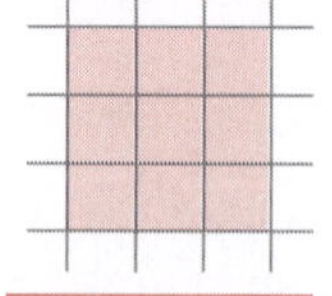

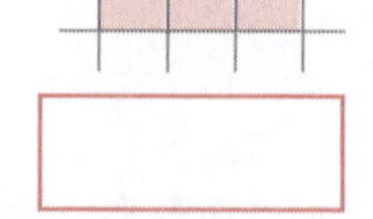

What is the length of each side of the square?

10 Circle the shapes that contain more than 1 litre.

11 1 L of milk has a mass of about 1 kg. Circle the best estimate of the mass of 6 L of milk.

16 kg   60 kg   6 kg

12 Brittany arrives at netball training at 10 to 4. Show this time on the clock face.

13 Eleni has four of each of these shapes. She tries to make a stack of the four shapes. Circle the shape that is easiest to stack.

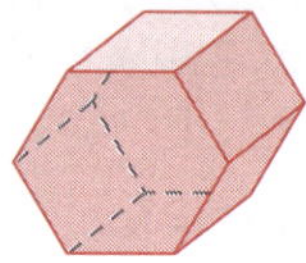
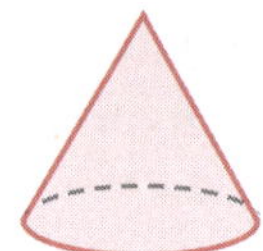

14 Which of these shapes has/have four equal sides?

rectangle   square   rhombus

15 Draw a rectangle and tick all the right angles.

16 Which shape is at D3?

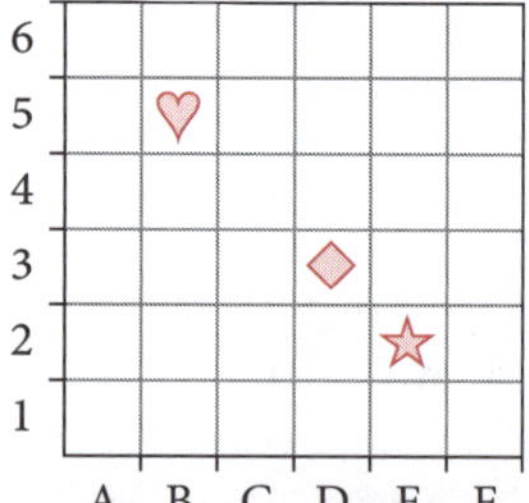

STATISTICS AND PROBABILITY

17 Circle the more likely event.

Lena will win the lottery.

Aldo will eat dinner tonight.

18 Here is a list of runs scored by Nicole.

Circle the tally which represents the number of runs.

NUMBER AND ALGEBRA

1 Boris uses these five numbered cards to make numbers.

3 0 8 2 6

What is the largest three-digit number he can make?

2 For the school market day, Pearl, Ruby and Ellie baked cupcakes. Pearl baked 20, Ruby 30 and Ellie 10. What was the total number of cupcakes they baked?

3 Oscar is given a box of chocolates for his birthday. He eats 16 chocolates. If there were originally 24 chocolates, how many remain in the box?

4 On each of five mornings Ruben cycled 8 km. What is the total distance he cycled?

5 Margot has washed the team jerseys. She uses two pegs for each jersey. If 24 pegs have been used, how many jerseys have been washed?

6 This shape is formed using five squares. Some of the squares are shaded.

Charlotte shades another two squares. What fraction of the shape is now shaded?

7 Zoe has these coins.

What is the total value of the money?

8 Emily writes this pattern of numbers.

49, 46, 43, 40 …

What will be the sixth number in the sequence?

MEASUREMENT AND SPACE

9 Mackenzie has a 1-metre roll of ribbon. She cuts 60 cm from the roll to wrap a present. What length of ribbon remains on the roll?

10 Tomi has two mugs. Each mug contains 120 mL of apple juice. What is the total amount of juice in Tomi's mugs?

11 One litre of milk has a mass of about 1 kg. Todd opens a 3-L container of milk and pours out 1 L. Which of these is closest to the mass of the remaining milk?

4 kg 2 kg 1 kg

12 Maeve leaves home at half past 8 and takes 20 minutes to walk to school. Show the time she arrives at school on the clock face.

13 Liana was given a cardboard model of a cone. She used a pair of scissors to investigate the net of the cone. Circle the two shapes that form the net.

14 Lola counted the number of sides of this shape.

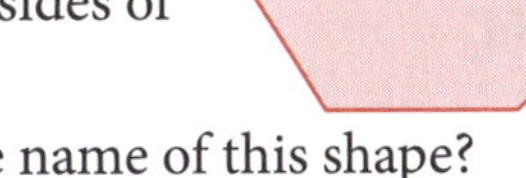

What is the name of this shape?

15 Draw a rhombus and tick all the angles that are smaller than a right angle.

16 Jack and Rosie are standing on the grid. Jack is located at B5.

Rosie is 3 squares from Jack. Which of these is a possible location of Rosie?

E6 E5 B3

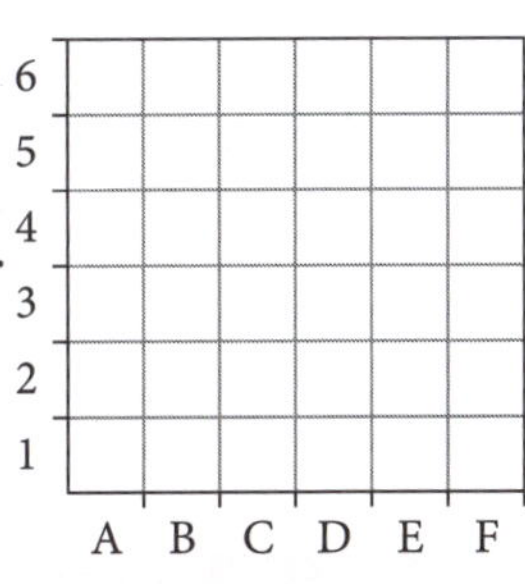

STATISTICS AND PROBABILITY

17 A bag contains six balls. Four balls are red and two are green. William chooses a ball without looking. Circle the more likely outcome.

William chose a red ball.

William chose a green ball.

18 George was scoring goals in a netball game. Here is the score at half-time.

Wildcats	Bears
𝍸 𝍸 ||	𝍸 |||

Which team is winning and by how many goals?

NUMBER AND ALGEBRA

1 What is the next even number after 398?

2 What is the total of 12, 3 and 8?

3 Rosa fills a container with 24 biscuits. After a week there are only seven biscuits remaining in the container. How many biscuits have been eaten?

4 Isaiha multiplied six by five. What is her answer?

5 Chelsea's family swimming pool is 10 m long. She swims 100 m. How many laps does Chelsea swim?

6 Shade $\frac{3}{4}$ of this shape.

7 Caitlin needed $3.90 to buy a loaf of bread. She has these coins.

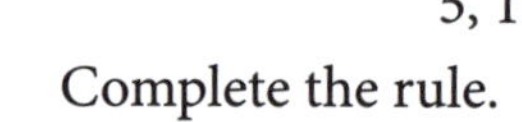

Does Caitlin have enough money?

8 Here is a sequence of numbers.

5, 11, 17, 23, 29 …

Complete the rule.

Start with 5 and add ______.

MEASUREMENT AND SPACE

9 Circle the longer length.

120 cm 87 cm

10 The jug contains juice.

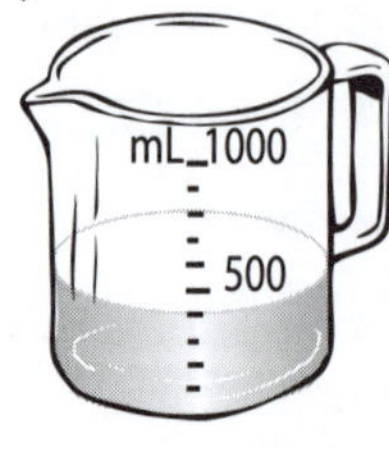

Which of these is the best estimate of the amount of juice?

40 mL 100 mL 400 mL

11 Two students compared their mass. Kye's mass was 37 kg. Brad was 4 kg heavier than Kye. What was Brad's mass?

12 The minute hand is pointing to 7 and the hour hand is between 10 and 11. Show the time on the clock face.

13 Circle the correct word to complete the statement.
On a 3D shape, an edge is where two ________ meet.

faces bases

14 Which of these shapes must have four right angles?

parallelogram rectangle rhombus

15 Circle the time(s) when the hands of the clock form a right angle.

16 The diagram shows a shape which has been translated down.

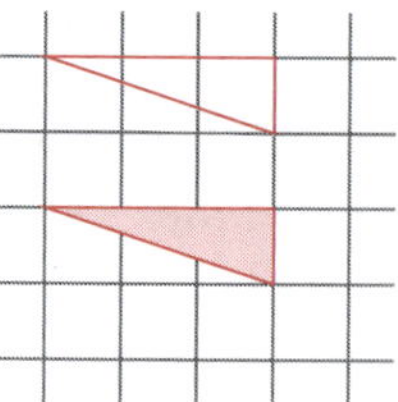

How many units has the shape been translated?

STATISTICS AND PROBABILITY

17 Elijah rolled a normal dice. How many different outcomes are possible?

18 Students were asked what their favourite fruit was. The results are shown below.

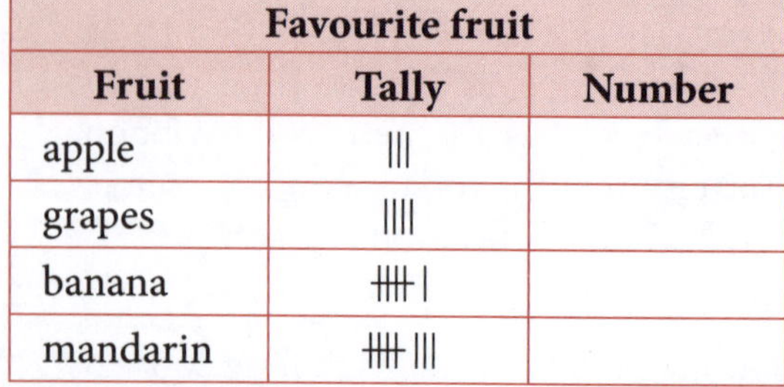

Favourite fruit		
Fruit	**Tally**	**Number**
apple	|||	
grapes	||||	
banana	𝍸		
mandarin	𝍸 |||	

Complete the table by writing the numbers.

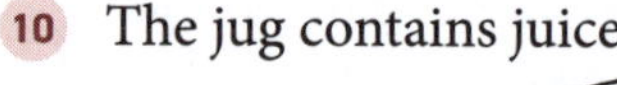

NUMBER AND ALGEBRA

1 How many odd numbers are between one hundred and five and one hundred and ten?

2 What is the total of 36, 14 and 9?

3 Anne opens a packet which contains nine biscuits. She gives one each to each of her four friends and eats one herself. How many biscuits remain in the packet?

4 Cans of soft drink are sold in boxes of eight. How many cans are in five boxes?

5 Brandan gives away all his 50 marbles. He gives 10 marbles to each of his friends. How many of Brandan's friends received marbles?

6 Shade $\frac{3}{4}$ of this shape.

7 Declan bought a glue-stick for $2. He used 50-cent coins to pay for the glue-stick. How many coins did he use?

8 Here is a sequence of numbers.
23, 32, 41, 50, 59 …
Complete the rule.

Start with ________ and ________.

MEASUREMENT AND SPACE

9 Circle the longest length.

120 cm   1 m   86 cm

10 The jug contains juice.

Which of these is the best estimate of the amount of juice?

500 mL   700 mL   1000 mL

11 Tomatoes are priced at $4 per kg. What is the cost of 3 kg of tomatoes?

12 The minute hand is pointing to 8 and the hour hand is between 3 and 4. What is the time?

13 Circle the correct word to complete the statement.
On a 3D shape, a vertex is where three or more ________ meet.

faces   bases

14 Helen cut a quadrilateral into these two triangular pieces.

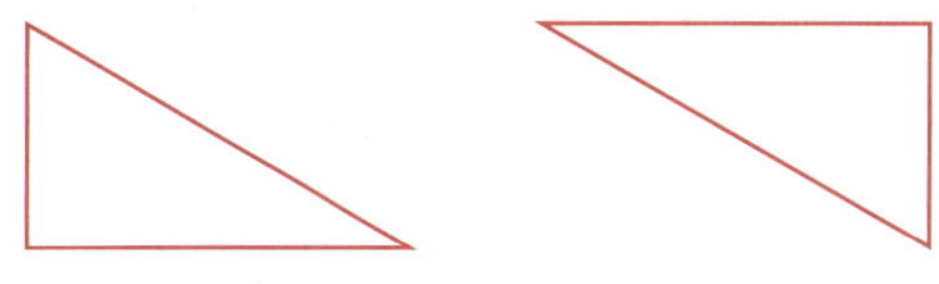

What was the original quadrilateral?

15 Circle the time(s) when the hands of the clock form an angle less than a right angle.

10 o'clock   7 o'clock   2 o'clock

16 The diagram shows a shape which has been translated left.

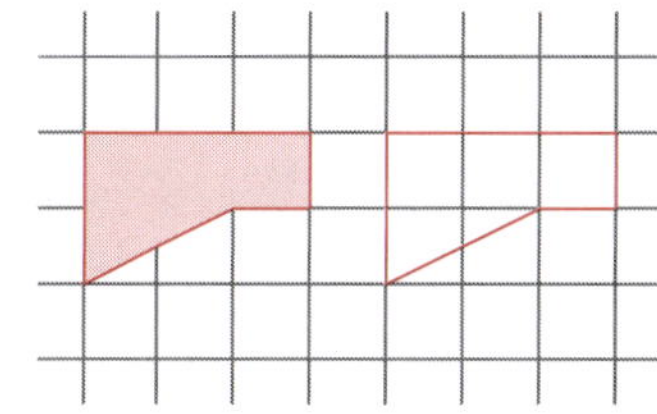

How many units has the shape been translated?

STATISTICS AND PROBABILITY

17 Elijah rolled a normal dice. How many different outcomes are less than 5?

18 Students were asked what their favourite fruit was. The results are shown below.

Favourite fruit		
Fruit	**Tally**	**Number**
apple		4
grapes	~~||||~~ ||||	
banana		8
mandarin	~~||||~~ ~~||||~~ ||	

Complete the table.

NUMBER AND ALGEBRA

1 Bryan is counting by even numbers and starts at 2. What is the third number counted? ☐

2 For Easter, Holly's aunt gave her a bag of 12 eggs. Her parents gave her a box of six eggs and her brother gave her two eggs. How many eggs did Holly receive? ☐

3 Mel and Scotty counted their merit cards. Mel has 28 cards which is seven more than Scotty. How many merit cards has Scotty? ☐

4 Hot-cross buns are sold in packets of six. How many buns are in 10 packets? ☐

5 There are four tables set up in the library. A total of 24 students are sitting at the tables. Each table has the same number of students. How many students are sitting at each table? ☐

6 Here are two equal-sized circles.

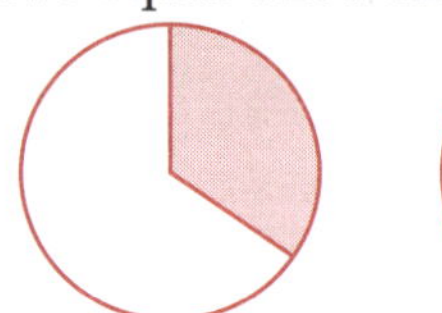
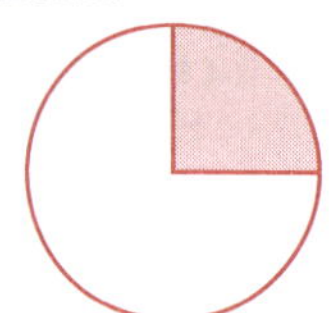

Tick the circle with the greatest area shaded.

7 A bottle of shampoo is priced at $6.91. Round the price to the nearest 5 cents. ☐

8 What is the next number? ☐

24, 20, 16, 12, ?

MEASUREMENT AND SPACE

9 Circle the shorter length.

53 mm 6 cm

10 Jackson has two jugs. Each jug can hold 2 L. He fills each jug with juice. What is the total amount of juice? ☐

11 A bag of potting mix is half the mass of a bag of sand. A bag of sand has a mass of 20 kg. What is the mass of a bag of potting mix? ☐

12 Here are two clocks. How many minutes are there between the two times? ☐

13 Here is a rectangular prism.

Three of the edges are hidden from view. Use dotted lines to draw the three edges.

14 How many pairs of parallel sides does a rectangle have? ☐

15 Here is an angle.

Circle the vertex of the angle.

16 The diagram shows a rectangle which has been translated. The image is shaded.

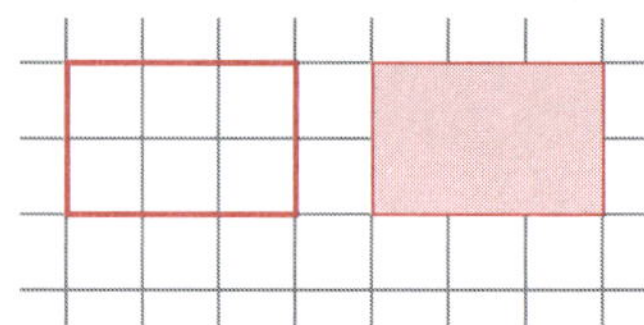

The rectangle has been translated to the left. True or false? ☐

STATISTICS AND PROBABILITY

17 Ravi said, 'It is possible to toss a coin six times and always land on heads'. Is the statement true or false? ☐

18 Students were asked about their favourite season. The results are shown below.

Favourite season		
Season	**Tally**	**Number**
summer	卌	
autumn	||	
winter	|||	
spring	卌 ||	

Complete the table by writing the numbers.

NUMBER AND ALGEBRA

1 Alyson is counting the numbers from 1 to 1000. What is the second-last number called out?

2 The final score in a basketball game was 47 to 32. What was the total number of points scored in the match?

3 Twenty-six birds were in a tree. Nineteen birds were in another. How many more birds were in the first tree than the second?

4 How many legs do 30 seagulls have?

5 Carla buys a packet of 24 balloons. The balloons are to be inflated and tied into bunches of three. How many bunches can be made?

6 Here are two equal-sized circles.

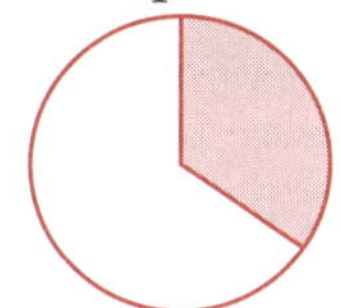
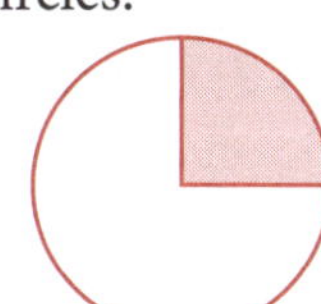

Cross the circle with the greatest area **not** shaded.

7 Brodie purchased a toothbrush costing $2.98. Round the price to the nearest 5 cents.

8 What is the next number?

110, 107, 104, 101, 

MEASUREMENT AND SPACE

9 Circle the shortest length.

8 cm   1 m   60 mm

10 How many millilitres are in 1 litre?

11 How many grams are in half a kilogram?

12 Here are two clocks. How many minutes are there between the two times?

13 Here is a triangular prism.

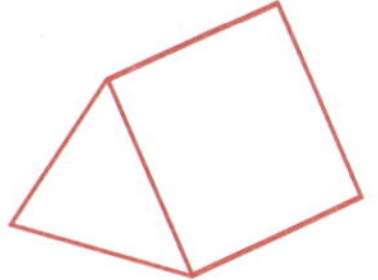

Some of the edges are hidden from view. Use dotted lines to draw the edges.

14 How many pairs of parallel sides must a trapezium have?

15 Here is an angle.

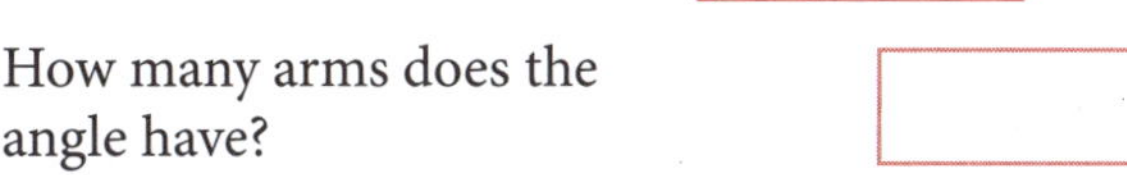

How many arms does the angle have?

16 The diagram shows a triangle which has been translated. The image is shaded.

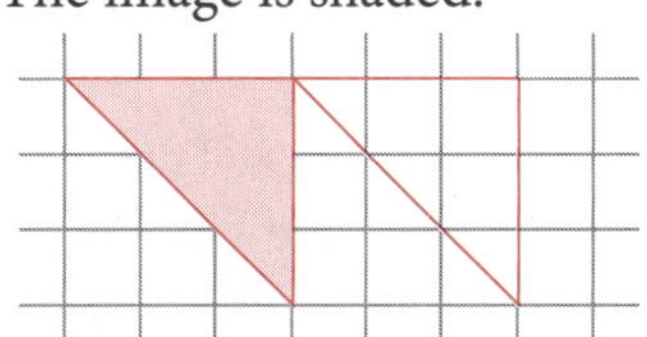

The triangle has been translated 4 units to the left. True or false?

STATISTICS AND PROBABILITY

17 Letters have been written on the sections of a spinner.

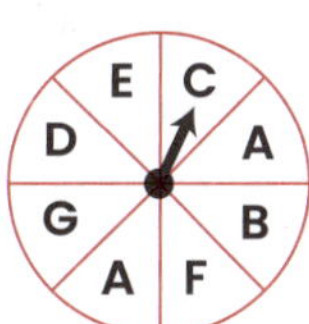

Which letter is most likely to be spun?

18 Students were asked about their favourite season. The results are shown below.

Favourite season		
Season	**Tally**	**Number**
summer	卌 |||	
autumn	|||	
winter	卌	
spring	卌 ||||	

How many more students liked spring than autumn?

NUMBER AND ALGEBRA

1 Elijah makes four-digit numbers using these cards.

 5  1  2 0

How many of these numbers can be formed?

5210 2051 3501

2 Anna plays a game where she rolls four normal dice and adds the numbers on top of each dice. What is the total if she rolls 6, 2, 5 and 3?

3 Emily baked 24 cupcakes. She gave 11 away to her friends. How many cupcakes remained?

4 There are nine pairs of socks in a drawer in Thomas's bedroom. What is the total number of socks?

5 Six children shared a bowl containing 30 cherries. Each child ate the same number of cherries and all cherries were eaten. How many cherries were eaten by each child?

6 Here is a sequence:

$\frac{1}{5}, \frac{2}{5}$, ? , $\frac{4}{5}$

What is the missing fraction?

7 Archer purchased \$59.43 worth of petrol. He paid cash for the petrol. What was he charged when the amount was rounded to the nearest 5 cents?

8 What is the missing number?

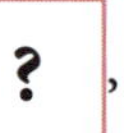

? , 20, 14, 8, 2

MEASUREMENT AND SPACE

9 Danielle's father measured her height as 1 m 38 cm. What is this height in centimetres?

10 An empty container can hold 8 L. Grace pours 6 L of water into the container. How much more water is needed to fill the container?

11 Donald has six blocks. Each block has a mass of 2 kg. What is the total mass of the blocks?

12 Here are two clocks. How many minutes are there between the two times?

13 Here are some 3D shapes.

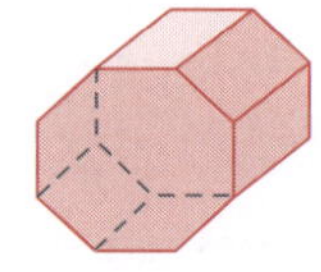

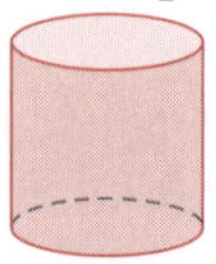

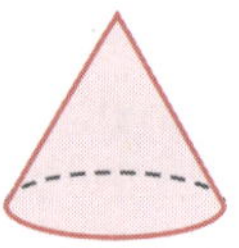

Draw a circle around the prism(s).

14 Circle the names of the shapes that must have all angles equal.

parallelogram kite rectangle

15 Here is a line.
Draw another line which is perpendicular to this line.

16 Mia has drawn two triangles. She says that the triangle on the left has been translated to the image triangle on the right. Is Mia correct?

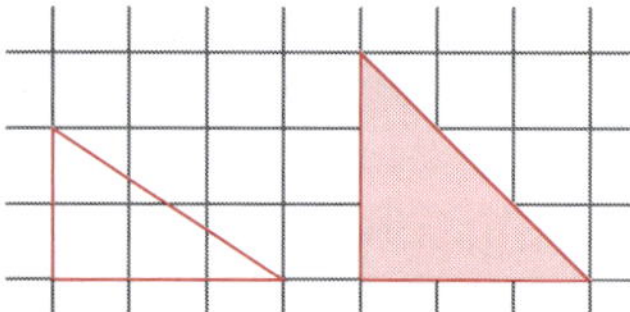

STATISTICS AND PROBABILITY

17 The diagram shows a box of coloured balls which are either red (R) or blue (B).

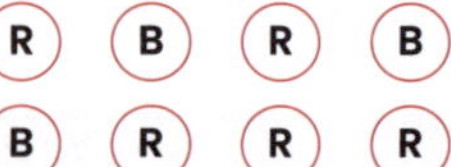

How many blue marbles are in the box?

18 Students were asked for the number of times they had tidied their bedroom in the past week.

Tidy bedrooms	
Child	**Number**
Eloise	4
Sebastian	2
Daphne	3

How many times did Daphne tidy her bedroom?

NUMBER AND ALGEBRA

1 Jordan used these cards to form the number three thousand, five hundred and thirty.

7 ? 3 5

What is the missing number?

2 Mrs Rhys has 14 coloured pencils in one jar and 26 in another. What is the total number of coloured pencils?

3 Emma has 35 marbles. She has 13 more marbles than Ben. How many marbles does Ben have?

4 Noah kicked five goals for his Aussie Rules team. If each goal is worth 6 points, what is the total number of points scored?

5 A grocer is selling small buckets of plums. There is a total of 90 plums and there are 10 plums in each bucket. How many buckets are for sale?

6 Here is a sequence:

$0, \frac{1}{2}, 1,$? $, 2$

What is the missing number?

7 Round $14.27 to the nearest 5 cents.

8 What is the missing number?

? , 45, 39, 33, 27

MEASUREMENT AND SPACE

9 Keira used a ruler to measure the length of a single strand of her hair. It was 6 cm 3 mm. What is this length in millimetres?

10 Three containers have capacities of 40 mL, 60 mL and 80 mL. What is the total capacity of the three containers?

11 Will has four steel balls. The mass of each ball is 5 kg. What is the total mass?

12 Here are two clocks. How many minutes are there between the two times?

13 Here are some 3D shapes.

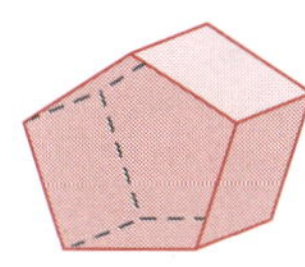
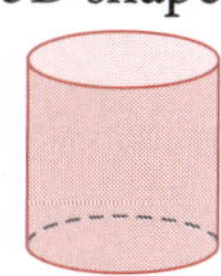
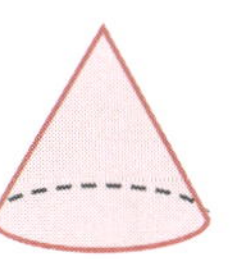

How many of the shapes are not prisms?

14 Circle the name of the shape(s) that can be irregular.

square regular hexagon kite

15 Here is a line.
Draw another line which is perpendicular to this line.

16 Symon has drawn two triangles. He says that the triangle on the left has been translated to the image triangle on the right. Is Symon correct?

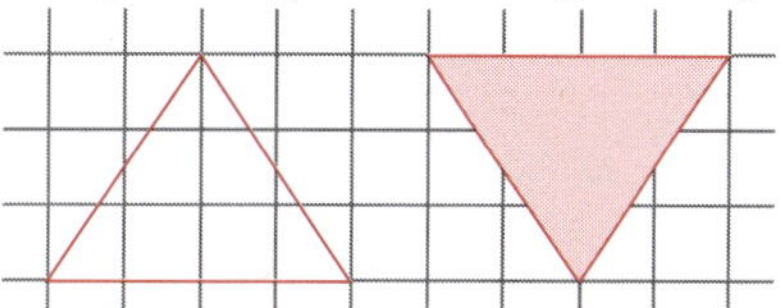

STATISTICS AND PROBABILITY

17 The diagram shows a box of coloured balls which are either red (R) or blue (B).

R	B	R	B	R
B	R	R	R	R

Charlotte chooses a ball from the box without looking. Circle the colour she is more likely to choose.

red blue

18 Students were asked how many times they had tidied their bedroom in the past week.

Tidy bedrooms	
Child	**Number**
Eloise	4
Sebastian	2
Daphne	3

How many more times did Eloise tidy her bedroom than Sebastian?

NUMBER AND ALGEBRA

1 An orchardist picked 1429 oranges. What is the number of oranges, to the nearest hundred?

2 George works for 6 hours on Monday, 4 hours on Wednesday and 5 hours on Saturday. What was the total hours worked?

3 There are 18 horses in a paddock. Jess moves 10 of the horses to another paddock. How many horses remain?

4 Eleanor babysits for 3 hours on four afternoons each week. What is the total number of hours?

5 Zac buys a dozen doughnuts. The doughnuts are shared equally between six children. How many doughnuts are given to each child?

6 On the number line use a dot to locate the fraction $\frac{3}{5}$.

0 $\frac{1}{5}$ $\frac{2}{5}$ $\frac{3}{5}$ $\frac{4}{5}$ 1

7 What is the total of the money shown?

8 What is the missing number?

18, 23, 28, **?** , 38, 43

MEASUREMENT AND SPACE

9 Stephanie used a ruler to measure the length of a USB drive.

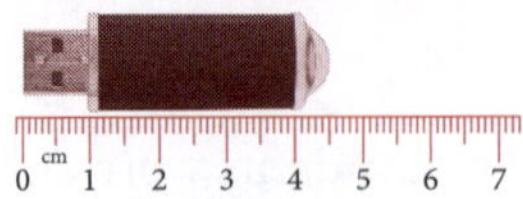

What is the length in millimetres?

10 This shape is made using cubic-centimetre blocks.

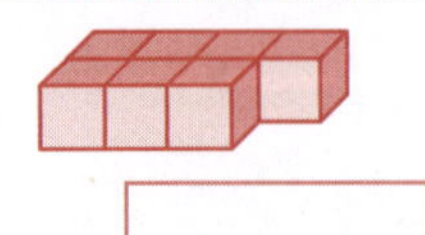

What is the volume of the shape?

11 Andrew buys an 18-kg bag of fertiliser. He uses half of the fertiliser on his garden. What is the mass of fertiliser used?

12 Circle the digital clock showing 20 past 7.

13 Carissa built a 3D model with six rectangular faces. Circle the name of the shape.

hexagon rectangular prism pentagonal prism

14 Here is a rectangle. Draw the two diagonals.

15 This shape is formed by joining two squares. How many right angles are inside the shape?

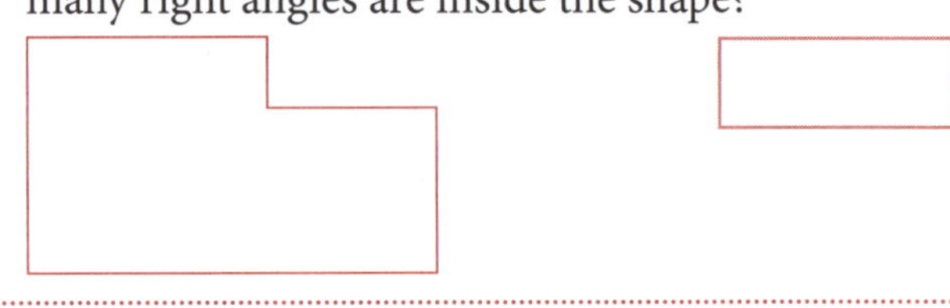

16 From P move 5 spaces up and ________ to the right to Q. What is the missing number?

Q

P

STATISTICS AND PROBABILITY

17 Here are five balls. Some of the balls are blue (B) and the others are yellow (Y).

B Y B Y B

There are more blue balls than yellow balls. True or false?

18 Students were asked about their favourite juice. The results are shown in the table.

Favourite juice	
Juice	**Students**
orange	11
apple	6
pineapple	7
lemon	2

How many students liked orange juice?

NUMBER AND ALGEBRA

1 There are 12 879 spectators at a match. What is this number, to the nearest thousand?

2 Shane is 12 years old. His father is 38 years older than Shane. What is the total of their ages?

3 Jenny has read 61 pages of her book. Michael has read 37 pages of his book. How many more pages has Jenny read?

4 A netball club has three under-9 teams. If there are 10 players on each team, what is the total number of players?

5 There are 30 crayons on the classroom floor. The crayons are to be placed evenly back into three boxes. How many crayons fit into each box?

6 On the number line use a dot to locate the fraction $\frac{3}{4}$.

0 1

7 What is the total of the money shown?

8 What is the missing number?

65, ?, 77, 83, 89

MEASUREMENT AND SPACE

9 Lea has two lengths of timber. Both pieces are 2 m 30 cm long. What is the total length of the timber?

10 Each layer of a prism has six cubic-centimetre blocks. There are three layers. What is the volume of the prism?

11 Three balls have a total mass of 6 kg.

What is the mass of each ball?

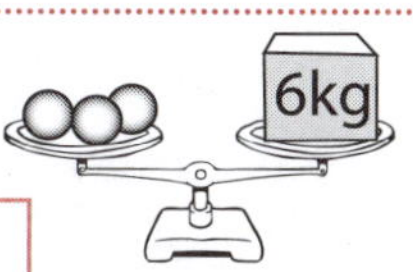

12 Circle the digital clock showing 10 to 5.

04:50

13 Jordan built a prism with faces. The faces were triangular and rectangular. Circle the name of the shape.

triangular prism rectangular prism pentagonal prism

14 Here is a parallelogram.

Circle the correct word in this statement: The diagonals of a parallelogram are equal/unequal.

15 What is the highest possible number of right angles in a quadrilateral?

16 Aleesha placed a coin on X. She moved the coin down and then right to finish on Y. How many spaces did she move the coin?

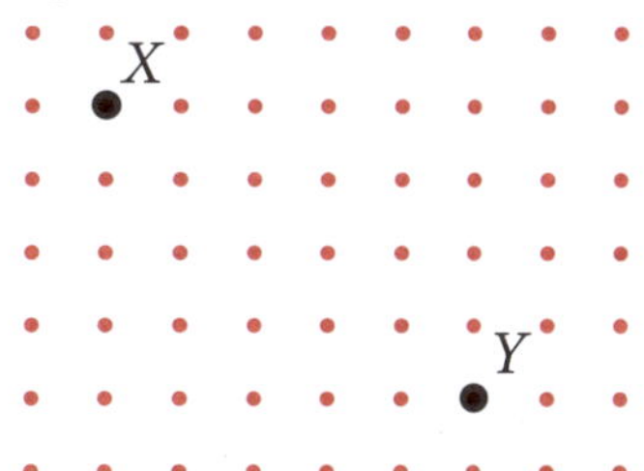

STATISTICS AND PROBABILITY

17 Here are five balls. Some of the balls are blue (B) and the others are yellow (Y).

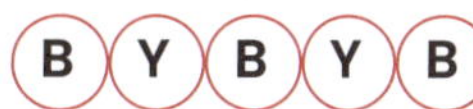

A ball is chosen without looking. Which coloured ball is more likely?

18 Students were asked about their favourite juice. The results are shown in the table. What was the total number of students who said apple or pineapple?

Favourite juice	
Juice	**Students**
orange	11
apple	6
pineapple	7
lemon	2

NUMBER AND ALGEBRA

1 Here are three numbered cards.

  8

How many different numbers can be made?

2 Stewart swam 400 m on Wednesday and 500 m on Friday. What was the total distance he swam in the two days?

3 Charles invited 18 children to his birthday party. Four boys and two girls could not come. How many children were at the party?

4 A spider has eight legs. What is the total number of legs on three spiders?

5 Sara can make 10 doll's dresses in 20 days. How many dresses can she make each day?

6 How many quarters are in one whole?

7 What is the total of the money shown?

8 Here is a sequence of numbers.
45, 41, 37, 33, 29 …

Complete the rule.

Start with 45 and subtract

MEASUREMENT AND SPACE

9 A rectangle is drawn on a centimetre grid.

How many small squares are inside the rectangle?

10 Alma takes a drink bottle to school. Which of these is closest to the capacity of the bottle?

6 mL 60 mL 600 mL

11 Julian had two rocks with a combined mass of 14 kg. The mass of one rock was 5 kg. What was the mass of the other rock?

12 Here is a clock with the hour hand missing.

Circle a possible time on the clock.

10 o'clock 10 past 4 10 to 4

13  Here is a rectangular prism. How many faces are hidden?

14 What 2D shape am I? I have four equal sides and four equal angles.

15 Circle the smaller angle.

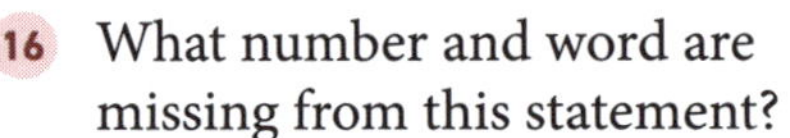

16 What number and word are missing from this statement?

On the dot paper, *C* is ________ spaces to the ________ of *A*.

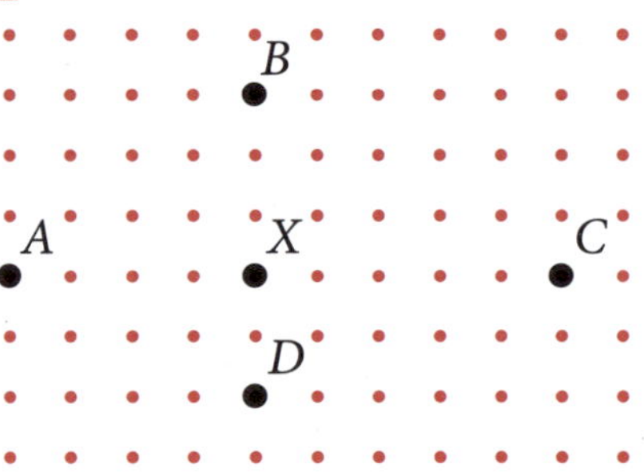

STATISTICS AND PROBABILITY

17 Millie tossed a coin 20 times and recorded the results in a table.

Outcome	Tally
Heads	卌 III
Tails	卌 卌 II

How many times did the coin land on tails?

18 A pizza restaurant opens from Thursday to Sunday and the number of pizzas sold each day is recorded. How many days is the pizza shop open?

Pizza sales	
Day	**Pizzas**
Thursday	20
Friday	28
Saturday	36
Sunday	20

NUMBER AND ALGEBRA

1 Here are three numbered cards.

6 4 2

What is the second smallest three-digit number that can be formed using the digits?

2 On a cruise ship there were 1600 adults and 1200 children. What was the total number of passengers?

3 There are 27 students standing in one line. Forty students are standing in a second line. How many more students are in the second line?

4 Brendan planted three rows of beans. In each row there were six plants. What was the total number of bean plants?

5 A selection night is held to choose a representative team. Seventy players were present and were split into seven teams. How many players were in each team?

6 How many hundredths are in one whole?

7 What is the total of the money shown?

8 Here is a sequence of numbers: 47, 58, 69, 80, 91 …
Complete the rule.

Start with ______ and ______.

MEASUREMENT AND SPACE

9 A rectangle is drawn on a centimetre grid. How many small squares are inside the rectangle?

10 Brooklyn bought some paint. She bought two 4-L tins and a 1-L tin. How much paint did she buy?

11 Grapes are priced at $4.99 per kilogram. Which of these is closest to the cost of 3 kg of grapes?

$12 $15 $8

12 Here is a clock with the minute hand missing.
Circle the most likely time.

quarter to 9 8 o'clock quarter past 8

13 
Here is an octagonal prism.
How many faces are hidden?

14 What shape am I? I have four equal sides but I am **not** a square.

15 Here are three angles labelled *A*, *B* and *C*.

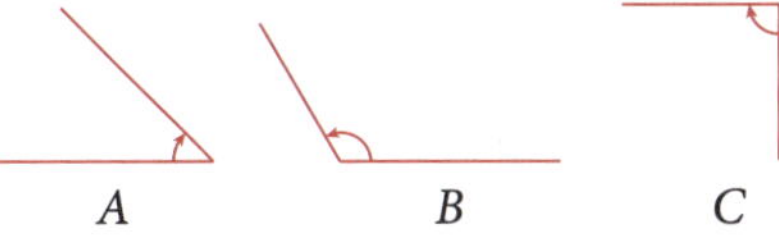

Arrange the angles from smallest to largest.

16 A coin was placed on *A*. The coin can only be moved up and right. Callum moves the coin a total of 8 spaces.
Where does the coin finish?

X *Y* *Z*

STATISTICS AND PROBABILITY

17 Chloe tossed a coin many times and recorded the results in a table.

Outcome	Tally
Heads	卌 卌 ||||
Tails	卌 卌 卌 |

How many times did Chloe toss the coin?

18 A pizza restaurant opens from Thursday to Sunday and the number of pizzas sold each day is recorded.

Pizza sales	
Day	**Pizzas**
Thursday	20
Friday	28
Saturday	36
Sunday	20

How many pizzas were sold on the weekend?

NUMBER AND ALGEBRA

1 On a holiday Jackson drives 3469 km on a trip to outback Queensland. What is this distance to the nearest 10 km?

2 The Henderson family has eight fish, three birds, two cats and a dog. How many pets do they have?

3 Here are three numbers.

27 58 67

What is the difference between the two odd numbers?

4 Donald is collecting cards. Each packet he buys contains four cards. How many cards are in 10 packets?

5 Four equally sized bags of rice have a combined mass of 40 kg. What is the mass of each bag?

6 Shade two-thirds of the shape.

7 Brodie was given this amount of money as a Christmas bonus. How much did he receive?

8 Callum writes the first five numbers in a sequence.

12, 15, 18, 21, 24

If the sequence continues, which of these numbers will Callum write?

25 31 26 27

MEASUREMENT AND SPACE

9 Meilani drew a rectangle on a centimetre grid. She shaded six of the small squares inside the rectangle.

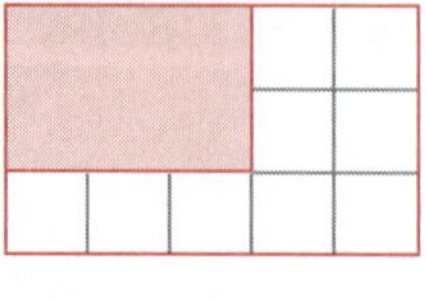

How many small squares are **not** shaded?

10 Tom has an empty bucket that can hold 10 L. He fills the bucket and pours half the water around a tree. How much water remains in the bucket?

11 The mass of the ball is 8 kg. Circle a possible mass of the cube.

5 kg 8 kg 13 kg

12 Write this time on the digital clock.

13 Riley was given a model of a cone. How many flat surfaces are on Riley's cone?

14 How many pairs of parallel sides has a trapezium?

15 Circle the letter(s) with perpendicular lines.

E S F

16 Tick every square that is on this path: From the start square, go right 5 squares, up 5 squares and to the left 3 squares.

Start

STATISTICS AND PROBABILITY

17 There are 24 students in a class. Which of these words describes the chance that a student has their birthday today?

impossible possible certain

18 Students were asked what their favourite pet was. The results are shown in the table.

Student pets	
Pet	**Students**
cat	8
fish	4
dog	12
rabbit	2

What pet did most students say was their favourite?

NUMBER AND ALGEBRA

1 One Saturday morning a cafe made 380 coffees, to the nearest 10. Which of these could be the exact number?

390 386 375 37

2 Donald picked 62 cucumbers from his farm on Wednesday. He picked another 45 on the following Sunday. What was the total number of cucumbers?

3 Justin is 41 years old. He is 12 years older than his cousin Kenrick. How old is Kenrick?

4 Emma is playing a game using five normal dice. She rolls the dice and they all land on 6. What is the total of the five dice?

5 Jazlyn doubled a number. Her answer was 18. What was Jazlyn's original number?

6 Here are four fractions.

$\frac{3}{10}$ $\frac{3}{5}$ $\frac{3}{8}$ $\frac{3}{4}$

What is the largest fraction?

7 Filip received money for his birthday. The amount of money is shown.

What is the total amount?

8 Bianca writes the first five numbers in a sequence: 63, 70, 77, 84, 91.

If the sequence continues, which of these numbers will Bianca write?

99 105 106 108

MEASUREMENT AND SPACE

9 A rectangle is drawn on a centimetre grid. How many squares each with an area of 4 cm² can fit into the rectangle?

10 Lincoln pours water into two containers. Which container has more water? Circle your answer.

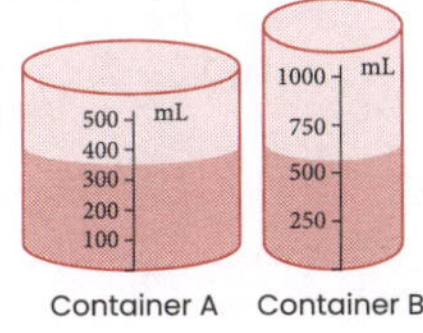

Container A Container B

11 An apple has a mass of 80 g and a banana has a mass of 90 g.
What is the total mass?

12 Write this time on the digital clock.

13 Beka was given a model of a pentagonal prism. He counts the number of faces on the model. How many faces does he count?

14 Albert measured the lengths of the sides of a triangle. Two of the sides were each 6 cm. Which of these is **not** a possible length of the third side? Circle the length(s).

4 cm 7 cm 13 cm

15 How many of these letters have perpendicular lines?

H T A N

16 Tick every square that is on this path: From the start square, go up 5 squares, to the right 4 squares, down 3 squares and to the left 4 squares and then back to the start. How many squares were ticked at least once?

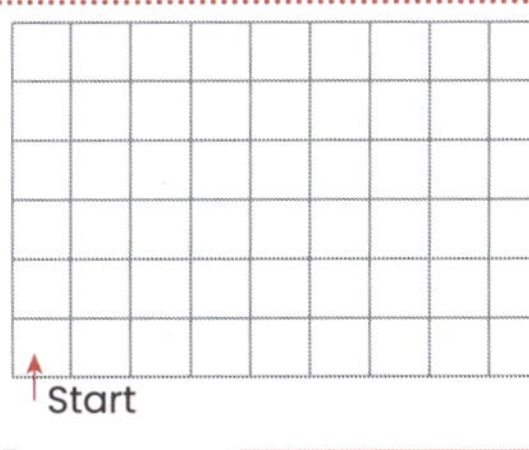

STATISTICS AND PROBABILITY

17 Jaime rolls a normal dice. Which of these words describes the chance that Jaime rolls a number less than 7?

impossible possible certain

18 Students were asked what their favourite pet was. The results are shown in the table.

Student pets	
Pet	**Students**
cat	8
fish	4
dog	12
rabbit	2

How many students said a dog or a cat?

NUMBER AND ALGEBRA

1 Phoebe uses increasing consecutive digits to write a four-digit number. What is the largest possible number she can write?

2 Evan sold 16 cups of homemade lemonade on Saturday and another 20 cups on Sunday. What was the total number of cups sold?

3 At 9:30 there were 18 people at the skatepark. A half hour later no one had left but another 13 people had arrived. What was the total number of people at the skatepark?

4 A store sells boxes containing 10 coloured pencils. How many pencils were in four boxes?

5 Ellie-Dee has 30 counters. She arranges them into groups of 5. How many counters are in each group?

6 What is the numerator in the fraction $\frac{7}{10}$?

7 Romeo buys a chocolate bar for 65c. How much change will he receive from a $1 coin?

8 Om wrote these numbers.

167 380 449 118 572

How many even numbers did Om write?

MEASUREMENT AND SPACE

9 Daphne drew a rectangle. She drew and shaded two identical squares inside the rectangle. How many more of these squares would fit into the rectangle?

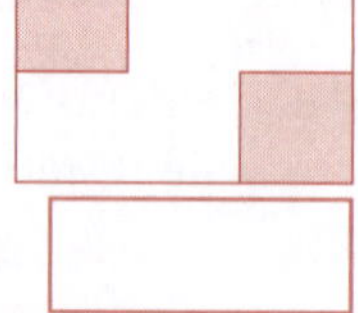

10 This shape is made using cubic-centimetre blocks. What is the volume of the shape?

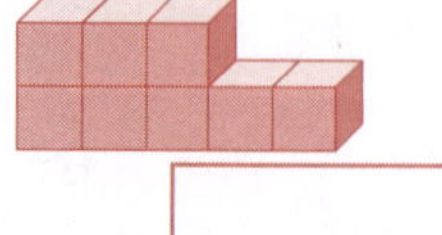

11 Potatoes are sold in 3-kg bags. What is the total mass of four bags of potatoes?

12 Write this time on the digital clock.

:

13 How many triangular faces has a triangular prism?

14 How many pairs of parallel sides does a square have?

15 Pictured is a line with a dot.

Draw another line through the dot which is perpendicular.

16 Move the smiley face 4 spaces to the right and 5 spaces up.

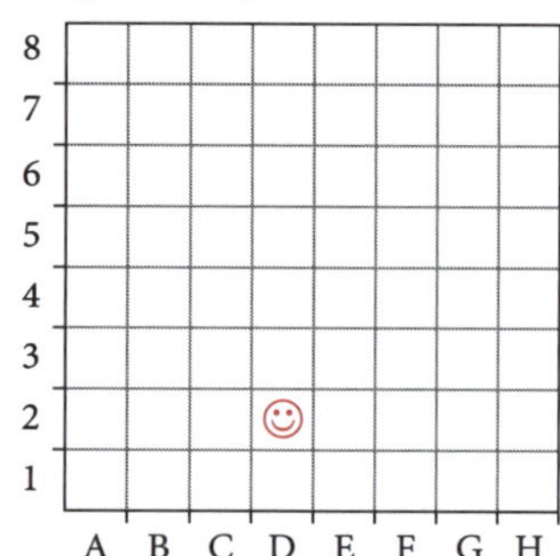

Where is the smiley face now?

STATISTICS AND PROBABILITY

17 A bag contains some numbered cards. There are four 3s, six 4s and two 5s. A card is chosen from the bag without looking. Which number is most likely to be chosen?

18 The favourite colours of a group of students are recorded in the table.

Favourite colours	
Colour	**Students**
blue	3
green	7
purple	12
red	10
yellow	4

What is the most popular colour?

NUMBER AND ALGEBRA

1 Francis uses consecutive odd digits to write a number larger than 2000. What is the smallest possible number he can write?

2 Jarrod is a birdwatcher and spotted 23 different bird species on Saturday morning. In the afternoon he recorded another 19 species. What was the total number?

3 Kacey had 60 beads. She lost 10 and gave 20 to Megan. How many beads did she keep?

4 How many sides are on five squares?

5 A 30-metre length of rope is cut into five equal pieces. How long is each piece of rope?

6 Circle the fraction(s) with a numerator two less than the denominator.

$\frac{3}{5}$ $\frac{4}{2}$ $\frac{1}{3}$ $\frac{5}{10}$

7 Juliet buys a peach which costs 85c. What change will she receive from a $2 coin?

8 Annona wrote the smallest odd three-digit number. She subtracted 9 from her number. What was the new number?

MEASUREMENT AND SPACE

9 What is the difference between the lengths of the two pencils?

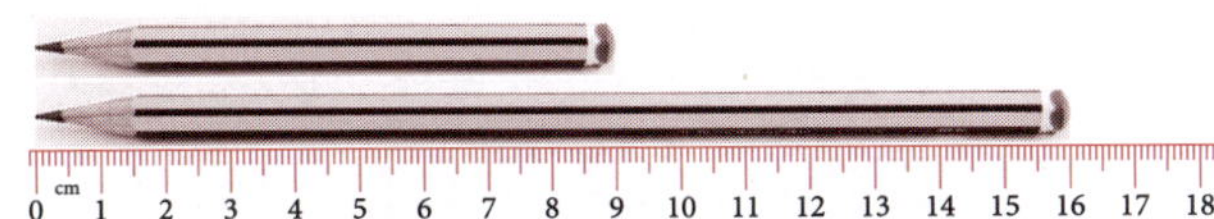

10 This shape is made using cubic-centimetre blocks.

What is the volume of the shape?

11 A baker buys 35 kg of flour online. He orders the flour in 5-kg bags. How many bags did he order?

12 Write this time on the digital clock.

13 How many rectangular faces does an octagonal prism have?

14 Rob used the dotted line to cut a square into two shapes.

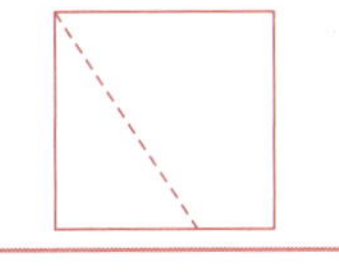

One shape was a quadrilateral. What was the other shape?

15 A line with a dot is pictured.

Draw a perpendicular line through the dot.

16 Simon placed a coin on one of the squares. He moved it up 5 squares and then to the right 4 squares. The coin is now on G7.

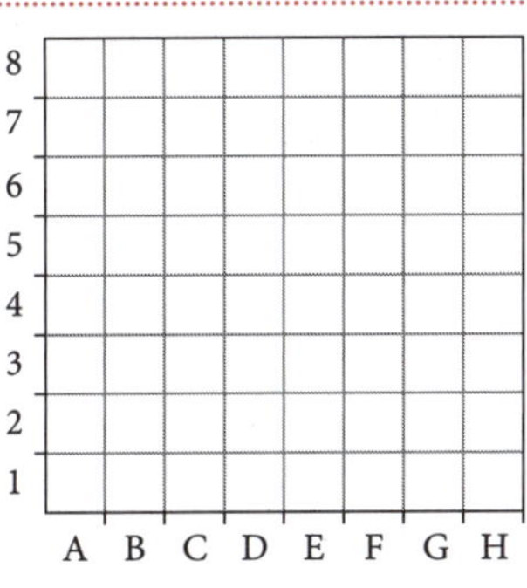

On what square did the coin start?

STATISTICS AND PROBABILITY

17 A bag contains some numbered cards. There are four 3s, three 4s, two 5s and a 6. A card is chosen from the bag without looking. Which number is least likely to be chosen?

18 The favourite colours of a group of students are recorded in the table.

Favourite colours	
Colour	**Students**
blue	3
green	7
purple	12
red	10
yellow	4

How many students said their favourite colour was purple or red?

NUMBER AND ALGEBRA

1 Holly used four different digits smaller than 8 to make the largest possible number. What is Holly's number?

2 Leo scored 12 points in one game of basketball, 9 points in a second game and 11 points in a third. What is the total number of points scored?

3 Jenny cooked 24 sausages on her barbecue. If 18 sausages were eaten, how many remained?

4 Elliot has five boxes. In each box there are seven books. What is the total number of books in the boxes?

5 There are four wheels on a car. Olivia counted 20 wheels on cars that were parked in the school car park. How many cars were in the car park?

6 Lilah writes these four fractions.

$\frac{1}{3}$ $\frac{1}{10}$ $\frac{1}{4}$ $\frac{1}{5}$

Circle the smallest fraction.

7 A supermarket self-service register dispenses change using the smallest possible number of coins. How many coins are dispensed for change of $3.40?

8 What is the next number in this pattern?

0, 7, 14, 21, 28, ?

MEASUREMENT AND SPACE

9 Blake's handspan is 18 cm. Andrea's handspan is 15 cm. What is the difference between the length of their handspans?

10 A leaking tap wastes 3 L of water every day. How much water is wasted in a week?

11 A Christmas ham has a mass of 7 kg. A watermelon has a mass of 5 kg. What is the total mass?

12 Here is a time on a digital clock. Draw the time on the clock face.

13 Annalise drew the shapes of the faces of a square pyramid. How many squares did she draw?

14 Draw a regular quadrilateral.

15 Scott has started to draw a rectangle.

Complete the rectangle.

16 Complete the directions used to move from the triangle to the circle.

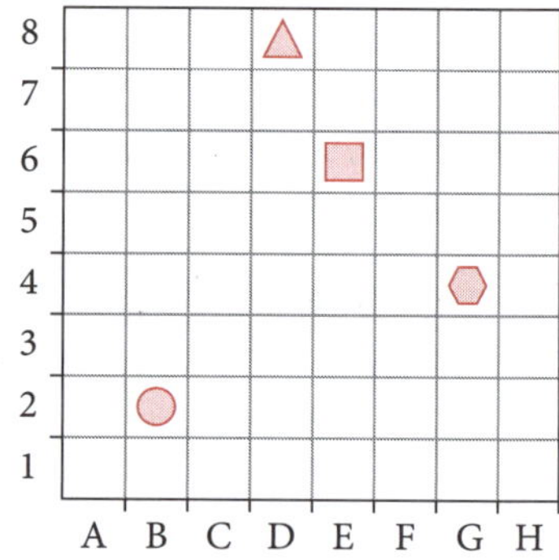

Move ________ squares left and ________ squares down.

STATISTICS AND PROBABILITY

17 A box contains five numbered balls. A ball is chosen without looking. Circle the certain result.

3 5 4 1 2

The number is odd.

The number is less than 6.

18 Here is a table recording the type of vehicle that passed the school at recess.

Vehicles passing the school	
Colour	**Students**
bus	1
truck	3
car	21
motorbike	3
bicycle	4

How many motorbikes went past the school?

NUMBER AND ALGEBRA

1 Isaac wrote the number for forty-nine thousand, eight hundred and six. He then swapped the digits in the thousands and tens places. He subtracted 3 from the digit in the hundreds place. What is Isaac's new number?

2 Tahlia played in six games in a soccer gala day. She scored 2 goals in one game and a goal in two other games. How many goals did she score in total?

3 There were 24 chocolates in a packet. If a chocolate was given to each of seven friends, how many were left?

4 Jacob wants to put three lemons in each of eight bags. How many lemons does he need?

5 Taj has been given 40 stickers on a chart. He draws circles on the chart which each hold eight stickers. How many circles did he draw?

6 On Tuesday Stella bought two milk containers. Her family uses half a container of milk each day. How many days will the milk last?

7 A supermarket self-service register dispenses change using the smallest possible number of coins. How many coins are dispensed for change of $4.95?

8 Melanie wrote down a sequence of all the odd numbers starting with 1. What was the tenth odd number in the sequence?

MEASUREMENT AND SPACE

9 Hayden measured the length of his desk as 10 handspans. He used a ruler to measure his handspan. It was 18 cm. What is the length of his desk?

10 Ava owns a coffee shop. Each day a dozen 2-L milk containers are ordered. How many litres of milk does Ava order each day?

11 How many grams are in 5 kg?

12 Here is a time on a digital clock. Draw the time on the clock face.

13 Aly drew the shapes of the faces of a triangular pyramid. How many triangles did she draw?

14 Circle the shapes with at least four sides.

parallelogram triangle octagon

15 Lisa has started to draw a square.
Complete the square.

16 The map shows where students *P*, *Q*, *R* and *S* live.

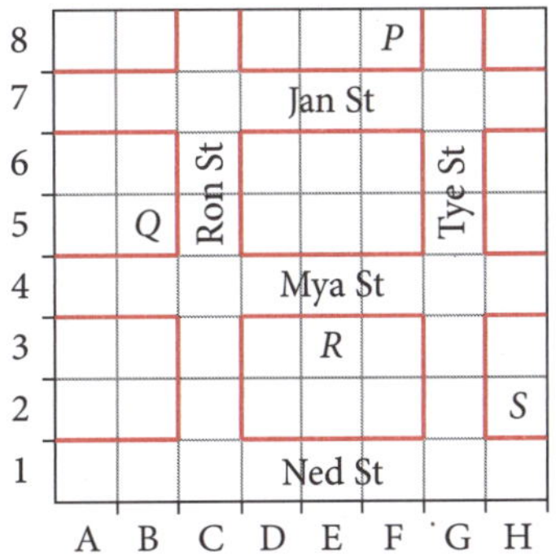

Who lives on the corner of Tye Street and Ned Street?

STATISTICS AND PROBABILITY

17 A box contains five numbered balls. A ball is chosen without looking. Circle the more likely result.

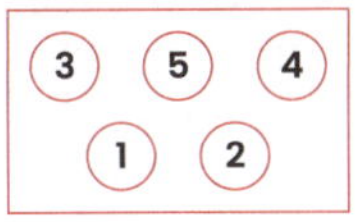

The number is even.

The number is odd.

18 Here is a table recording the type of vehicle that passed the school at recess.

Vehicles passing the school	
Colour	**Students**
bus	1
truck	3
car	21
motorbike	3
bicycle	4

What was the total number of buses and trucks?

NUMBER AND ALGEBRA

1 Agnes used blocks to represent a number. She had 7 thousands, 8 tens and 3 ones. What is the number she has represented?

2 Ethan has two boxes of matchbox cars. In one box there are 26 cars. In the other box there are 23 cars. What is the total number of cars?

3 There are 27 students enrolled in 3K. Two students are absent today. Three students are in the library. How many students are in class?

4 Wesley bought two dozen eggs. How many eggs did he buy?

5 Courtney has 18 dolls. She organises the dolls into pairs. How many pairs of dolls are there?

6 Here is a number line.

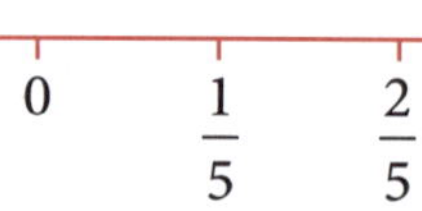

What number is located at A?

7 Shae bought two ice creams at $2.20 each. What is the total cost of the ice creams?

8 Liana adds two odd numbers together. Is her result odd or even?

MEASUREMENT AND SPACE

9 The length of Rohan's bed is 188 cm long. Rohan is 148 cm tall. How much longer is his bed than him?

10 Jayne purchased a 200-mL bottle of soy sauce. After a month she had used half of the soy sauce. How much remains in the bottle?

11 Sasha bought a 5-kg bag of potatoes, a 3-kg bag of oranges and a 1-kg bag of carrots. What was the total mass of the purchases?

12 Here is a time on a digital clock. Draw the time on the clock face.

13 How many of these shapes can roll down a gentle slope?

sphere triangular pyramid cylinder

14 Here is a regular hexagon. How many pairs of sides are parallel?

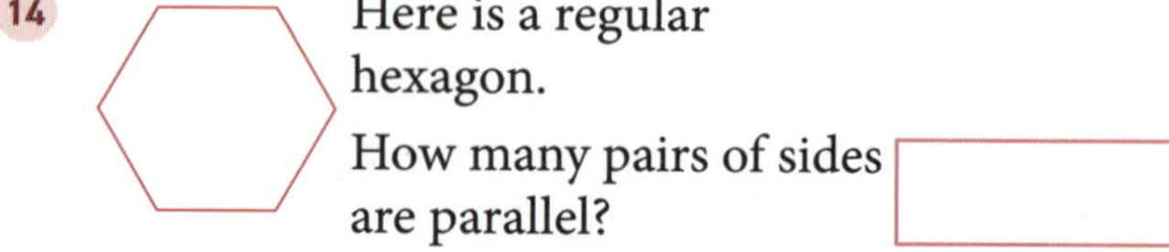

15 Conrad drew a line across a horizontal line. Are these lines perpendicular?

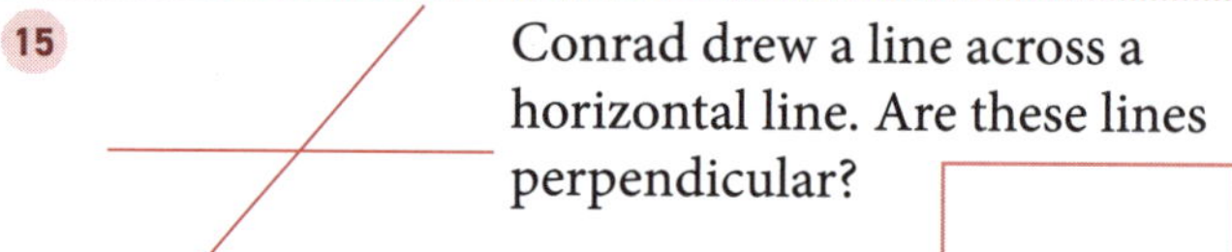

16 A dot is located at F3.

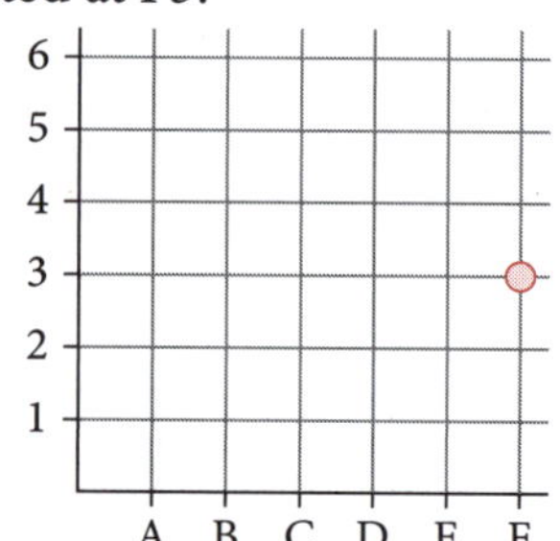

Place a dot on C5.

STATISTICS AND PROBABILITY

17 A bag contains jelly beans. There are eight red jelly beans and four black jelly beans in the bag. Without looking, a jelly bean is removed from the bag. What is the more likely colour chosen?

18 At the sports carnival, students wore house colour T-shirts. Here is a table for the students in class 3P.

T-shirt colours	
Colour	**Number**
red	6
green	4
blue	7
yellow	5

How many students in the class wore green T-shirts?

NUMBER AND ALGEBRA

1 Kristin used blocks to represent 148. She did not have any hundreds blocks. If she had 8 ones, how many tens blocks did she use?

2 There are 16 girls in class 3P and 15 girls in class 3M. How many girls are in the two classes?

3 A shop had 26 T-shirts for sale. After a week there were 15 still not sold.

How many T-shirts had been sold?

4 A roller-coaster has nine rows of three seats. How many people can ride the roller-coaster at the same time?

5 Rosie has 36 cards. She lays the cards on a table in three equal rows. How many cards are in each row?

6 Here is a number line.

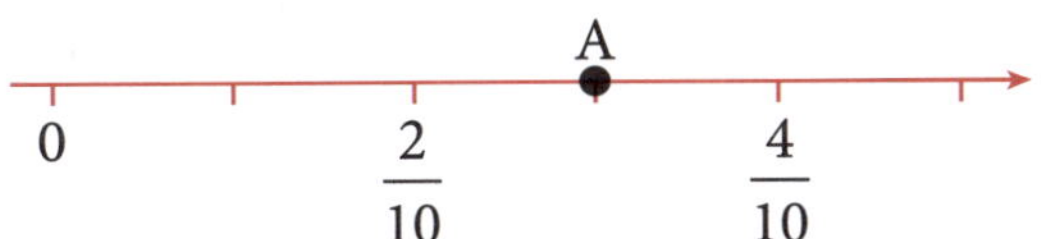

What number is located at *A*?

7 What is \$1.50 + \$1.50 + 90c?

8 Isla adds an odd number of odd numbers together. Is her result odd or even?

MEASUREMENT AND SPACE

9 How many millimetres are in 1 m 5 mm?

10 In a bucket there is 3 L of water. The capacity of the bucket is 9 L.

How much more water is needed to fill the bucket?

11 Orion bought two 5-kg bags of potatoes, a 3-kg bag of oranges and three 1-kg bag of carrots. What was the total mass of the purchases?

12 Here is a time on a digital clock. Draw the time on the clock face.

13 What shape am I? I have an apex and one of my two surfaces is curved.

14 Maddy drew a regular octagon. How many pairs of sides are parallel?

15 A 2D shape has 10 sides. How many angles has the shape?

16 How many units are between D1 and D6?

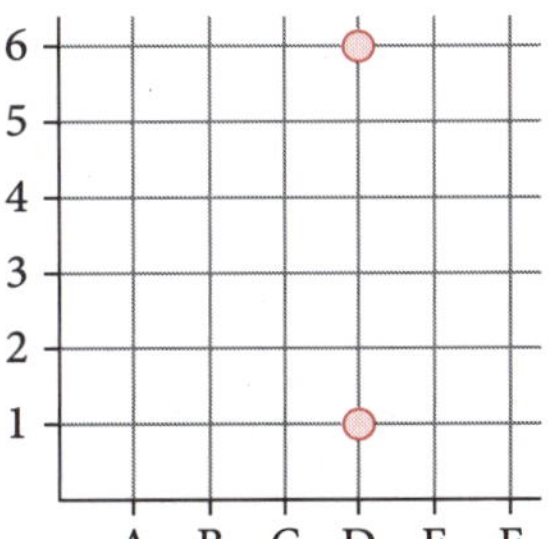

STATISTICS AND PROBABILITY

17 A bag contains 20 jelly beans. There are nine red jelly beans and the remainder are black.

Without looking, a jelly bean is removed from the bag and eaten. What is the more likely colour chosen?

18 At the sports carnival, students wore house colour T-shirts. Here is a table for the students in class 3P.

T-shirt colours	
Colour	**Number**
red	6
green	4
blue	7
yellow	5

How many students wore red or green T-shirts?

NUMBER AND ALGEBRA

1 What number is 20 more than 379?

2 Indie's mother is 42 years old and her grandmother is 26 years older than her mother. How old is Indie's grandmother?

3 An environmental group has 50 small trees to plant. On Saturday 23 trees were planted. The rest were planted on the following day. How many trees were planted on Sunday?

4 Stuart baked a batch of cookies. He placed five cookies in each of six boxes. What was the total number of cookies?

5 Fifteen cards are to be shared equally between five children. How many cards will each child receive?

6 

Angus has drawn a rectangle around some of the balls. What fraction of the balls are inside the rectangle?

7 Amelia bought a calculator for $15 and a pen for $4. What is the total cost?

8 Erika is counting back by 10s. Here are the first three numbers: 125, 115, 105. What is the next number?

MEASUREMENT AND SPACE

9 A square is drawn on a centimetre grid.

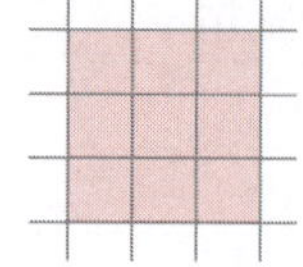

What is the distance around the outside of the square?

10 A jug holds more than 300 mL but less than 550 mL. Which of these is a possible amount of water in the jug?

288 mL 620 mL 510 mL

11 Firewood is sold in 15-kg bags. What is the mass of two bags?

12 How many seconds are in 1 minute?

13 True or false? A cylinder has two vertices.

14 How many lines of symmetry has a square?

15 Circle the larger angle.

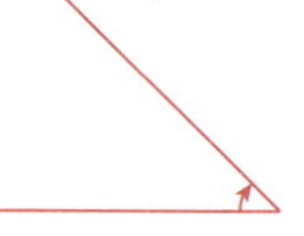

16 The shape is to be translated 3 units right.

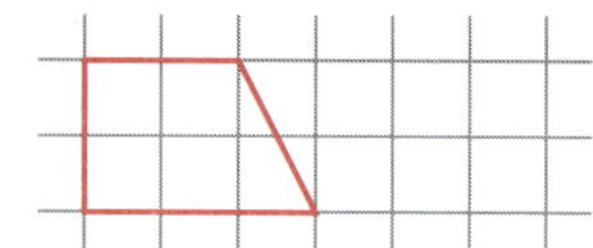

Draw the image of the shape.

STATISTICS AND PROBABILITY

17 Lauren cut these shapes out of cardboard.

Her friend closed her eyes and pointed to a shape. What is the chance she pointed at the triangle?

likely unlikely

certain impossible

18 Donald counted the animals on his farm.

Farm animals	
Animal	**Number**
chicken	12
cow	6
sheep	10
pig	8

How many cows were on the farm?

NUMBER AND ALGEBRA

1 Rachel purchased a new car. After a week the car's odometer showed 000389 km. In the following week she drove another 400 km. What did the odometer show then?

2 Last night Anthony spent 17 minutes reading and 29 minutes watching television. What was the total time?

3 Andrew has a herd of 85 cows. If 45 have already been milked, how many remain to be milked?

4 A shop is selling bags containing 10 oranges. How many oranges are in seven bags?

5 Bryan thinks of a number. He multiplies it by 10 to get 90. What was Bryan's original number?

6 A rectangle has been drawn around some of the balls. What fraction of the balls are outside the rectangle?

7 Thomas bought two paintbrushes. Each paintbrush was priced at $19. What was the total cost?

8 What is three more than the largest even two-digit number?

MEASUREMENT AND SPACE

9 A rectangle is drawn on a centimetre grid.

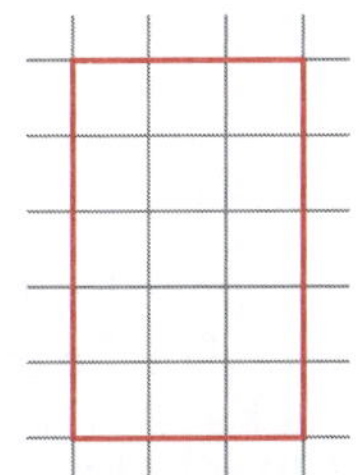

How much shorter is the width than the length?

10 Ethan has two glasses of iced tea. In one glass there is 250 mL and in the other 220 mL. What is the total amount of iced tea?

11 Prawns are sold in 5-kg boxes. Michael bought two boxes of prawns and 2 kg of calamari. What is the total mass of the seafood?

12 How many seconds are in 5 minutes?

13 What is the name of a prism with identical faces?

14 How many lines of symmetry does this parallelogram have?

15 Here are three angles labelled *P*, *Q* and *R*.

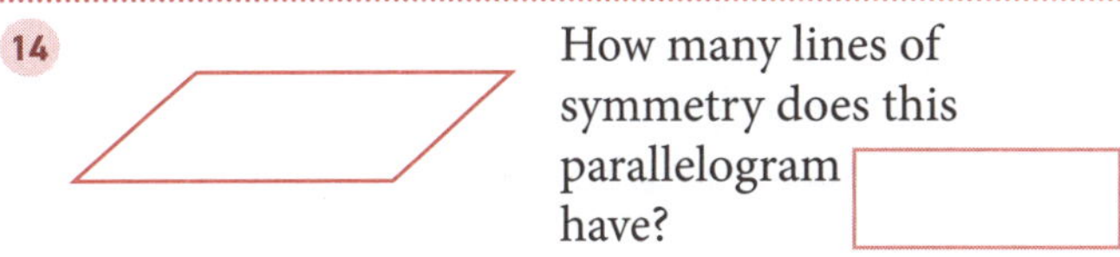

Arrange the angles from largest to smallest.

16 This shape is to be translated 3 units right.

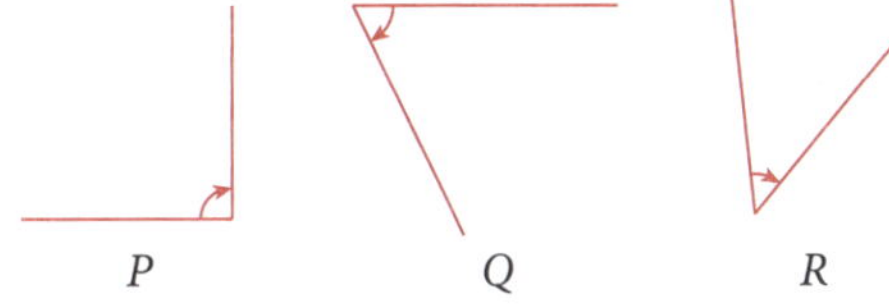

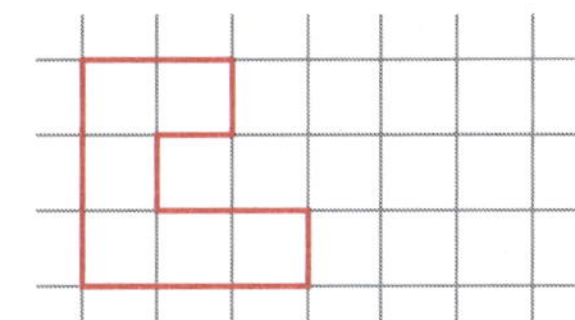

Draw the image of the shape.

STATISTICS AND PROBABILITY

17 At the official opening of a store, every tenth shopper is given a voucher. Harry visits the store. Circle the chance that he is given a voucher.

impossible unlikely likely certain

18 Donald counted the animals on his farm.

Farm animals	
Animal	**Number**
chicken	12
cow	6
sheep	10
pig	8

How many more sheep than cows did Donald have on his farm?

NUMBER AND ALGEBRA

1 Amalie counted 47 cars in the school car park. Thirty minutes later there were only 37 cars. If no new cars had arrived, how many cars left the car park?

2 Ethan has 26 footy cards. His friend William gave him another 30 cards. How many cards does Ethan have?

3 Lawrence added two numbers together and the answer was 46. If the bigger number was 32, what was the smaller number?

4 Tayla tied three balloons together to make a bunch. How many balloons are in 10 bunches?

5 Eight pies are needed to fill one tray. There is a total of 24 pies. How many trays are full?

6 Shade half the squares.

7 Lane has $2 in 20-cent coins. Archer has $2 in 5-cent coins. Which person has more coins?

8 What is the next number?

61, 71, 81, 91, ?

MEASUREMENT AND SPACE

9 A rectangle is drawn on a centimetre grid. What is the distance around the outside of the rectangle?

10 Peyton takes 5 mL of medicine three times a day. What is the total amount of medicine she will take in one day?

11 Sean buys some meat for a barbecue. He buys 4 kg of sausages, 3 kg of steak and 2 kg of chicken wings. What is the total mass of meat?

12 Dawn looked at these clocks in the afternoon and the evening. How many hours are between the times shown on the clocks?

13 Eva has a packet of round biscuits. Each biscuit is the same size. She makes a stack of 12 biscuits. What 3D shape does Eva make?

14 Carmel drew a quadrilateral with no pairs of parallel lines. Circle the shape she could have drawn.

rectangle kite trapezium

15 Tick the angle that is smaller than a right angle.

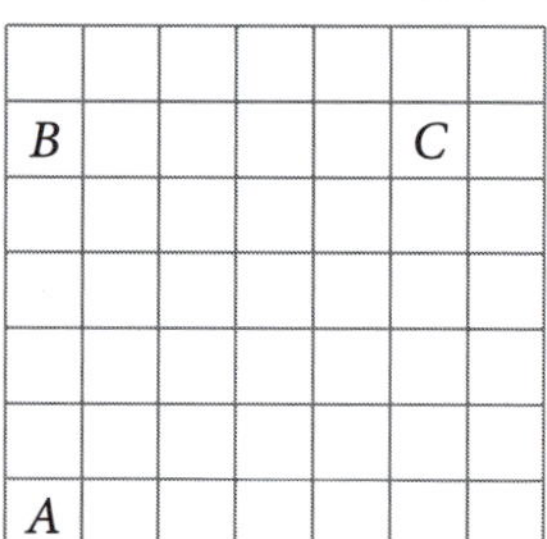

16 Alison is in square *A*. She moves to *B*. She turns right and moves to *C*. How many units has she moved from *A* to *C*?

B					*C*	
A						

STATISTICS AND PROBABILITY

17 These numbered cards are placed in a bag.

7 3 9 5 1

One card is chosen from the bag without looking. What is the chance that the card is odd?

likely unlikely certain impossible

18 The way students travelled to school this morning is recorded in the table.

Transport to school	
Method	**Students**
walk	4
car	12
bus	16
bicycle	7

How many students travelled by bus?

NUMBER AND ALGEBRA

1 Half an hour before a concert was scheduled to start there were 297 people seated. In the next 20 minutes another 3000 people arrived. How many were then at the concert?

2 Jahal collects stamps. In one box he has 120 and in another 78. How many stamps are in the two boxes?

3 There are 200 sheep to be shorn. By lunchtime 120 have been shorn. How many more sheep need to be shorn?

4 Hannah drew eight rows of hearts. Each row had five hearts. How many hearts did Hannah draw?

5 Abby counted 21 days until her birthday. How many weeks are there until her birthday?

6 Here are 12 triangles.

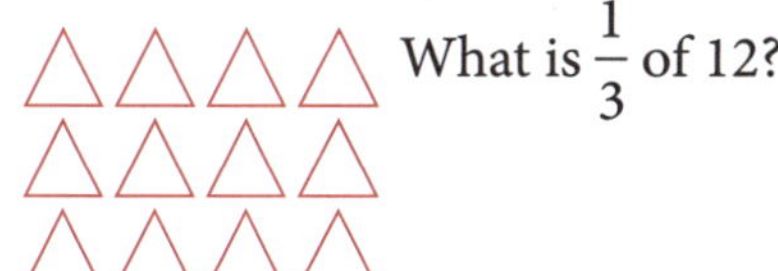

What is $\frac{1}{3}$ of 12?

7 A restaurant dinner cost $65. Caitlin paid for the meal with two $50 notes.

How much change did she receive?

8 ☐, 79, 89, 99, ☐

What are the two missing numbers?

MEASUREMENT AND SPACE

9 Kaiden drew a rectangle where the length was twice the width. The width of the rectangle was 6 cm. What was the length?

10 This jug contains some water. Victoria says there is 250 mL of water in the jug. Is she correct?

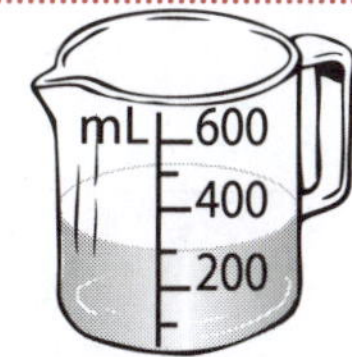

11 An orange has a mass of 120 g. Theo uses a knife to cut the orange into two halves. What is the mass of half an orange?

12 Shannon looked at these clocks in the afternoon and the night. How many hours are between the times shown on the clocks?

13 The cross-section of a 3D shape is a circle. The area of the cross-section is smaller than the area of its base. Circle the name of the shape.

cone cylinder

14 What 2D shape am I? All my sides are equal. I have exactly two lines of symmetry.

15 Draw a quadrilateral with four right angles.

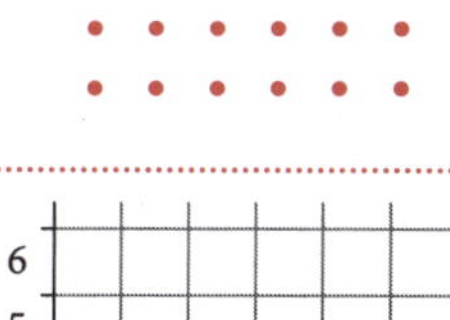

16 Dwayne starts at E3. He moves up 2 units and 4 units to the left.

What is Dwayne's location?

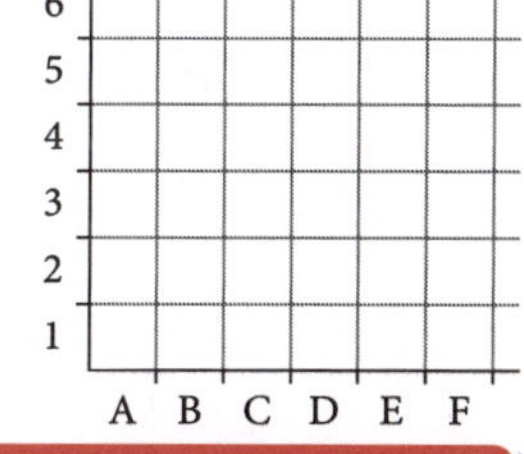

STATISTICS AND PROBABILITY

17 Tommi rolled three normal dice and added the top numbers. What is the chance that the total was 18?

impossible very unlikely
very likely certain

18 The way students travelled to school this morning is recorded in the table.

Transport to school	
Method	**Students**
walk	4
car	12
bus	16
bicycle	7

What was the total number of students who walked or travelled by car?

NAPLAN-STYLE TEST 1

1 Here are five numbers: 873 387 738 378 783
Rewrite the numbers from smallest to largest.

smallest largest

2 17 + **?** = 50. What is the missing number?

A 27 **B** 33 **C** 37 **D** 43

3 Here is a pattern of numbers: 9, 13, 17, 21, 25, 29, **?** .
What is the missing number?

A 32 **B** 33 **C** 34 **D** 35

4 Choose the **two** number sentences that do **not** equal 12.

A 4 + 4 + 4 **B** 2 + 2 + 2 + 2 + 2 + 2 + 2 **C** 3 + 3 + 3 + 3 **D** 6 + 2

5 How many cubic-centimetre cubes are in this solid?

A 8 **B** 10
C 12 **D** 13

6 Which of these is **not** a quadrilateral?

A **B** **C** **D**

7 A rectangle is drawn on a grid. The rectangle is translated to the right 3 units and then up 2 units. After the translations, which of these are covered by the image of the rectangle?

A E6 **B** F2 **C** F5
D G3 **E** G7

8 The clock shows the time Latanna woke this morning.
She needed to leave for school three-quarters of an hour later.
Which of these clocks shows the time she needed to leave home?

A 07:55 **B** 08:15 **C** 08:30 **D** 08:45

9 A supermarket sells lemons in small bags. A bag of five lemons costs $3.
What is the most lemons Jannah can buy for $10?

A 7 **B** 13 **C** 12 **D** 15

10 Linsey used a ruler to measure a pen and a USB.
How much longer is the pen than the USB?

A 6 cm **B** 7 cm
C 8 cm **D** 9 cm

11 What number is two more than six thousand and ninety-eight?

12 Theo and Agnes have a total of $40. Theo has $10 more than Agnes.
How much money has Agnes?

A $15 **B** $25 **C** $30 **D** $35

13 Daisy rolls a normal dice once.
Which **three** of these outcomes are possible?

A Daisy rolls a 6.
B Daisy rolls a number less than 4.
C Daisy rolls a 9.
D Daisy rolls a 3 and a 4.
E Daisy rolls an even number.

14 These shapes are the faces of a solid.
How many edges will the solid have?

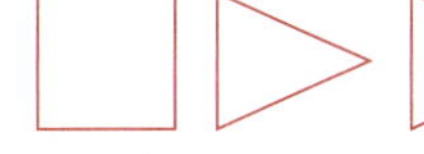

A 5 **B** 16 **C** 8 **D** 12 **E** 9

15 Xander used the grid to draw a shape.
Half of the shape is drawn.
The dotted line is a line of symmetry of the completed shape.
How many sides has Xander's final shape?

A 8
B 9
C 10
D 12

16 Joaquin is practising basketball in his backyard. He counts his shots and the number of times he scores.
He works out that he scores in $\frac{2}{5}$ of his shots. In what fraction of his shots does he **not** score?

A $\frac{1}{5}$ **B** $\frac{2}{5}$ **C** $\frac{3}{5}$ **D** $\frac{4}{5}$ **E** $\frac{5}{5}$

17 There are 24 coloured pencils on the teacher's desk.
The pencils are to be placed evenly back into three boxes.
How many pencils fit into each box?

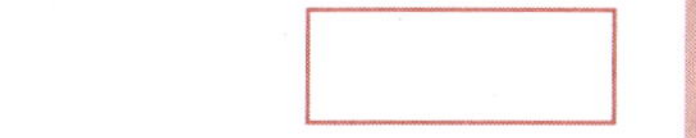

18 The graph shows the maximum temperatures during one week in Melbourne.
On what day was the temperature 2 degrees warmer than the maximum temperature on Monday?

A Wednesday
B Thursday
C Friday
D Saturday

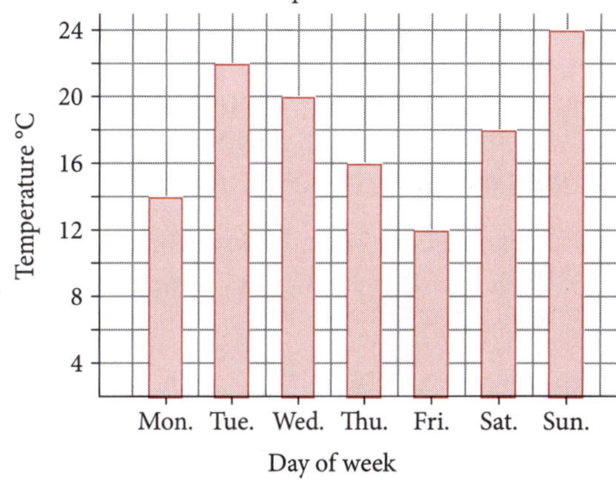

19 Oscar fills four identical jugs with water.
Each jug holds 2 L. He pours all the water from the jugs into an empty container with a capacity of 9 L when full.
How much more water is needed to fill the container?

A 1 L **B** 2 L **C** 3 L **D** 5 L

20 Frank spun the arrow on this spinner twice.
He added both numbers the arrow pointed to.
Which of these totals is **not** possible?

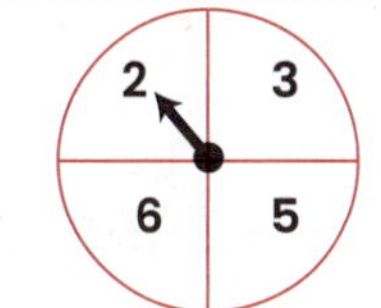

A 3 **B** 4 **C** 7 **D** 9 **E** 11

NUMBER AND ALGEBRA

1 Use numbers and a symbol to rewrite 'Two hundred and six is less than three hundred and forty'.

2 What number is 23 less than 40?

3 In a cricket match Jackie scored 65 runs and Mim scored 35 runs. What is the total number of runs scored by the two players?

4 Thomas buys 55 tomato plants. He arranges the plants in his garden equally in five rows. How many plants are in each row?

5 When she attends the fitness centre, Katja swims for 20 minutes. In one week she visits the fitness centre four times. For how many minutes did she swim during the week?

6 What fraction of the shape is **not** shaded?

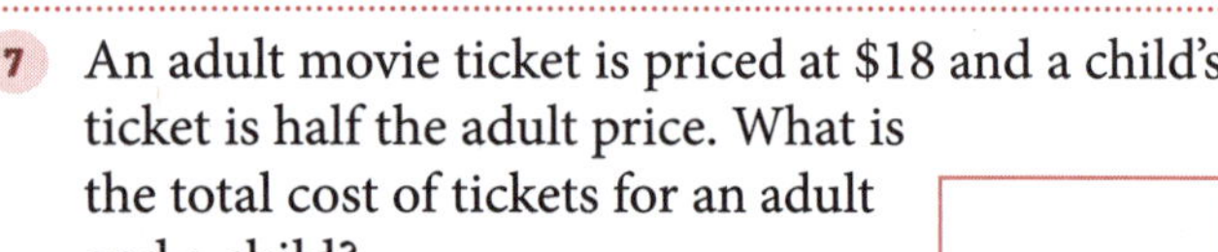

7 An adult movie ticket is priced at $18 and a child's ticket is half the adult price. What is the total cost of tickets for an adult and a child?

8 Alex starts at 20 and counts backwards by 4. Which of these numbers is on Alex's list?

18 14 12 10

MEASUREMENT AND SPACE

9 Three sides of a rectangle are 8 cm, 3 cm and 8 cm. What is the length of the other side?

10 A 10-L bucket is filled with water. How many 2-L containers can be filled with water from the bucket?

11 A bag of rice has a mass of 3 kg. Lena needs to buy 12 kg of rice. How many bags does she need to buy?

12 How many seconds have passed between the two digital clocks?

06:18 06:20

13 How many edges has a cube?

14 Mo has started to draw a rectangle on a grid.

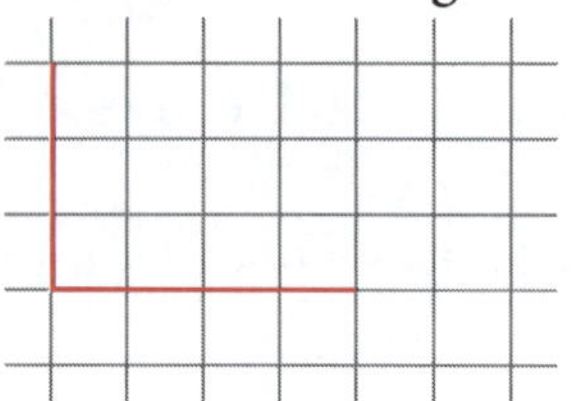

Complete the rectangle.

15 The diagram has four labelled angles.

a b c d

Which letter is the name of the smallest angle?

16 Shane is driving north along a straight road. Which direction is on his left?

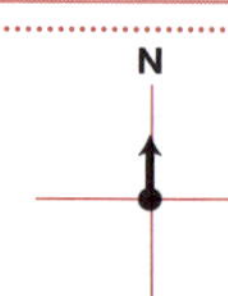

STATISTICS AND PROBABILITY

17 A small ball is hidden under one of the cups.

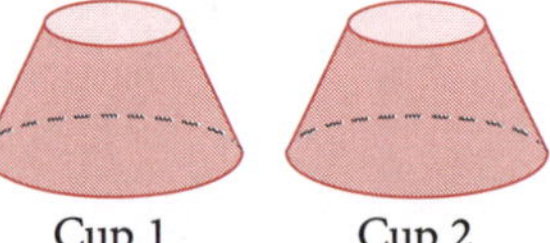

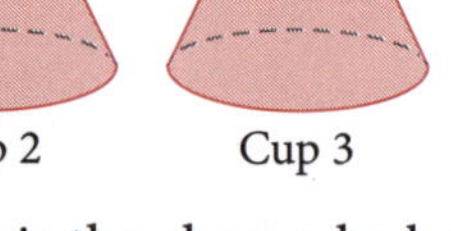

Jack chooses Cup 2. What is the chance he has chosen the cup which contains the ball?

certain unlikely impossible

18 The number of animals in a nature park is recorded in a graph.

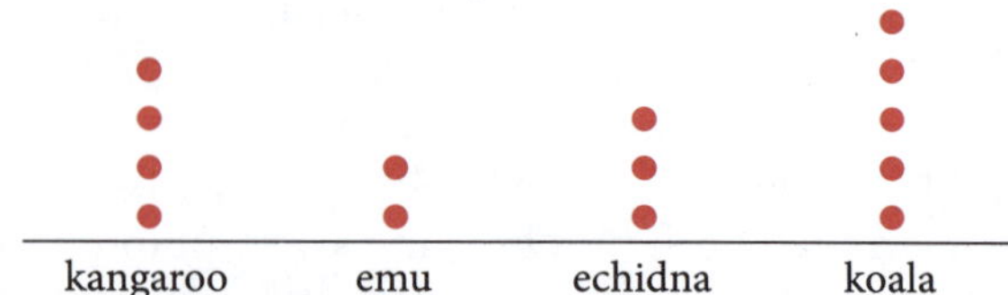

How many kangaroos and koalas were counted?

NUMBER AND ALGEBRA

1 Theodore wrote a number which was less than seven thousand and fifty. Which of these could be his number?

7400 7009 7401 7060

2 George has walked 8000 steps. How many more steps does he need to walk to reach his daily goal of 11 000 steps?

3 A family ate 16 apples in one week and another 19 apples in the following week. How many apples were eaten in the fortnight?

4 A warning light flashes every 3 seconds. If it flashes now, how many more times will it flash in 30 seconds?

5 Jemima buys half a dozen packets of toilet paper. Each packet contains 10 rolls. What is the total number of toilet paper rolls purchased?

6 Laylah records the number of netball goals scored.

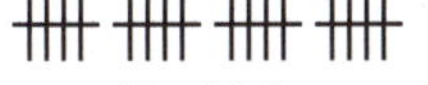

Her friend Ava scored half the goals. How many goals did Ava score?

7 Isaac buys a banana which costs 65 cents. What change is he given from a $2 coin?

8 What is the rule for this pattern of numbers?

74, 67, 60, 53 …

MEASUREMENT AND SPACE

9 What is the difference between the lengths of the two crayons?

10 These shapes are made using cubic-centimetre blocks.

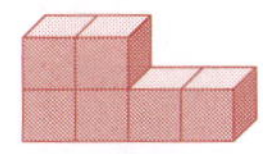
Shape A

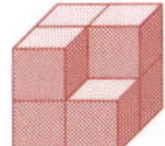
Shape B

Circle the shape with the greater volume.

11 The mass of a sphere is 13 kg. A sphere and a cube have a combined mass of 23 kg. What is the mass of two cubes?

12 How many seconds have passed between the two analog clocks?

13 How many edges does a hexagonal prism have?

14 Ruth has started to draw a parallelogram on a grid.

Complete the parallelogram.

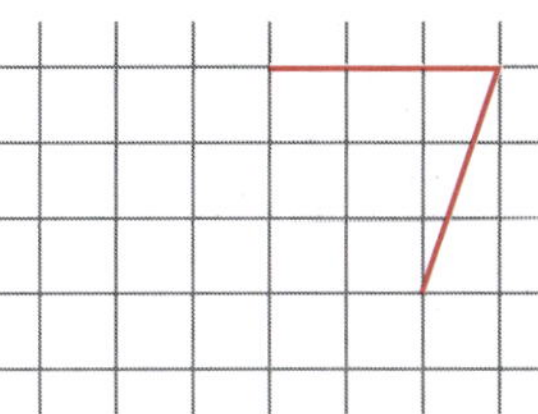

15 The angles in a parallelogram are named *a*, *b*, *c* and *d*.

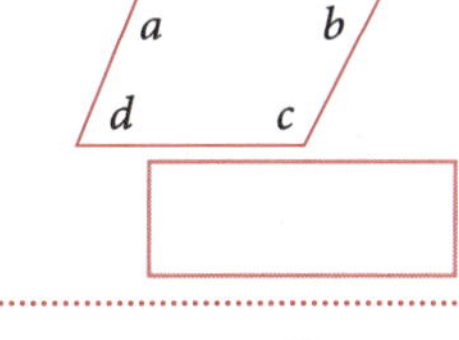

Name the angles that are less than a right angle.

16 Olivia is driving south along a straight road.

Which direction is on her left?

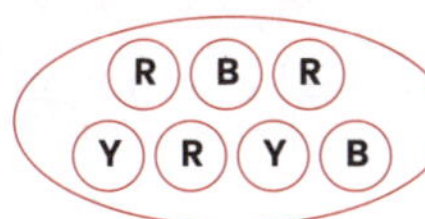

STATISTICS AND PROBABILITY

17 Balls coloured red (R), blue (B) and yellow (Y) are placed in a container.

A ball is chosen without looking.

What colours have an equal chance of being chosen?

18 The number of animals in a nature park is recorded in a graph.

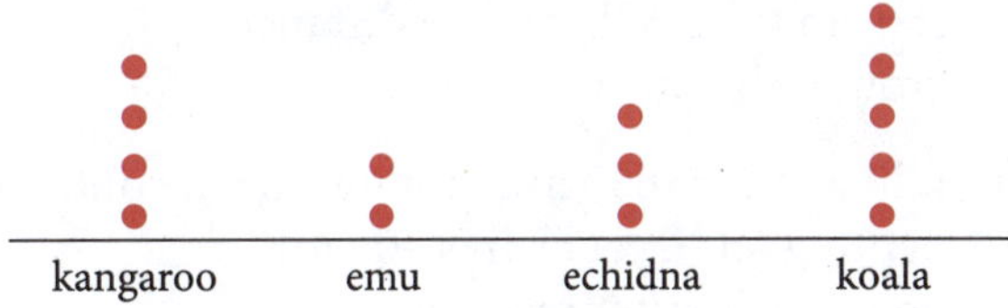

What was the total number of animals counted?

NUMBER AND ALGEBRA

1 Nate uploaded a video to a social media site. After a week it had 2973 views. Round the number of views to the nearest thousand.

2 A hockey team scored the same number of goals in each of five games. The team scored a total of 20 goals. How many goals did they score in the final game?

3 The temperature at 6 am was 14 °C. By 10 am it had risen 13 °C and by midday it had risen another 3 °C. What was the temperature at midday?

4 A supermarket displays 24 cans in a box. After 2 days there are nine cans remaining. How many cans have been purchased?

5 At a concert the first five rows have 10 seats each. How many seats are in the first five rows?

6 Here are two circles. Shade $1\frac{1}{2}$ circles.

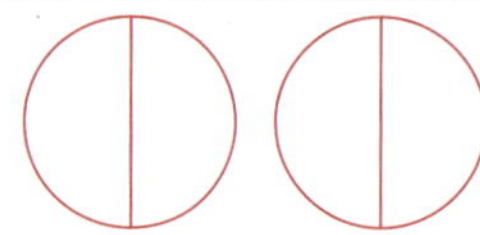

7 On Mother's Day, a roadside stall was selling flowers for $10 a bunch. Illiana bought two bunches and handed over a $50 note. How much change did Illiana receive?

8 The numbers in the boxes form a pattern.

16	22	28	34			X

What is the number in box X?

MEASUREMENT AND SPACE

9 Phoenix drew a square. Each side of the square is 6 cm long. What is the distance around the outside of the square?

10 Lillian pours 600 mL of water into a container for her dog Jet. If Jet drinks 100 mL, how much water remains?

11 Here are four blocks. The mass of each block is shown. What is the total mass of the blocks?

12 What time is 30 minutes after the time shown on the clock?

13 Circle the net of a cube.

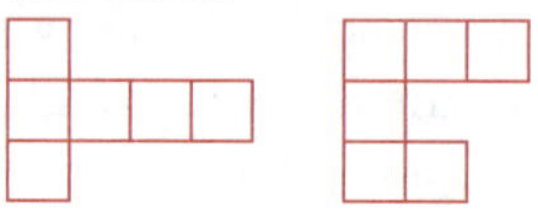

14 Felix has started to draw a trapezium on a grid.

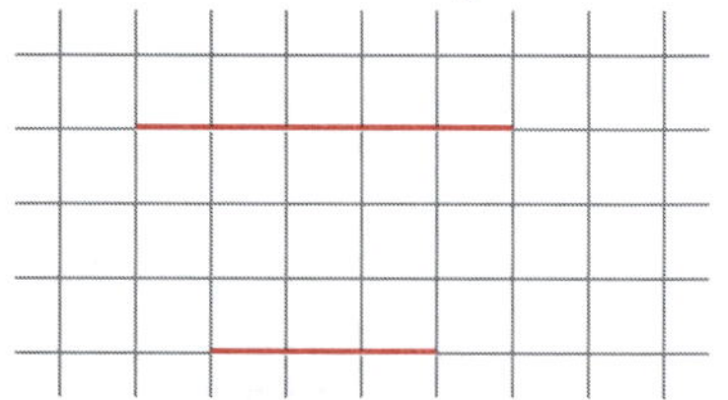

Complete the trapezium.

15 How many right angles are in this diagram?

16 The grid shows the location of five students.

Jessica is standing on C3.

Troy is east of Jessica. What is the location of Troy?

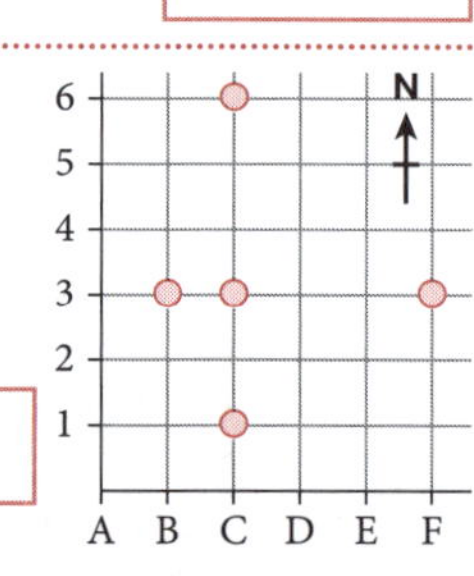

STATISTICS AND PROBABILITY

17 The arrow on this spinner is spun.

True or false? There is no chance that the arrow lands on purple.

18 The number of pies sold by a bakery in one hour is recorded.

Pie sales

beef, chicken, mushroom, meat-free

What was the total number of beef and chicken pies sold?

NUMBER AND ALGEBRA

1 What is 3007 rounded to the nearest hundred?

2 Each table in a restaurant has four chairs. There are 27 occupied and 13 vacant chairs. How many tables are in the restaurant?

3 A hotel has 38 rooms booked for Saturday night. There are 24 rooms still available. What is the total number of rooms in the hotel?

4 Theo is driving 100 km from his home to Forster. He stops for petrol after driving 63 km. What distance does he still need to travel?

5 There are 12 chairs around a large table. Each chair has 4 legs. What is the total number of chair legs?

6 This shape consists of three rows of rectangles.

Shade $1\frac{1}{3}$ rows of rectangles.

7 How much less than $5 is the total value of these coins?

8 The numbers in the boxes form a pattern.

X			68	72	76	80

What is the number in box *X*?

MEASUREMENT AND SPACE

9 A length of wire is one and a half metres. How long is the length of wire in centimetres?

10 Charlotte and Emily are bushwalking for 2 days. They both plan to drink 10 L of water each day. What is the total amount of water they should carry?

11 A tub of margarine has a mass of 500 g. Jen bought two tubs. What is the total mass, in kilograms?

12 What time is half an hour after the time shown on the clock?

13 Here is a net. Circle the name of the 3D shape formed.

square pyramid triangular pyramid triangular prism

14 Tori has started to draw a kite on a grid.

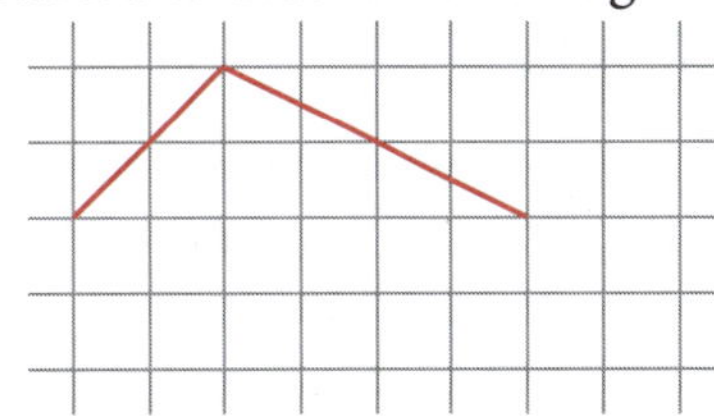

Complete the kite.

15 Here is a quadrilateral. Tick the largest angle.

16 The grid shows the location of five students. Jessica is standing on C3. If Jessica faces east, Jane is on her right. What is Jane's location?

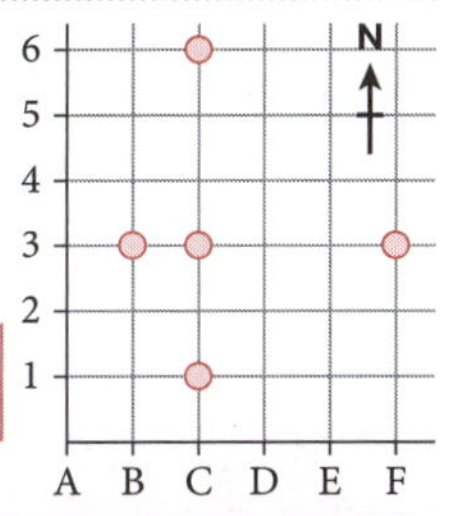

STATISTICS AND PROBABILITY

17 The arrow on this spinner is spun. True or false? It is more likely that the arrow will land on blue than green.

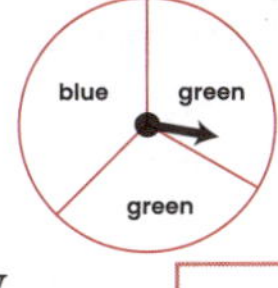

18 The number of pies sold by a bakery in one hour is recorded.

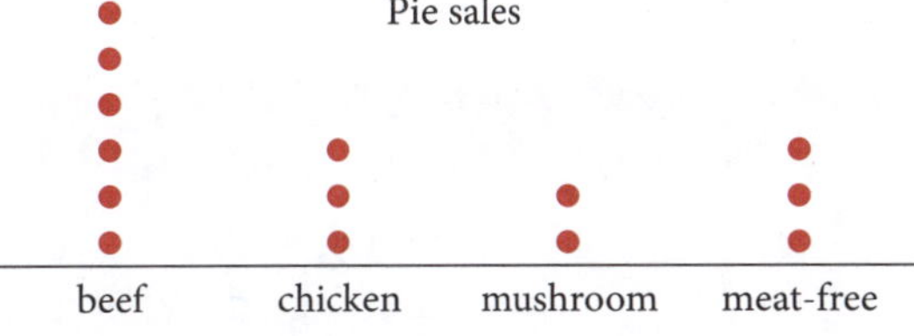

How many pies that were **not** beef or chicken were sold?

NUMBER AND ALGEBRA

1 Lachlan wrote a number with odd digits in the thousand and tens place and even digits in the hundreds and ones place. Which of these could be Lachlan's number?

3871 7282 9876

2 A small gift was given to every tenth customer who walked into a shop. After an hour 80 customers had entered the shop. How many gifts had been handed out?

3 In 2020 there were 68 koalas in a colony. Three years later there were 13 fewer koalas. How many were in the colony in 2023?

4 A hardware store sold packets containing eight screws. If Ellie bought five packets, how many screws did she buy?

5 On Saturday nights Baylee babysits for her parents' friends. Over four Saturdays she babysits for 3 hours, 5 hours, 4 hours and 5 hours. What is the total number of hours?

6 Here is a number line.

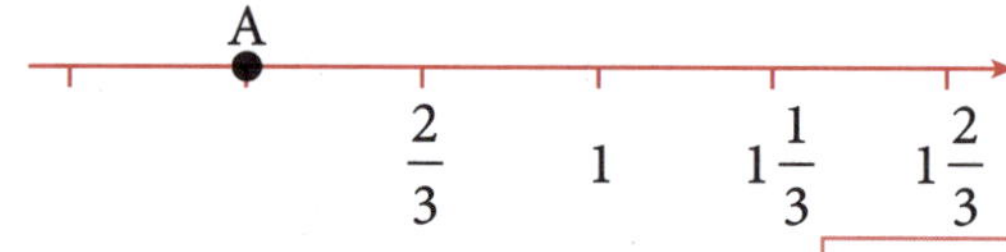

What number is located at *A*?

7 Hannah bought a mathematics book online which was priced at $18. She then paid $3.50 for postage. What was the total cost?

8 A rule links the numbers in the bottom row with numbers in the top row. Write the missing numbers in the boxes.

Top	5	6	7	8	9
Bottom	13	14			17

MEASUREMENT AND SPACE

9 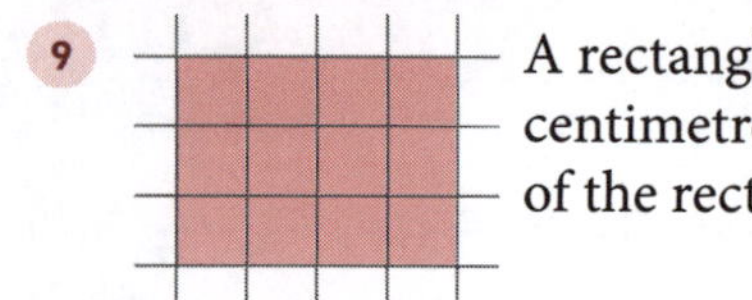
A rectangle is drawn on a centimetre grid. What is the area of the rectangle?

10 Petrol costs $2 per litre. What is the cost of the petrol if Cindy buys 40 L?

11 A box of apples has a mass of 20 kg. If 13 kg of apples are removed, what is the mass of the box with the remaining apples?

12 Circle the digital clock showing 10 past 12.

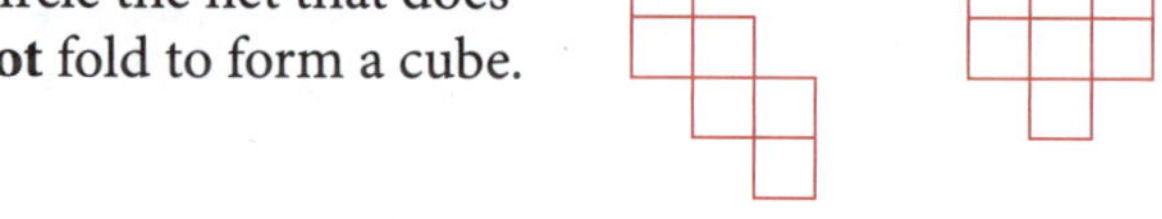

13 Circle the net that does **not** fold to form a cube.

14 Draw the lines of symmetry on this shape.

15 The circle has been cut into quarters.

How many right angles are shown?

16 Ariana leaves D2 and moves 4 units north and then 2 units west.

What is Ariana's new location?

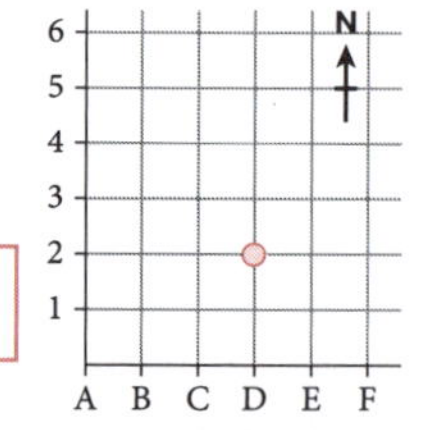

STATISTICS AND PROBABILITY

17 Here are two spinners.

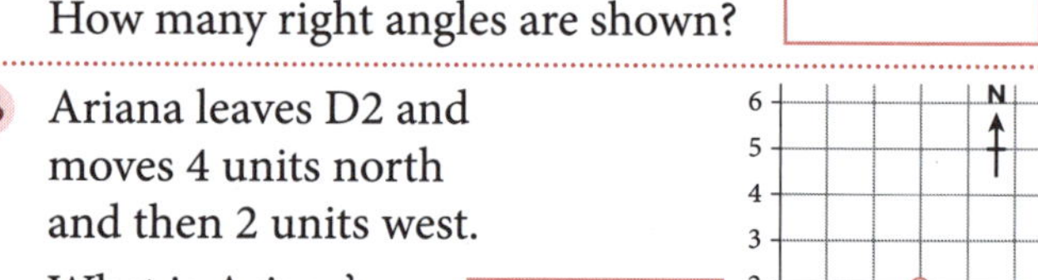

Circle the spinner that has a chance of stopping on a 5.

18 The savings of four students are shown on the graph.

Who saved the most amount of money?

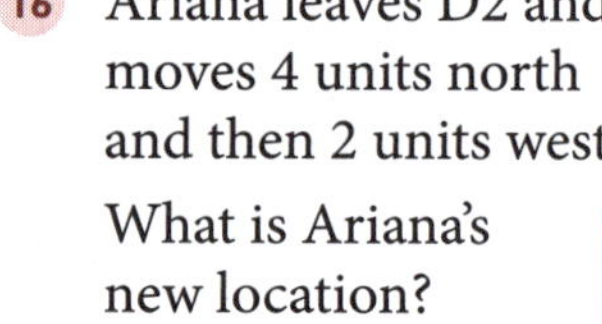
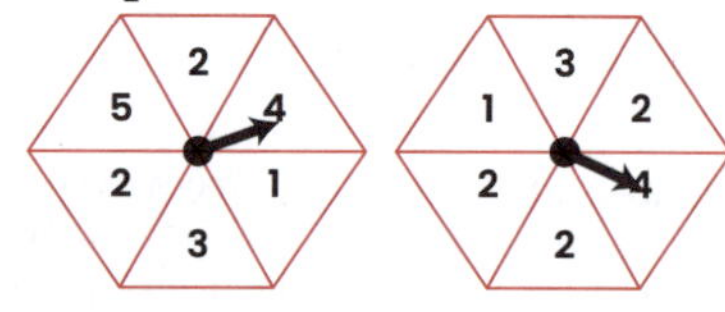
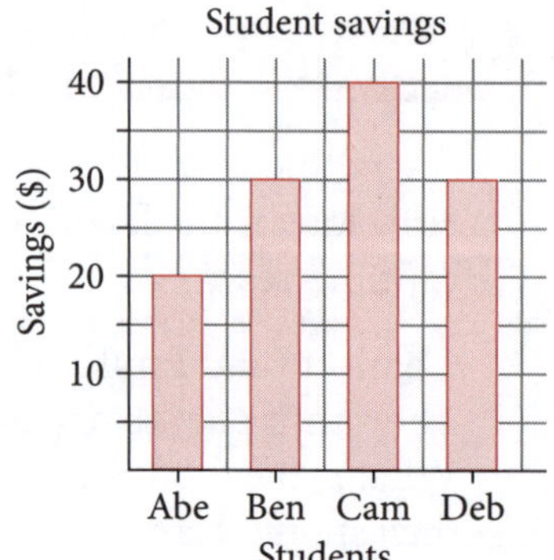

NUMBER AND ALGEBRA

1 What number is one less than a four-digit number which has identical digits that add to 8?

2 Boxes contain one dozen mangoes. Nathan buys two boxes. The mangoes are to be shared between four people. How many mangoes does each person receive?

3 The total distance from Jackson to Thorpe is 53 km. Finlay left Jackson and has driven 36 km on his way to Thorpe. What distance remains?

4 The principal formed groups of 10 students. There was a total of 12 groups. How many students had been arranged into groups?

5 A playroom has a pit containing 170 plastic balls. Another 65 balls are added to the pit. How many balls are now in the pit?

6 Here is a number line.

$\frac{1}{4}$ $\frac{2}{4}$ A

What number is located at *A*?

7 Violet purchased \$3.88 worth of salami. She handed \$4 to the cashier. How much change was she given?

8 A rule links the numbers in the bottom row with the numbers in the top row. Write the missing numbers in the boxes.

Top	7	11	14	20	
Bottom	12	16		25	37

MEASUREMENT AND SPACE

9 The dimensions of a single mattress are 188 cm by 92 cm. A double mattress has dimensions 188 cm by 138 cm. How much wider is the double mattress?

10 Soft drink is available in a 375-mL can or a 600-mL bottle. What is the difference between the two quantities?

11 The mass of a litre of water is about 1 kg. At the start of the day Jaclyn fills a bottle with a litre of water. During the day she drinks half the water. Estimate the mass of the remaining water.

12 What time is half an hour after 20 to 3?

13 Complete the statement.
The net of a cylinder has 2 ________________ and 1 ________________.

14 Draw the line(s) of symmetry on this shape.

15 The angles in a triangle are named *a*, *b* and *c*.

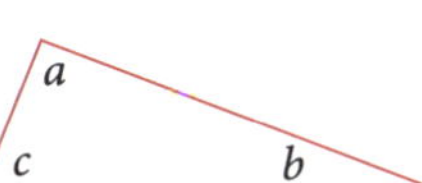

Write the names of the angles, from smallest to largest.

16 Katie left *X* and moved 4 units east and then north to F5.

How many units north did Katie move?

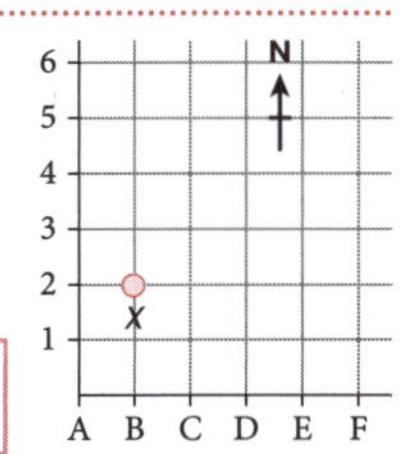

STATISTICS AND PROBABILITY

17 Here are two spinners.

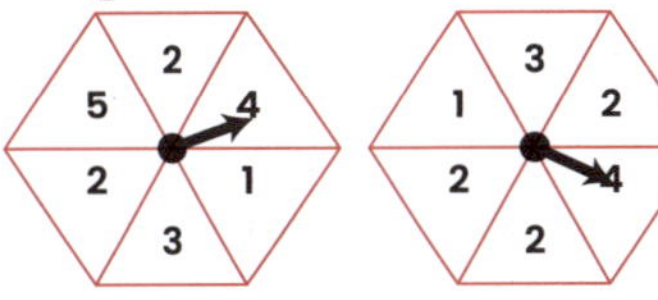

Circle the spinner that has a greater chance of stopping on a 2.

18 The savings of four students are shown on the graph.

What was the total amount saved by Cam and Abe?

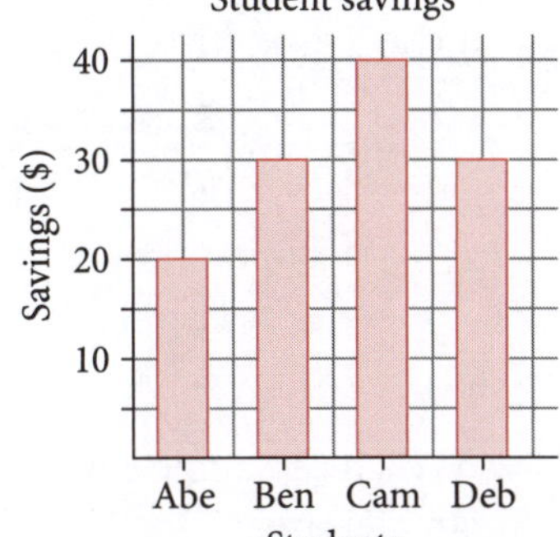

NUMBER AND ALGEBRA

1 Cameron started with 137 and counted forward by 10s. Which of these numbers did he count?

173 187 203

2 Silas makes stacks of eight coins. He makes a total of five stacks. How many coins did he use?

3 Four athletes are running in a relay race. Each athlete takes turns to run the same distance. The total distance of the relay is 20 laps of a park. How far will each athlete run?

4 A supermarket sold 900 packets of toilet paper in one day. The next day it sold another 700 packets. What was the total number of packets sold?

5 Amy is reading a book containing 60 pages. She has already read 39 pages. How many pages has she still to read?

6 Divide this rectangle into halves and shade $\frac{1}{2}$ of the rectangle.

7 Finn was given a $150 gift card for Christmas. He bought a tennis racquet for $120. How much money value has he remaining on the card?

8 Peter thinks of an odd number. He adds 6, then subtracts 5. Is his answer even or odd?

MEASUREMENT AND SPACE

9 Rectangles *A* and *B* are drawn on a centimetre grid.

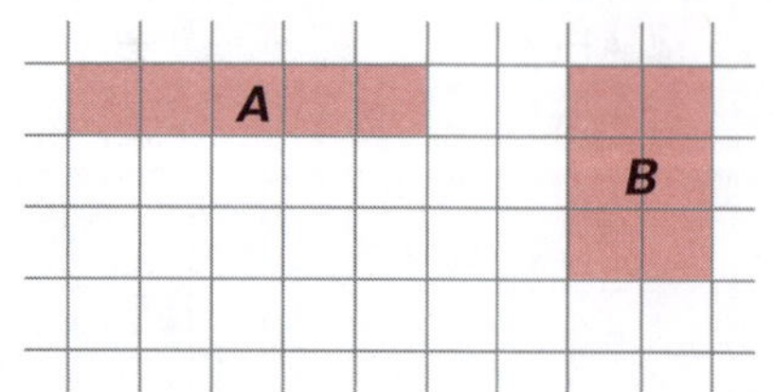

Which rectangle covers the greater area?

10 Levi has a drum of petrol containing 40 L. He has a small container with a capacity of 10 L.

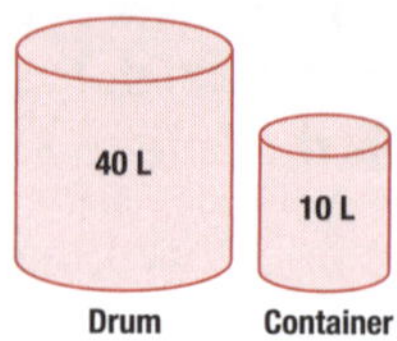

How many small containers can be filled using the drum?

11 Ariana had a mass of 47 kg. Her brother Kale had a mass 4 kg more than his sister. What was Kale's mass?

12 Eloise arrives at the bus stop at 8:40. She is 12 minutes early for her bus. What time does her bus arrive?

13 Circle the net that would fold to a rectangular prism.

14 Marcus drew three hexagons and two pentagons. What was the total number of sides?

15 The diagram has four labelled angles. What is the name of the largest angle?

16 The sun sets in the west. Hugh is looking at the sunset. What direction is on his left?

STATISTICS AND PROBABILITY

17 A bag contains a red ball, a green ball and a blue ball. Two balls are drawn out at the same time. Kristy listed two out of the three possible pairs.

red and green red and blue

What is the missing pair?

18 The number of bikes sold in four days is recorded in the dot plot.

What was the total number of bikes sold?

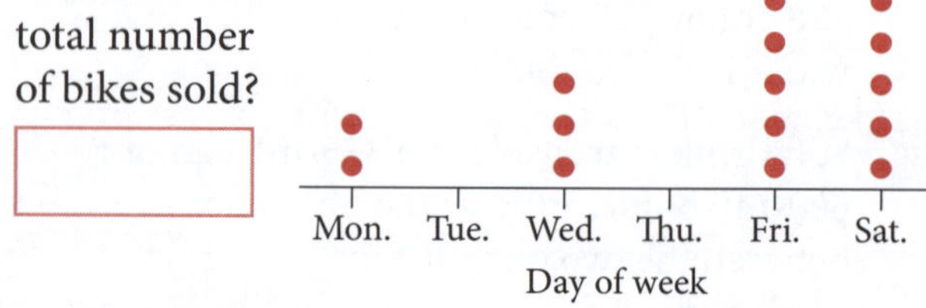

NUMBER AND ALGEBRA

1 Erin started at 193 and counted backwards by 20s. Which of these numbers will she count?

191 183 123 113

2 Monique bought three dozen bananas. What is the total number of bananas?

3 Twenty-four chocolates are to be shared equally between Alice, Emma and Terri. What is the total number of chocolates given to Alice and Emma?

4 Saraya is 3 years older than Erin and 2 years younger than Harrison. If Erin is 8 years old, what is the sum of their ages?

5 At the end of a football match there were 84 people waiting for a bus. A bus arrived and 52 people got on the bus. How many people were left waiting for the next bus?

6 Divide this rectangle into quarters and shade $\frac{3}{4}$ of the rectangle.

7 Esther makes 50 cents for every bag of cookies she sells. How much will she make if she sells 12 bags?

8 Mandy writes the first five numbers in a sequence: 120, 112, 104, 96, 88.

If the sequence continues, which of these numbers will Mandy write?

72 70 68 56

MEASUREMENT AND SPACE

9 Jade started to draw a rectangle on a centimetre grid. The rectangle will have an area of 15 cm^2.

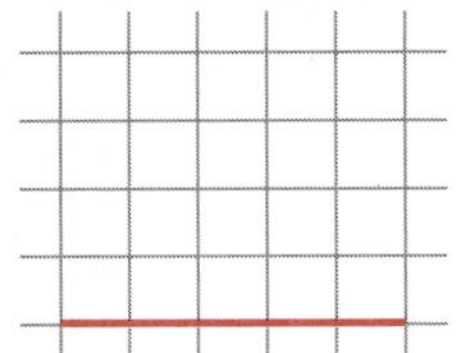

Complete the rectangle.

10 Jacob heats two cans of tomato soup. Each can contains 420 mL of soup. What is the total amount of soup?

11 How many kilograms are in 13 000 g?

12 It is now 7:36 and the game starts in 24 minutes. At what time is the game expected to start?

13 Here is a 3D shape. Pepe picks up the shape and looks at it from all sides.

How many faces does the shape have?

14 The sides of a triangle are each 5 cm. How many lines of symmetry has the triangle?

15 Draw a pentagon with three right angles.

16 Cooper is facing south. He makes a quarter turn in a clockwise direction. What direction is he now facing?

STATISTICS AND PROBABILITY

17 Brittney has three T-shirts and two pairs of shorts. The T-shirts are white, yellow and red. Her shorts are blue and black. How many different outfits of T-shirt and shorts are possible?

18 The number of bikes sold in four days is recorded in the dot plot.

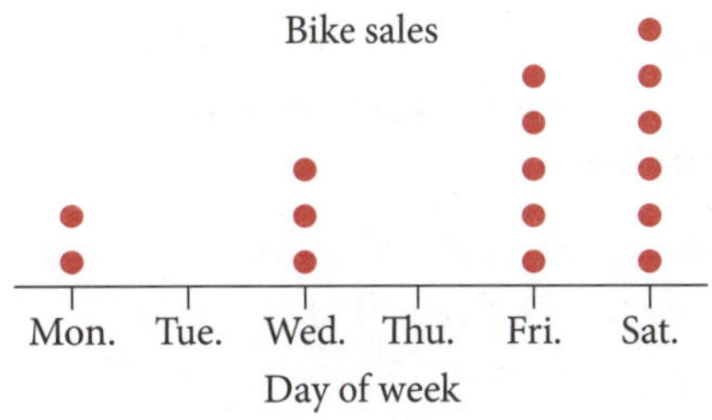

How many more bikes were sold on Friday and Saturday than on Monday and Wednesday?

NUMBER AND ALGEBRA

1 Jason is counting backwards by 2s, starting at 20. What is the third number?

2 A library has 430 fiction and 500 non-fiction books. What is the total number of books?

3 A game is played using a special set of 30 cards. Each of the five players receives an equal number of cards. How many cards will each player receive?

4 Ruby has 26 balloons. 17 balloons popped. How many balloons remain?

5 Lemons are sold in bags of five. How many lemons are in nine bags?

6 There are 20 students on a bus. Half of the students are girls. How many girls are on the bus?

7 The price of a hose at one store was $36. Another store had the same hose priced at $33.50. How much cheaper is the hose at the second store?

8 Tom thinks of an even number. Bob thinks of an odd number. Which of these could be the result of adding their numbers?

8 11 6 2

MEASUREMENT AND SPACE

9 Josie drew two lines which were 2 cm and 12 mm in length. What is the difference between the two lengths, in millimetres?

10 A plastic bottle contains 600 mL of water. Macey drinks 100 mL of water from the bottle. How much remains in the bottle?

11 A box of avocados has a mass of 3 kg. A cafe orders five boxes. What is the total mass of the boxes of avocados?

12 Ezra's music lesson lasted half an hour. If the lesson started at 4:20, at what time did it finish?

13 Here is a net.

Circle the name of the 3D shape formed.

square pyramid triangular pyramid triangular prism

14 William has started to draw a shape. The dotted line is a line of symmetry. Complete the shape.

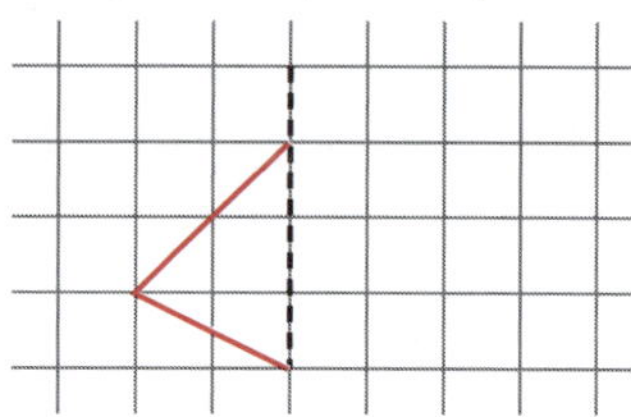

15 Adrian drew a regular triangle. Each angle is ______________ a right angle.

Circle the correct phrase.

less than equal to more than

16 Marley starts at D1 and walks 5 units north. She turns right and walks 2 units.

What is Marley's new location?

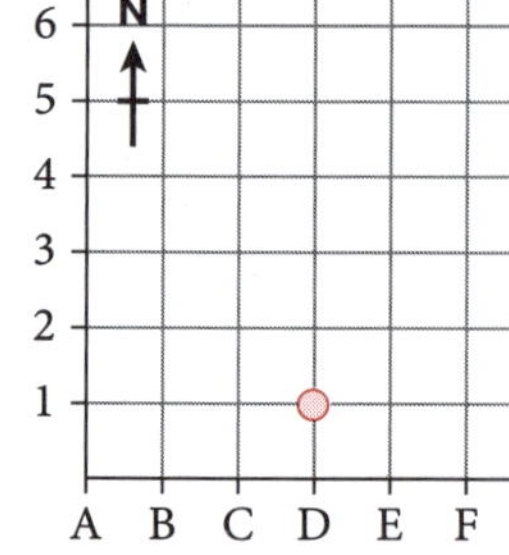

STATISTICS AND PROBABILITY

17 Balls coloured red (R), blue (B) and yellow (Y) are placed in a container.

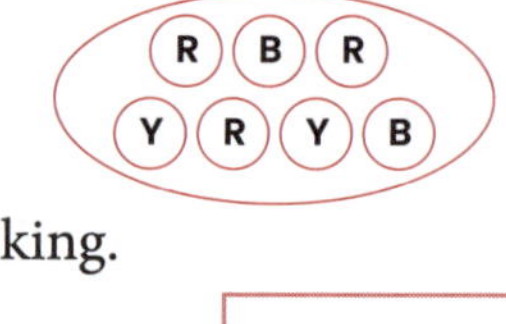

A ball is chosen without looking. What colour is most likely to be chosen?

18 The graph shows the number of Friday nights attended by members of a youth group.

How many nights did Dee attend?

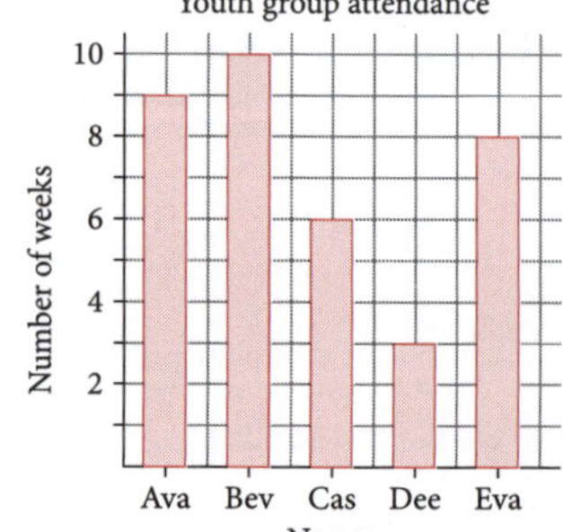

NUMBER AND ALGEBRA

1 Aaron is counting by fives. His first number is 20 and his last number is 50. What was the middle number he counted?

2 A bike-hire business had 38 customers on Saturday and 29 on Sunday. What was the total number of customers?

3 A game takes 10 minutes to play. How many games can be played in one hour?

4 Max has 46 trading cards and Jordan has 19 fewer than Max. How many trading cards has Jordan?

5 Each bus can transport 50 students to the swimming pool. How many students are on four buses?

6 One-third of the students in a group walked to school this morning. If there are 12 students in the group, how many walked to school?

7 An apple is 10c cheaper than a banana and 10c more expensive than a mandarin. If the cost of an apple is 60c, what did Ian pay for an apple, a banana and a mandarin?

8 Kathleen is calling out numbers in a pattern. Her third number is 12, her fifth number is 16 and her sixth number is 18. What was the first number Kathleen called out?

MEASUREMENT AND SPACE

9 Ella uses a ruler to measure the length of a paper clip.

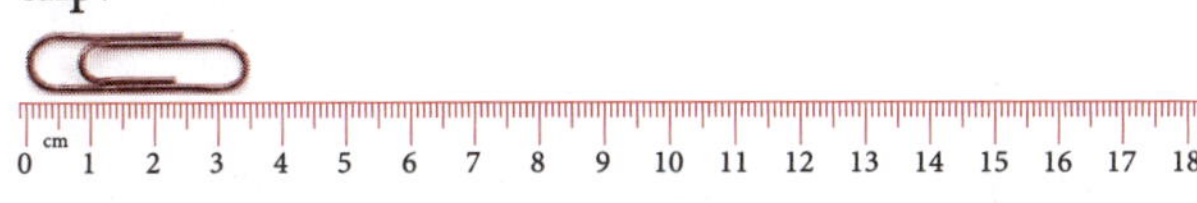

Which of these is closest to the length of two paperclips?

4 cm 7 cm 8 cm 35 cm

10 A bucket contains 8 L of water. The bucket is leaking 1 L of water every hour. How much water is in the bucket after 2 hours?

11 Three identical steel balls, a 10-kg block and a 2-kg block are placed on a pan balance.

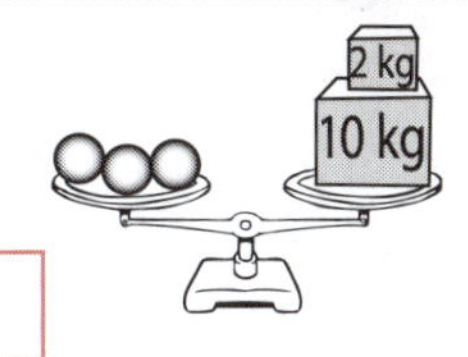

What is the mass of each steel ball?

12 Hudson arrived at work at 8:40. It had taken 25 minutes for him to drive from home to work. At what time had Hudson left home?

13 How many vertices has a pyramid with a hexagonal base?

14 Andy has started to draw a shape. The dotted line is a line of symmetry. Complete the shape.

15 Emmy drew these three triangles.

How many angles measure less than a right angle?

16 Charlyze starts at C5 and walks 3 units south. She turns left and walks 2 units.

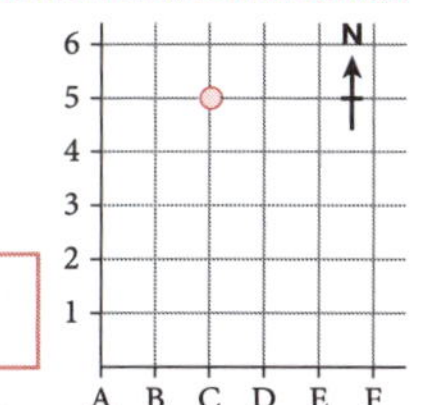

What is Charlyze's new location?

STATISTICS AND PROBABILITY

17 Freddie rolled a normal dice 20 times and the results are recorded in a table. The number of times Freddie rolled a 5 is not shown. What will be the missing number?

Results	Number of times
1	|||
2	||
3	||||
4	𝍸
4	?
6	|||

18 The graph shows the number of Friday nights attended by members of a youth group. How many more nights did Ava attend than Cas?

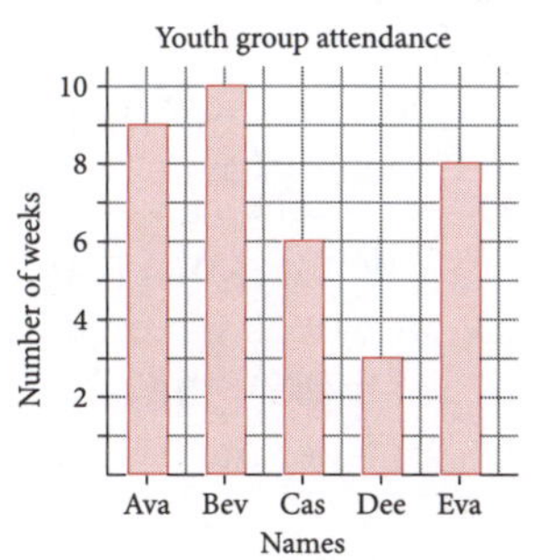

NUMBER AND ALGEBRA

1 Here are three numbers: 309 372 458
Circle the number that rounds to 400, to the nearest hundred.

2 How many 3s are in 27?

3 Ms Jackson reminded the class that there were only 4 more weeks in the school term before the holidays. How many schooldays are in 4 weeks?

4 One morning 76 students travelled to school by bus. In the afternoon only 65 of the students caught the bus home. How many did **not** travel home by bus?

5 On Saturday Buddy left home and drove 240 km to his grandmother's house. On Sunday he drove back home. What was the total distance travelled?

6 Violet drew these six stars. Shade $\frac{1}{2}$ of the stars.

☆ ☆ ☆ ☆ ☆ ☆

7 Mia was given \$80 for her birthday. She purchased three items costing \$30, \$20 and \$25. How much money remained?

8 Tom writes a sequence by starting with 14 and adding 2. Circle the two numbers that are in Tom's sequence.

15 17 18 40

MEASUREMENT AND SPACE

9 Two pencils were placed end to end. Hunter used a ruler to measure the total length of the two pencils as 23 cm. One pencil was 12 cm. What was the length of the other pencil?

10 Isaiah bought a 600-mL carton of chocolate milk. He poured an equal amount into two glasses. How much milk is in each glass?

11 The mass of a paper clip is about 1 g. Craig buys a box of 50 paperclips. He uses 10 paper clips. Which of these is the best estimate of the mass of the remaining paper clips?

40 g 4 kg 40 kg

12 Otis has a wall clock and an oven clock in his kitchen.

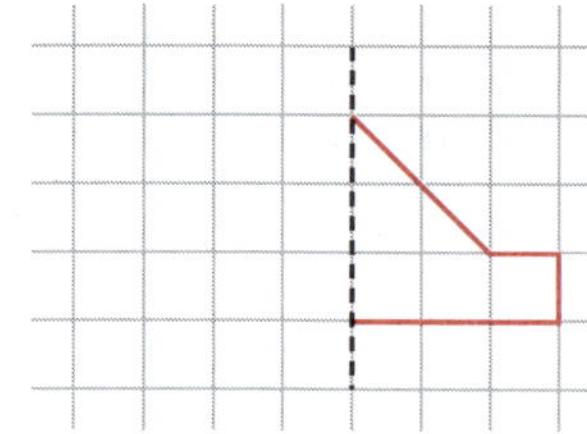

What is the difference in time between the two clocks?

13 A 3D shape has 12 edges. Each face is the same shape. Circle the name of the shape.

square pyramid cone cube

14 Rory has started to draw a shape. The dotted line is a line of symmetry. Complete the shape.

15 A right angle is a ______________ turn. Circle the correct word.

quarter half three-quarter

16 Here is a classroom plan. Gracie sits at desk *J*. She moves two rows to the front and one desk to the right. What is her new desk?

Front			
A	B	C	D
E	F	G	H
I	J	K	L

STATISTICS AND PROBABILITY

17 Here are three spinners which have sections coloured red (R) and yellow (Y).

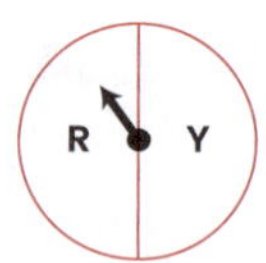

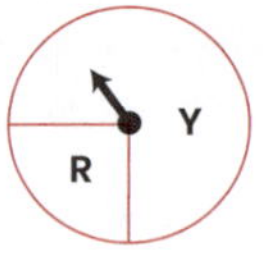

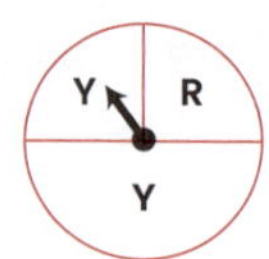

Circle the spinner that has an equal chance of spinning a red or a yellow.

18 The graph shows the number of pages Olivia read during the week.

How many pages were read on Thursday?

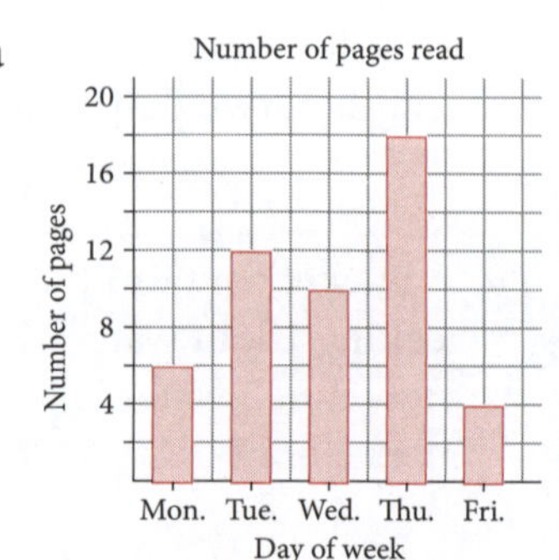

NUMBER AND ALGEBRA

1 Brett has a large property of about 2000 hectares. Which of these is closest to his estimate?

1930 hectares 2040 hectares 3000 hectares

2 Tennis balls are sold in cylinders. There are three balls in each cylinder. A tournament will use 60 balls. How many cylinders of balls need to be purchased?

3 At a dog show Emmie counted three people grooming their three dogs. How many legs did she count?

4 After his holidays, Ben checked his emails. He had received 96 emails. He immediately deleted 68 emails. How many remained?

5 Two planes landed at an airport before 6 am. The first plane had 246 passengers and the second 230. What was the total number of passengers?

6 Helena drew these six stars. Shade $\frac{1}{3}$ of the stars.

☆ ☆ ☆ ☆ ☆ ☆

7 A wrap costs $3.90. What is the cost of two wraps?

8 Andrew writes a sequence by starting with 75 and subtracting 2. Circle the numbers that are in Andrew's sequence.

55 18 11 2

MEASUREMENT AND SPACE

9 A rectangle is drawn on a centimetre grid.

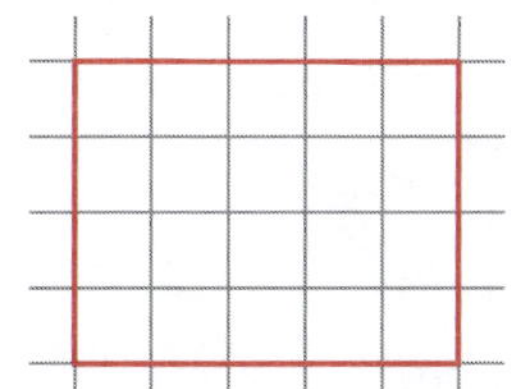

Benedict uses small, coloured rectangles to completely cover the shape. Each small rectangle has an area of 4 cm². What is the smallest number of coloured rectangles needed to cover the shape?

10 A teaspoon has a capacity of 5 mL. A syringe is filled with 20 mL of water. How many teaspoons of water can be filled using the syringe?

11 A can of soup weighs 440 g. What is the mass of ten cans?

12 Theo checks the times on his clock and his phone.

What is the difference between the two times?

13 Ava wrote different odd numbers on each face of a cube. What is the smallest possible total for her numbers?

14 Ellis has started to draw a shape. The dotted lines are lines of symmetry.

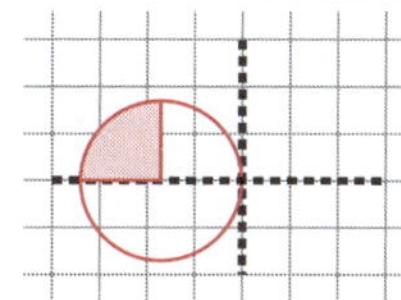

Complete the shape.

15 Draw a trapezium with two right angles.

16 Here is a classroom plan. Isaac sits at desk C. He moves a row back and two desks to the left. What is his new desk?

Front			
A	B	C	D
E	F	G	H
I	J	K	L

STATISTICS AND PROBABILITY

17 A coin is tossed six times. How many heads would you expect?

18 The graph shows the number of pages Olivia read during the week.

How many more pages were read on Wednesday than Friday?

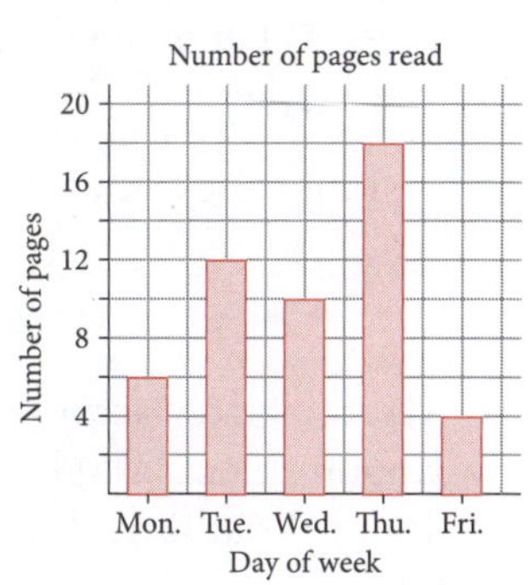

NUMBER AND ALGEBRA

1 Grace has four daughters. The girls were born in 2018, 2009, 2016 and 2011. In what year was her oldest daughter born?

2 Aisha is celebrating her 13th birthday today. Her mother was 28 when she was born. How old is Aisha's mother today?

3 Amy drew 40 stars. She coloured in 12 of the stars. How many were **not** coloured in?

4 In a grid there are seven rows of three squares. What is the total number of squares?

5 A class of students visited an art gallery. A guide was allocated to every eight students. If there were 24 students, how many guides were allocated?

6 Here are six apples. Draw a box around one-third of the apples.

7 Albert charges $15 to walk one dog and $25 to walk two dogs. On both Monday and Thursday, he walked two dogs. How much was he paid?

8 What is the tenth number in the sequence 3, 6, 9, 12, 15 … ?

MEASUREMENT AND SPACE

9 Fleur is 83 cm tall. How much more does she need to grow to be 1 m tall?

10 A shape is made using cubic-centimetre blocks. There are eight blocks in the bottom layer, six in the middle layer and three in the top layer. What is the volume of the shape?

11 Arrange these masses from lightest to heaviest.

65 g 9 g 532 g

12 Grace had a doctor's appointment at 9:20. The appointment lasted a quarter of an hour. What time did she leave?

13 Here is a net. Circle the name of the 3D shape formed.

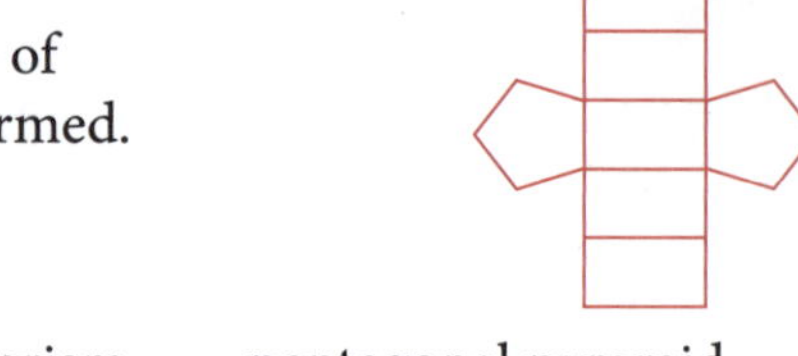

pentagonal prism pentagonal pyramid hexagonal prism

14 Draw the other half to make the picture symmetrical.

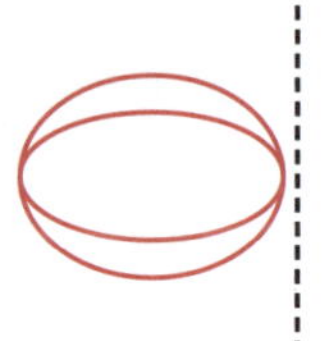

15 In these diagrams the arrow shows the movement of one arm of the angle to the other.

Circle the two angles that show a movement in a clockwise direction.

16 The shape is translated to the left 3 units.

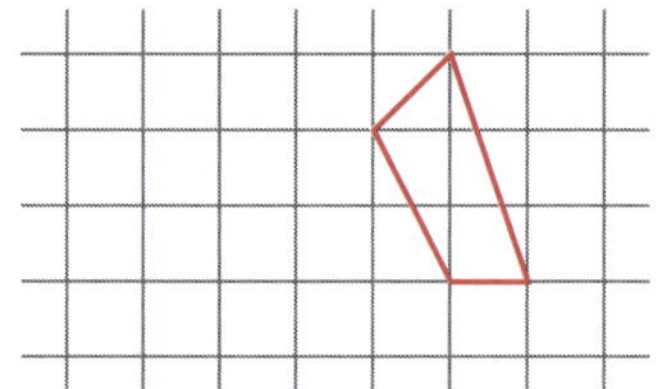

Draw the image of the shape.

STATISTICS AND PROBABILITY

17 Cameron's favourite ice cream flavours are strawberry, chocolate and caramel. He can choose scoops of two different flavours in a cone.

How many different combinations are possible?

18 The graph shows the number of dogs washed by DoggieClean.

On which day was the smallest number of dogs washed?

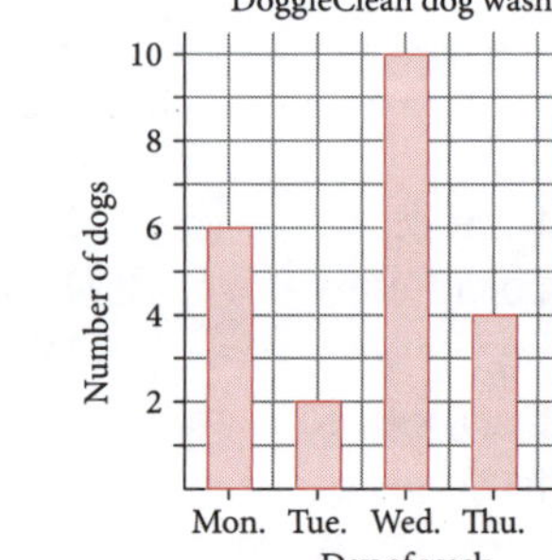

NUMBER AND ALGEBRA

1 Bella is 142 cm tall, Jessica 158 cm, Ethan 147 cm and Olivia 155 cm. Who is the second-tallest person?

2 Amy has nine balls. Keeley has 12 more balls than Amy. If Keeley gives all her balls to Amy, how many balls has Amy?

3 A bag contains 12 balls. Seven balls are red, three are blue and the remainder are green. How many green balls are in the bag?

4 In Bethany's wardrobe she has three shelves of shoes. On each shelf are four pairs of shoes. How many shoes are in the wardrobe?

5 There are 20 students in year 3 and 25 students in year 4. How many groups of five students can be made?

6 Indigo cut an orange into quarters. She ate two quarters. Circle the fraction of the orange that remained.

$\frac{1}{3}$ $\frac{1}{4}$ $\frac{1}{2}$

7 Erin is given $1.50 every day to empty the kitchen waste into the compost bin. How much will she earn in a week?

8 What is the hundredth number in the sequence 2, 4, 6, 8 … ?

MEASUREMENT AND SPACE

9 Nova measured the length of a wall to be 670 cm. What is this length rounded to the nearest metre?

10 Tomi has a 2-L jug and a 12-L container. How many jugs of water are needed to fill the container?

11 Arrange these masses from heaviest to lightest.

250 g 27 g 1 kg

12 Thomas arrived at the cinemas at 1:53. His movie started 12 minutes later. What time did Thomas's movie start?

13 Callie drew a prism. The base of the prism was a shape with 10 equal sides. How many faces has the prism?

14 Draw the other half to make the picture symmetrical.

15 In these diagrams the arrow shows the movement of one arm of the angle to the other.

Circle the two angles that show a movement in an anticlockwise direction.

16 The shape is translated to the left 2 units and down 3 units.

Draw the image of the shape.

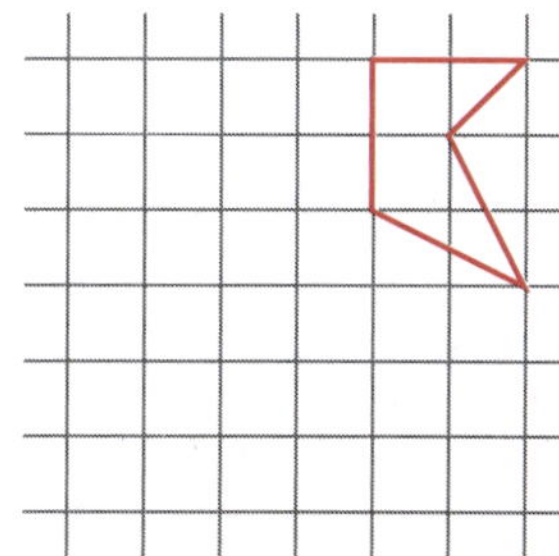

STATISTICS AND PROBABILITY

17 The spinner has red (R) and blue (B) sections.

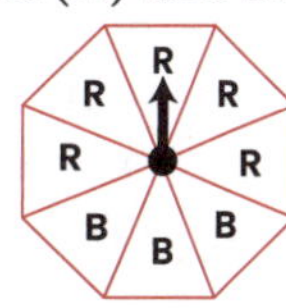

The arrow is spun twice and both times it stops on blue. If it is spun a third time, on which colour is the arrow likely to stop?

18 The graph shows the number of dogs washed by DoggieClean.

How many dogs were washed on Wednesday and Friday?

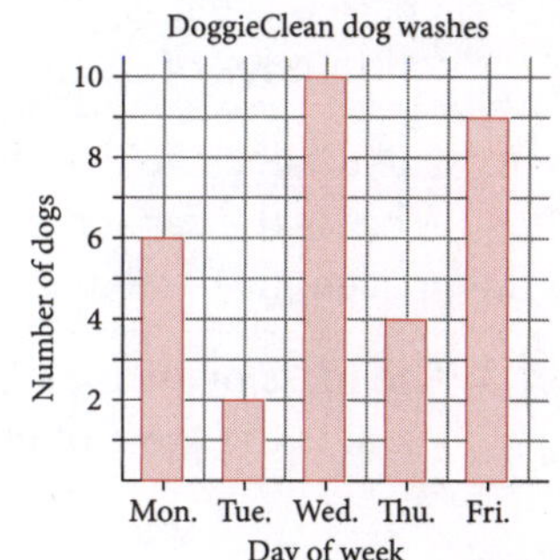

NUMBER AND ALGEBRA

1 Here is a four-digit number with the hundreds digit missing.

5 ? 20

If the digits add to 14, what is the four-digit number?

2 Charlize buys two dozen eggs. She uses 10 eggs to make some cakes. How many eggs remain?

3 Every night Ryan reads seven pages of his book. How many pages does he read in five nights?

4 Halle picked 16 strawberries on Tuesday and another 23 on Saturday. What was the total number of strawberries picked?

5 A group of students were holding up both hands. Mr Maudin counted 60 fingers. How many students were in the group?

6 There are eight cars in the car park. Half of the cars are white. How many white cars are in the car park?

7 Jackson bought a Lego set for $39.95. How much change did he receive from a $50 note?

8 A rule is applied to numbers in the Input row to give the numbers in the Output row. What is the missing number?

Input	3	7	10	13	16
Output	11	15	18	21	?

MEASUREMENT AND SPACE

9 Aspen cut a 120-cm long plank into two equal lengths. What is the length in centimetres of each new piece?

10 The total capacity of four identical jugs is 8 L. What is the capacity of each jug?

11 The mass of an apple is 200 g. What is the mass of two apples?

12 Dr James has four appointments: Len at 3:35, Jen at 3:10, Ben at 4:55 and Ken at 4.00. Who is the first person the doctor will see?

13 Here is a net. Circle the name of the 3D shape formed.

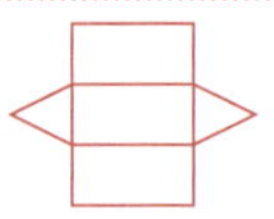

triangular pyramid triangular prism square prism

14 Dora needs the dotted line to be a line of symmetry for the squares on the grid. Shade the missing squares.

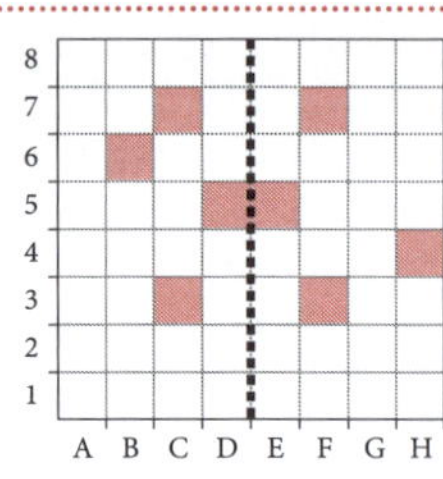

15 Morgan drew this diagram containing two vertical lines and two horizontal lines.

How many right angles can Morgan count?

16 Baxter placed a counter on X. He moved the counter up 5, 2 left, down 4 and right 3. What is the new location of the counter?

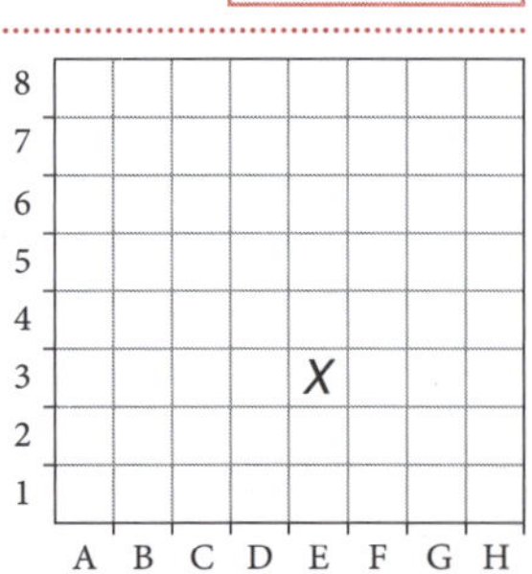

STATISTICS AND PROBABILITY

17 A box contains three cards. The cards are yellow (Y), green (G) and pink (P).

Rosie replaces the yellow card with another green card. She now selects a card from the box without looking. Which coloured card is she more likely to choose?

18 The dot plot shows the hair colour of students in Year 3.

How many students have black hair?

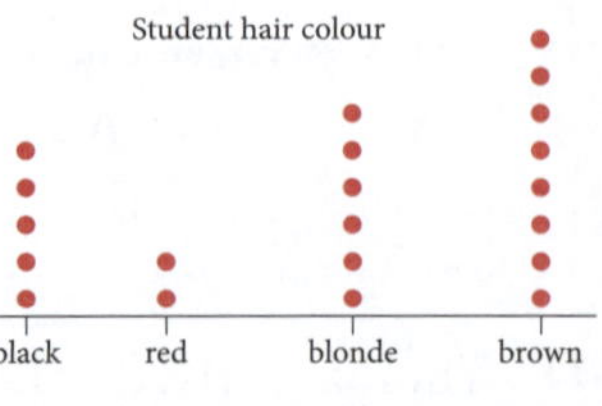

NUMBER AND ALGEBRA

1 The digits in a three-digit number add to 10. The digit in the hundreds place is 6 and is 5 more than the digit in the ones place. What is the number?

2 Aunt Sharon baked 36 cakes. She gave six to both Corey and Zidane and four to Elliott. How many cakes did Aunt Sharon keep?

3 Ariarne is three times the age of her niece Kiah. If Kiah is 9 years old, how old is Ariarne?

4 Jordan is playing a game and has earned 8700 points. When he defeats a dragon, he earns another 400 points. What are his total points now?

5 Frida brought two punnets of strawberries to school. Each punnet contains six strawberries. She shared them equally between herself and three friends. How many strawberries did Frida eat?

6 Part of this shape is shaded. Circle the fraction **not** shaded.

$\frac{1}{4}$ $\frac{3}{4}$ $\frac{1}{3}$

7 A sandwich press costs $39.90 and an electric kettle is priced at $70. What is the total cost?

8 On Sunday morning Geoff ran three laps of the local park. Every morning he plans to run two more laps than the previous day. How many laps does he plan to complete on the following Saturday?

MEASUREMENT AND SPACE

9 The television news reported that a town had received half a metre of rain. What is this amount in millimetres?

10 A bottle holds 1 L of water. Elke fills the bottle nine times and empties the water into a watering can. She then pours 2 L of water from the watering can on her roses. How much water remains in the watering can?

11 A jar contains 280 g of honey. If Trent uses 20 g of honey, how much remains?

12 A doctor has appointments scheduled every 20 minutes. Her next appointment is at 3:10. What time was the doctor's previous appointment?

13 Amelia used clay to make a sphere. She cut the sphere into two identical shapes.

Complete: Each new shape has ______ curved surface(s) and ______ flat surface(s).

14 Kamari needs the dotted line to be a line of symmetry for the shaded squares on the grid. How many more squares need to be shaded?

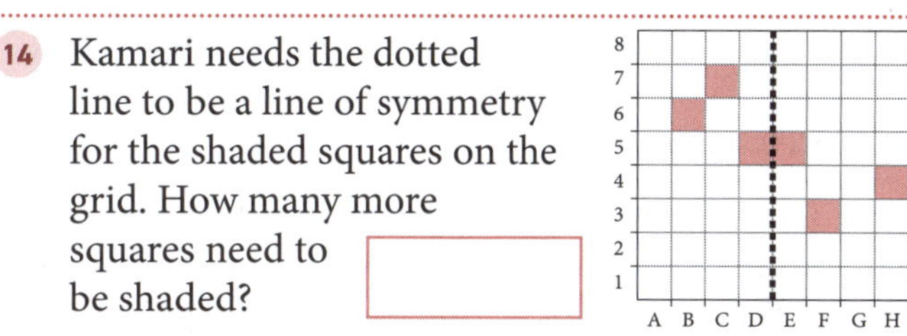

15 Josh looks at the kitchen clock. The time is 7 o'clock. What is the time when the minute hand has moved through a right angle?

16 Rory placed a disc on one square on the grid. He moved the disc down 2, to the right 2, up 4 and to the left 5. The disc is now on B7. Where was the disc placed at the start?

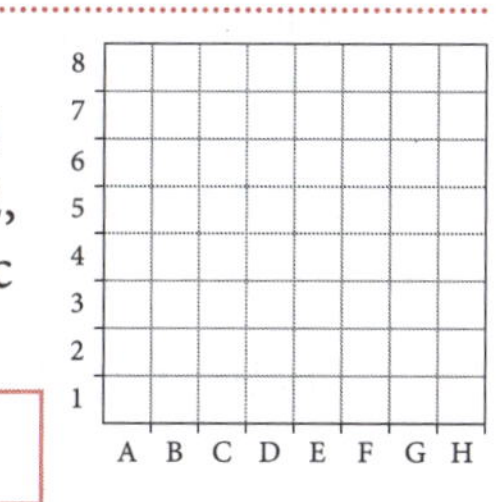

STATISTICS AND PROBABILITY

17 A box contains five coloured discs. The discs are blue (B), yellow (Y) and pink (P).

B Y
P B Y

Rosie replaces the pink disc with a yellow disc. Which coloured disc is she less likely to choose?

18 The dot plot shows the hair colour of students in Year 3. How many more students have brown hair than red hair?

Student hair colour

black red blonde brown

NUMBER AND ALGEBRA

1. Charlotte and Emma live on the same side of Smith St. House numbers on their side are even. If Charlotte lives at number 8 and Emma at 14, how many houses are between them?

2. Clyde has 43 toy soldiers. His friend Wesley has twice as many. How many toy soldiers has Wesley?

3. Joshua uses 32 squares to form a rectangle. He shades 20 squares. How many squares were **not** shaded?

4. Jack has a grid containing five rows. If there are 40 squares, how many columns are on the grid?

5. Imogen tosses a coin many times and records the results. The coin landed heads 38 times and tails 42 times. How many times was the coin tossed?

6. On Saturday Jaime caught 12 fish. A quarter of the fish were too small so he released them back into the water. How many fish were too small?

7. Henry is paid $20 each hour he works. On Tuesday he worked for 8 hours. How much will Henry be paid?

8. Phoebe started with 40 and counted backwards by 5. If 40 was her first number, what was her fourth number?

MEASUREMENT AND SPACE

9. Sawyer has a normal school ruler. It is about 30 cm long. Which of these is the best estimation of the width of his ruler?

   3 mm   3 cm   13 cm

10. Luke's dishwasher uses 10 L of water for each load. If he uses the dishwasher once a day, how much water does he use every week?

11. Anabelle was 3 kg when she was born. When she was 2 years old, her mass was 12 kg. What was the increase in Annabelle's mass?

12. How long does it take for the minute hand of an analog clock to move from pointing at 2 to pointing at 6?

13. Here is a net. Circle the name of the 3D shape formed.

   triangular pyramid   hexagonal pyramid   pentagonal prism

14. Complete the arrow using the dotted line of symmetry.

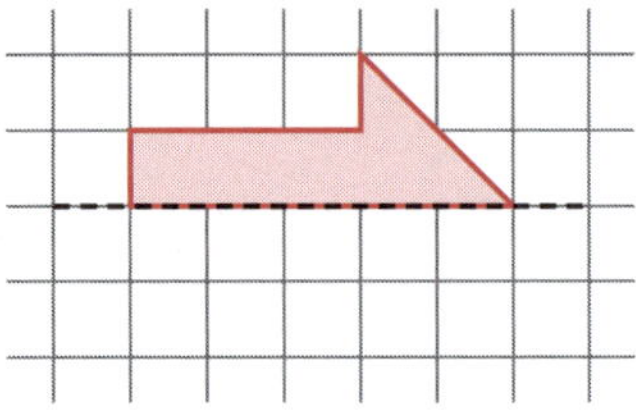

15. Lydia has shaded a quarter of a circle. Circle the phrase that best describes the size of the angle shown.

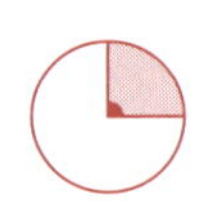

   less than a right angle   a right angle   more than a right angle

16. The shape is translated 3 units to the right. Draw the image.

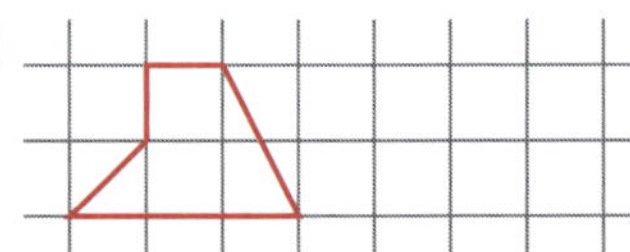

STATISTICS AND PROBABILITY

17. What are the three outcomes for the result in a game of soccer?

18. The number of goals scored by some teammates is recorded.

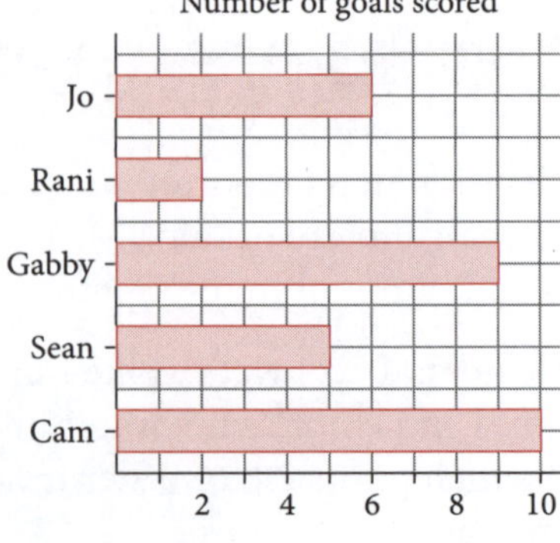

   Who scored the second highest number of goals?

NUMBER AND ALGEBRA

1 Jack lives at 3 Brown Street. His friend Jacob lives at 27 Brown Street. How many houses are between Jack and Jacob, if all house numbers on that side are odd?

2 There are five bags of balls. Each bag contains three red balls and two blue balls. What is the total number of balls?

3 There are 42 peaches on Eliza's tree and 18 are ripe. How many peaches are **not** yet ripe?

4 One hundred and twenty students are standing in the playground. They are arranged in groups of 10 students. How many groups have been formed?

5 A farmer has 500 sheep in one paddock and 670 in another. What is the total number of sheep?

6 Addison has four rows of three cards. She turns over the cards in one row. What fraction of the cards are turned over?

7 Oliver bought an apple costing 61 cents and a mandarin which cost 43 cents. What was the total cost, rounded to the nearest 5 cents?

8 Joseph is counting on by 4s. His first number is 102. What is his fifth number?

MEASUREMENT AND SPACE

9 How many millimetres are in 2 m 4 cm?

10 Peyton has a 3-minute shower every morning. She uses a total of 24 L of water. How much water does she use every minute?

11 An airline company allows each passenger to take a bag of luggage with a mass up to 22 kg and a carry-on bag up to 5 kg. What is the total kilogram allowance for each passenger?

12 How long does it take for the minute hand of an analog clock to move from pointing at 7 to pointing at 5?

13 Here is the net of a cube. When the net is folded, numbers on opposite faces multiply to the same result.

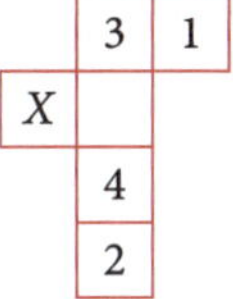

What is the number represented by X?

14 Complete the arrow using the dotted line of symmetry.

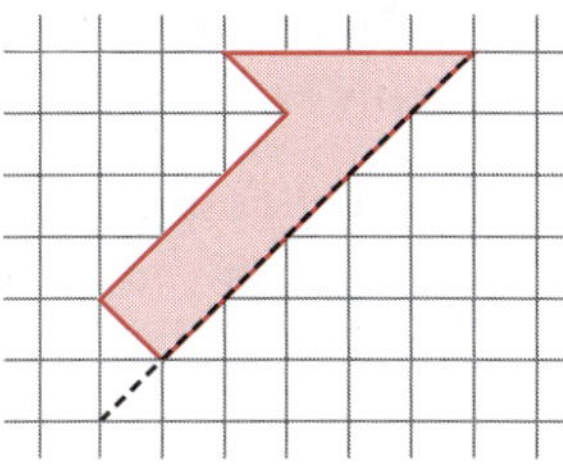

15 Nova drew these angles on dot paper.

How many angles are less than right angles?

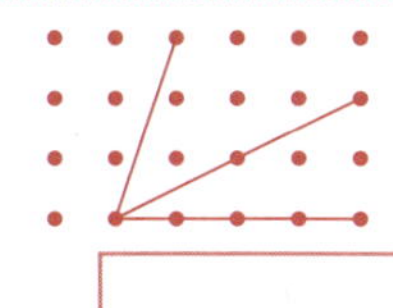

16 The shape is translated 3 units down and 2 units to the right.

Draw the image.

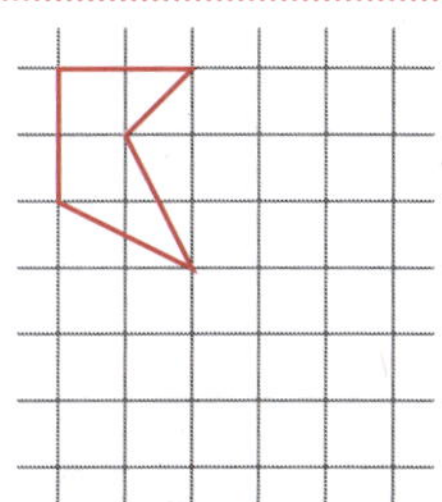

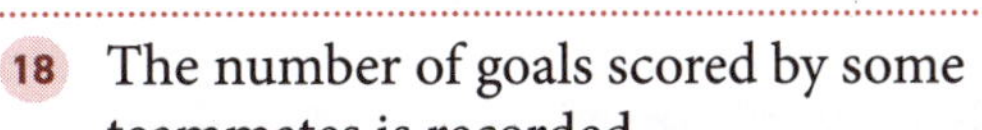

STATISTICS AND PROBABILITY

17 A 10-cent coin and a 20-cent coin are tossed. One of the outcomes is that both coins land on heads which can be written as head + head. What are the other three outcomes?

18 The number of goals scored by some teammates is recorded.

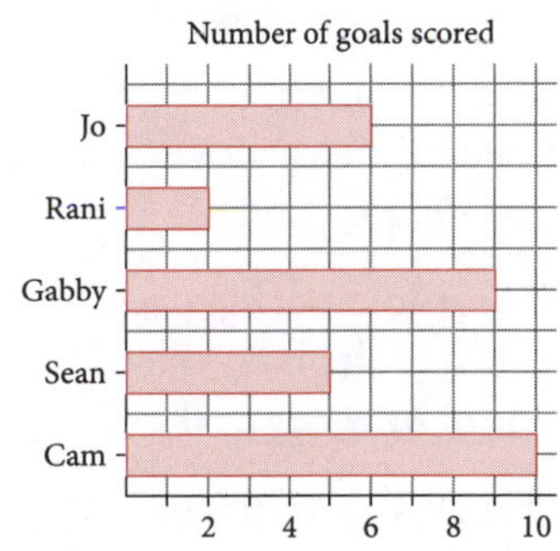

What was the total number of goals scored?

NUMBER AND ALGEBRA

1 Here are four numbers.

296 308 209 288

Circle the smallest number.

2 A bookcase has three shelves. There is an equal number of books on each shelf. If there is a total of 18 books in the bookcase, how many books are on each shelf?

3 Anabelle's grandmother is 97 years old. How old will she be if she lives another 5 years?

4 In a test of 50 questions, Kate answered 37 correctly. How many questions did Kate **not** answer correctly?

5 A florist placed six roses in each bunch. She made three bunches. What was the total number of roses used?

6 Here are eight oranges. Draw a box around $\frac{1}{2}$ of the oranges.

7 Ruby bought a calculator priced at \$18.60. What change did she receive from \$20?

8 Austin writes a sequence that uses the rule 'Start with 20 and add 7'. What is the fourth number in his sequence?

MEASUREMENT AND SPACE

9 Otis measured the length of his stride as 80 cm. Otis walked 10 steps. How many metres has Otis walked?

10 Ellie has four identical glasses. She pours 200 mL of water into each glass. What is the total amount of water in the glasses?

11 The mass of a slice of bread is 40 g. What is the mass of two slices of bread?

12 Here is a clock. What is the time 10 minutes later, written in digital form?

13 True or false? This is the net of a square pyramid.

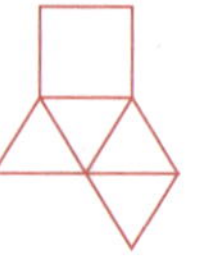

14 Here is a triangle with two sides equal in length.

Draw the line(s) of symmetry.

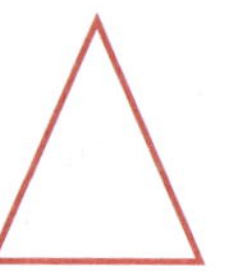

15 Use the grid to draw a line through the point which is perpendicular to the existing line.

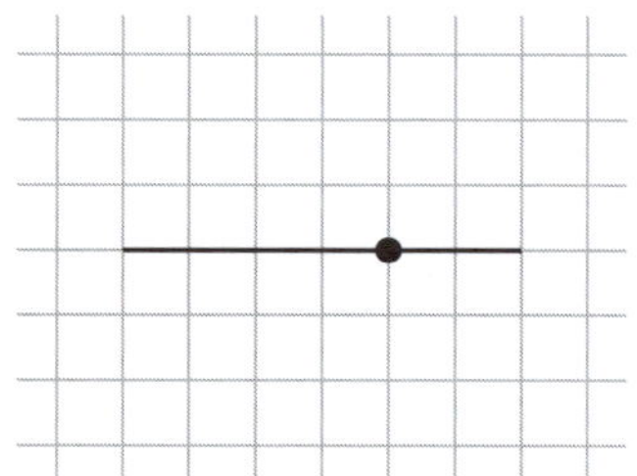

16 The map shows the roads built between eight towns.

How many roads have been built?

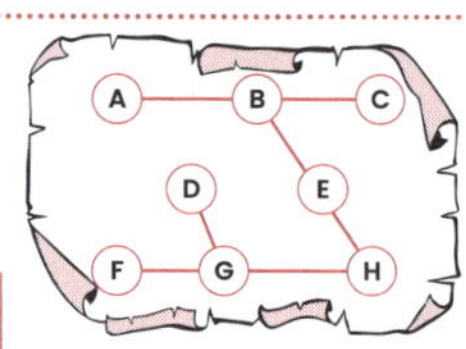

STATISTICS AND PROBABILITY

17 The table records the number of coloured counters in a box.

Colour	Number
blue	6
green	8
yellow	5
red	7

If a counter is chosen from the box without looking, what is the most likely colour selected?

18 A group of high-school students were asked to estimate the number of minutes they took to shower each day.

How many students showered for 4 minutes?

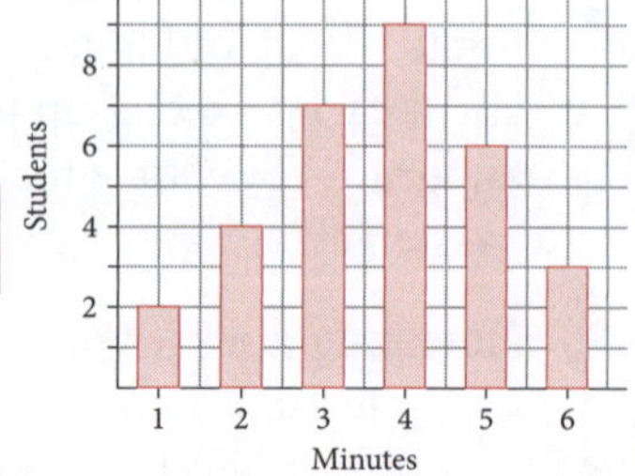

NUMBER AND ALGEBRA

1 Three friends are comparing the number of stamps in their collections. Mark has 2671, Mia has 2983 and Karl has 2967. Who has the most stamps?

2 There are 900 sheets of paper to be placed into stacks of 100. How many stacks are needed?

3 Kyle recorded the number of push-ups he completed each morning. On Monday and Tuesday he did 32 push-ups. On Wednesday he completed 35 push-ups. What was the total number of push-ups over the three mornings?

4 Two numbers add together to give 80. If one of the numbers is 46, what is the other number?

5 A team scored three goals in each of four games and two goals in another three games. What is the total number of goals scored?

6 Here is a sequence:

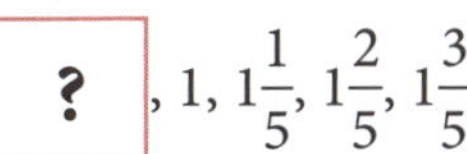

$?, 1, 1\frac{1}{5}, 1\frac{2}{5}, 1\frac{3}{5}$

What is the missing number?

7 Declan buys a packet of breakfast cereal priced at \$5.80. He pays the exact price in coins. What is the smallest number of coins he can use?

8 Adrian writes a sequence that uses the rule 'Start with 71 and subtract 5'. What is the tenth number in his sequence?

MEASUREMENT AND SPACE

9 Lottie places three identical glue sticks alongside a ruler. The total length of the three glue sticks is 33 cm. What is the length of each glue stick?

10 A bottle contains 500 mL of tomato sauce. Shannon pours 10 mL onto her plate. How much sauce remains in the bottle?

11 Blocks and balls are placed on a pan balance.

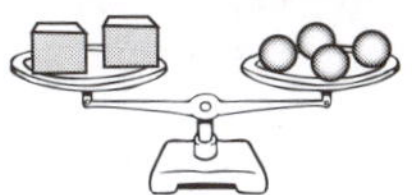

The mass of a ▢ is 10 kg. What is the mass of a ○?

12 Here is a clock. What was the time 25 minutes before the time shown, written in digital form?

13 Mabel is drawing the net of a cube. She has drawn five squares. Where will the sixth square be drawn?

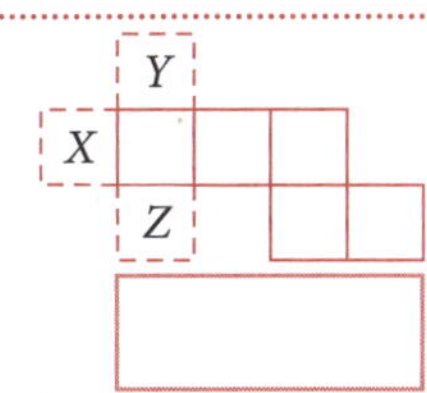

X *Y* *Z*

14 Siobhan drew a shape with four equal sides and four equal angles. How many lines of symmetry does the shape have?

15 Use the grid to draw through the point a line which is perpendicular to the existing line.

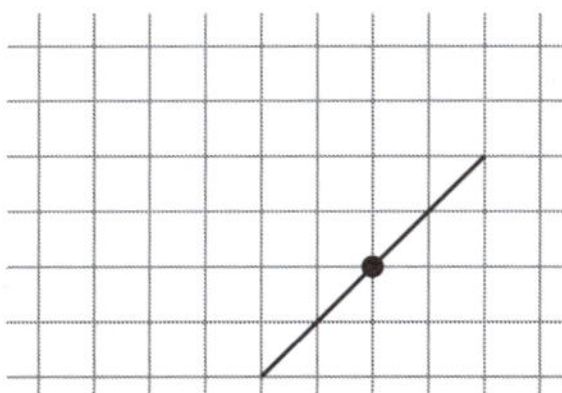

16 The map shows the roads built between eight towns.

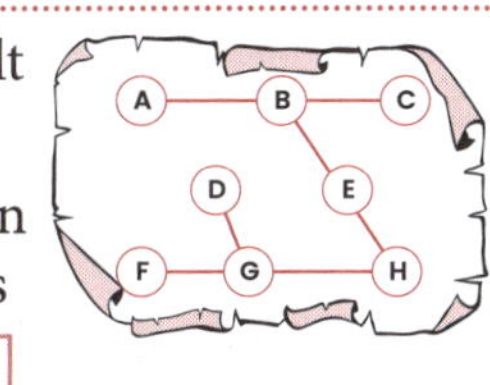

Ravi needs to travel from town *F* to town *C*. How many roads does he use?

STATISTICS AND PROBABILITY

17 The dots on the outside of a normal dice are changed. The numbers are now 2, 2, 2, 3, 3 and 4. The dice is rolled. Which number is most likely to be uppermost on the dice?

18 A group of high-school students were asked to estimate the number of minutes they took to shower each day.

How many students showered for more than 4 minutes a day?

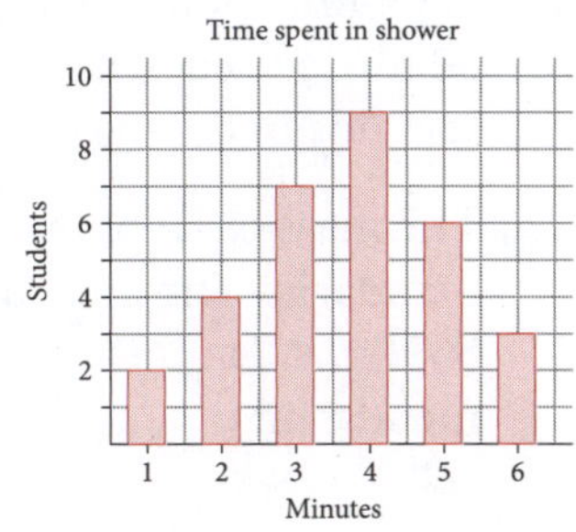

NUMBER AND ALGEBRA

1 Jason was born in 1957, Jeremy in 1983 and John in 1964. Who is the youngest person?

2 What is the total of all the dots on a normal dice?

3 Lucy cooks some pizzas and cuts each pizza into 6 slices. If she has a total of 18 slices, how many pizzas did Lucy cook?

4 Parents transported students in their cars on an excursion to the zoo. Three students travelled in each car. How many students went to the zoo in seven cars?

5 Thomas batted twice in a cricket match. He scored a total of 64 runs. He scored 41 runs when he batted first. How many runs did he score when he batted the second time?

6 Here are 10 circles. Shade $\frac{1}{2}$ of the circles.

○ ○ ○ ○ ○
○ ○ ○ ○ ○

7 Cooper has $40. Alexander has $20 more than Cooper. How much do the boys have altogether?

8 Here is a sequence of numbers.

80, 110, 140, 170, ?

What is the missing number?

MEASUREMENT AND SPACE

9 Justin used chalk to draw a line 160 cm long. Rylee drew a line which was 40 cm longer than Justin's line. How long was Rylee's line in metres?

10 Seraphina pours 300 mL of milk into a jug. If 50 mL is used, what amount remains in the jug?

11 The mass of an orange is 6 g more than a mandarin. The mass of the orange is 64 g. What is the mass of the mandarin?

12 Here is a clock without digits. What is the time, written in digital form?

13 Circle the name of the 3D shape with the most faces.

cube hexagonal prism octagonal pyramid

14 Abbie measures the length of each side of a rhombus. She adds the lengths and her total is 12 cm. What is the length of each side of the rhombus?

15 Shane used horizontal and vertical lines to draw this shape. How many right angles are **inside** the shape?

16 The homes of students *A*, *B*, *C*, *D* and *E* are shown on the map.

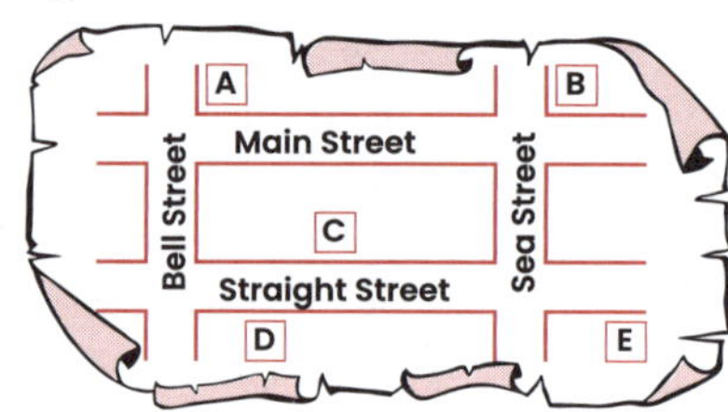

How many students live on Straight Street?

STATISTICS AND PROBABILITY

17 Nathan's birthday is in June. What is the chance that his birthday is on 17 June?

impossible very likely
certain unlikely

18 The graph shows the number of student votes for their favourite pet.

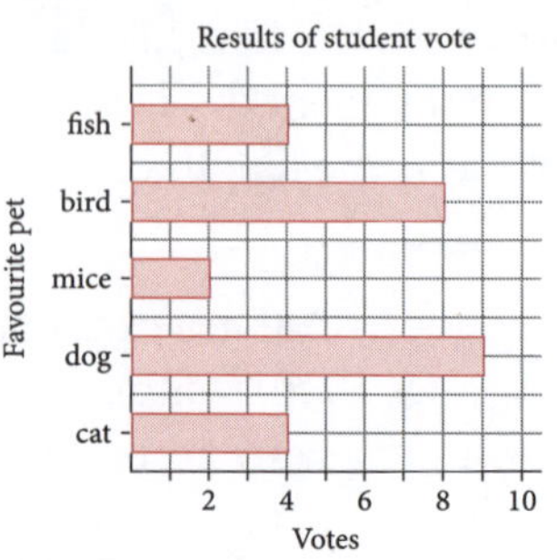

How many students voted for a dog?

NUMBER AND ALGEBRA

1 Here are five numbers.

748 824 794 489 842

The numbers are arranged in order. What is the middle number?

2 Lucy read six books during the holidays. Her friend Holly read four more books than Lucy. What was the total number of books read by the two girls?

3 Lani draws a row of triangles. She looks at the triangles and counts 60 sides. How many triangles have been drawn?

4 Joshua has two water tanks in his backyard. Each tank holds 3000 L when full. What is the total amount of water when the tanks are full?

5 A cinema has 180 seats. If 67 seats are being used, how many seats are empty?

6 Here are 10 circles. Shade $\frac{4}{5}$ of the circles.

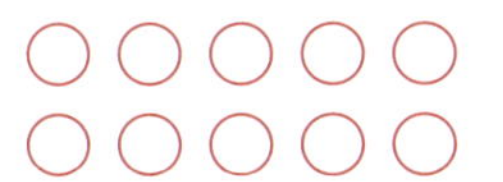

7 Declan has $20. Callum has $16 more than Declan but Beau has $4 less than Callum. How much money do they have altogether?

8 Bob and Jack are writing lists of numbers. Bob starts with 2 and is counting by 4s. Jack starts with 4 and is counting by 2s. What is the smallest two-digit number on both lists?

MEASUREMENT AND SPACE

9 Kessia has two erasers. The length of one eraser is 4 cm. The other eraser is 32 mm. What is the difference in the length of the two erasers in mm?

10 A prism is made using cubic-centimetre blocks. There are three layers on the prism. Each layer has 12 blocks. What is the volume of the prism?

11 A box contains 1 kg of flour. Josh uses 100 g of the flour. What mass of flour remains in the box?

12 Here is a clock without digits. What is the time, written in digital form?

13 Circle the names of the two 3D shapes with the same number of edges.

hexagonal pyramid pentagonal prism cube

14 Arthur has drawn a parallelogram. One side is 8 cm and another side is 3 cm shorter. What is the sum of the lengths of the sides of the parallelogram?

15 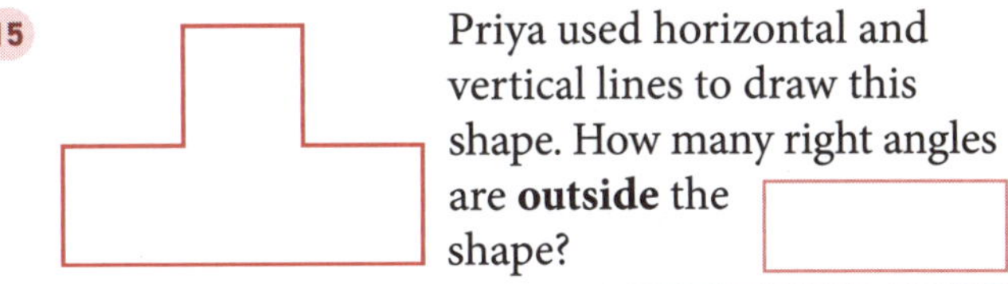

Priya used horizontal and vertical lines to draw this shape. How many right angles are **outside** the shape?

16 The homes of students *A*, *B*, *C*, *D* and *E* are shown on the map. Which two students live closest to each other?

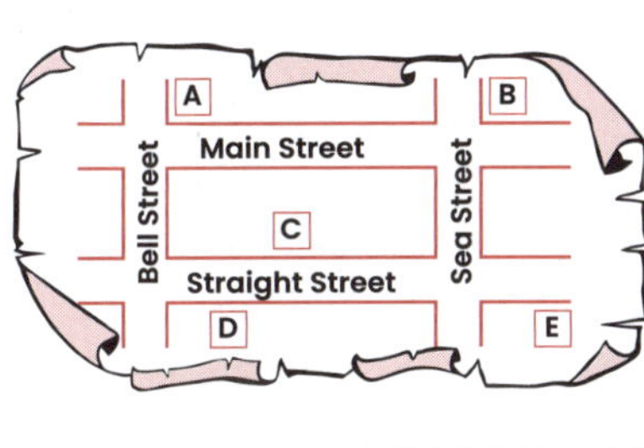

STATISTICS AND PROBABILITY

17 Here is a blank spinner. Use letters R (red), B (blue) and G (green) to label the four areas on the spinner if it is most likely to spin a blue and equally likely to spin red and green.

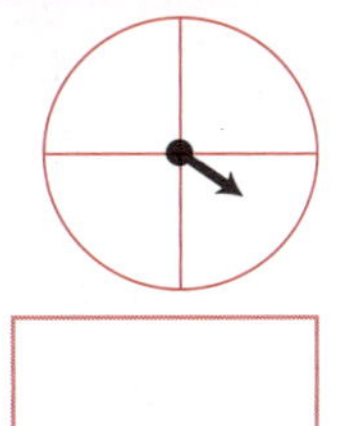

18 The graph shows the number of student votes for their favourite pet.

How many pets had more than five votes?

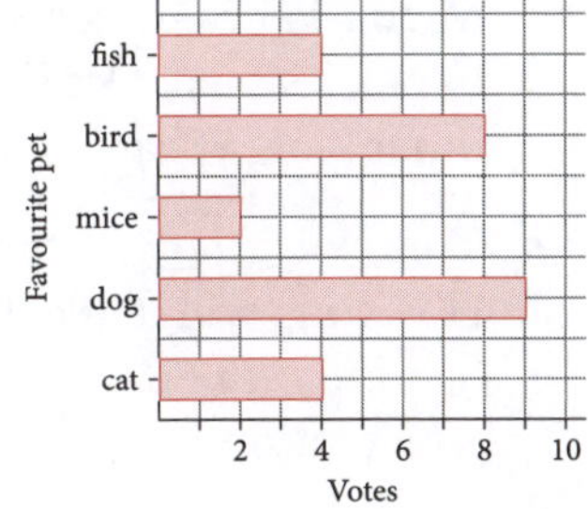

NUMBER AND ALGEBRA

1 Henry was counting by tens starting at 43. What is the fourth number he counts?

2 In a mathematics competition every correct answer is awarded 3 marks. If Lewis answered 7 questions correctly, what is his score?

3 Trent has two pieces of string. One length is 55 cm and the other 32 cm. What is the total length of string?

4 Lachlan is given a bottle of tablets to get well. He needs to take three tablets every day. There are 21 tablets in the bottle. How many days will Lachlan be taking the tablets?

5 What number is 10 less than the largest two-digit number?

6 Lucy is one-quarter the age of Eleanor. If Eleanor is 8 years old, how old is Lucy?

7 A stapler costs $4.80 and a pair of scissors $3.20. What is the total cost of the two items?

8 Pedro started with 11. He added an odd number and then subtracted an even number. Is his answer even or odd?

MEASUREMENT AND SPACE

9 Rupert drew this shape on a centimetre grid.

What is the area of the shape?

10 There is 30 L of petrol in Raphael's car. He adds another 20 L. How much petrol is now in the tank?

11 Michaela has three parcels to post. Two parcels have a mass of 3 kg each and the other 2 kg. What is the total mass?

12 This clock shows a time of 10:30. How long will it take the minute hand to make 2 revolutions?

13 Peyton made a 3D shape with two identical triangular faces on each end. Each other face was a rectangle. Circle the name of Peyton's shape.

triangle   triangular prism   triangular pyramid

14 Here are two pieces of cardboard.

Circle the two shapes that can be formed using the two pieces.

square   rectangle   parallelogram

15 Circle the two angles that are the same size.

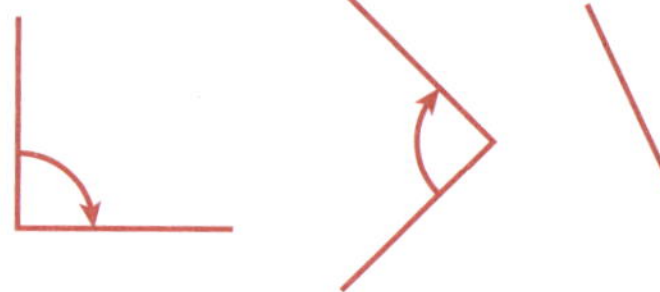

16 A map is drawn on a grid. Towns *P* and *Q* are shown on the map.

Town *R* is east of *P* and south of *Q*. Locate *R* on the map.

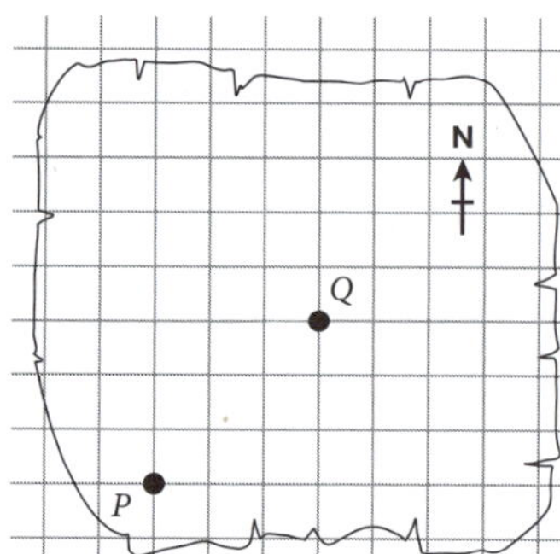

STATISTICS AND PROBABILITY

17 In a bowl there are four apples, two oranges and three bananas. Layla picks a piece of fruit without looking. What is the most likely fruit she picks?

18 The graph shows the number of after-school activities for a group of friends each week.

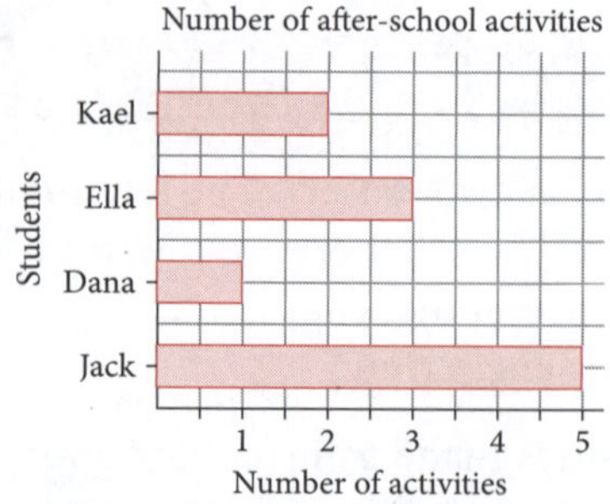

Who had the most after-school activities?

NUMBER AND ALGEBRA

1 Georgia wrote these numbers:
387, 397, ________, 417.
What is the missing number?

2 Kai placed four chocolates in each of five bags. He then removed a chocolate from each bag. What is the total number of chocolates in the bags?

3 Samara has 12 cousins and Olivia has 19 cousins. If the girls are not related, what is the total number of cousins?

4 Students are sitting in three lines. There are 10 students sitting in each line. All the students stand up and now sit in five equal groups. How many students are in each group?

5 Here are three numbered cards used to make a two-digit number.

3 6 1

What is the difference between the largest possible two-digit number and the smallest possible two-digit number?

6 There are 20 squares on a grid. Tate shades one-quarter of the squares. How many squares remain unshaded?

7 A 1-L container of milk costs $2.50. A 2-L container costs $4. Sloan wants to buy 3 L of milk. What is the cheapest price?

8 A rule is applied to numbers in the Input row to give the numbers in the Output row. What is the missing number?

Input	0	15	26	40	52
Output	7	22	33	?	59

MEASUREMENT AND SPACE

9 Mitchell competed in the shot-put. In his first attempt he threw 10 m 20 cm. What is this distance in centimetres?

10 A prism is made using cubic-centimetre blocks. The volume of the prism is 24 cm³. There are three layers in the prism. How many blocks are in each layer?

11 Lily balances two blocks on one side of a pan balance with three balls on the other side. Each ball has a mass of 6 kg. If the blocks are identical, what is the mass of each block?

12 James looked at this clock. The second hand goes around the clock 5 times before James looks at the clock again. What is the new time?

13 Here is the net of a cube. The cube is made and the square with the letter *X* is placed face down on a table. Label with *Y* the square that is facing up.

X

14 James looked at a regular hexagon. He added the number of sides, the number of angles and the number of lines of symmetry. What is James's total number?

15 Joe looked at a cube. He counted the right angles on each of the faces. What was the total number of right angles?

16 A map is drawn on a grid. Towns *P* and *Q* are shown on the map. Oliver leaves Town *Q* and drives south and then west to *P*. Draw the route that Oliver travelled.

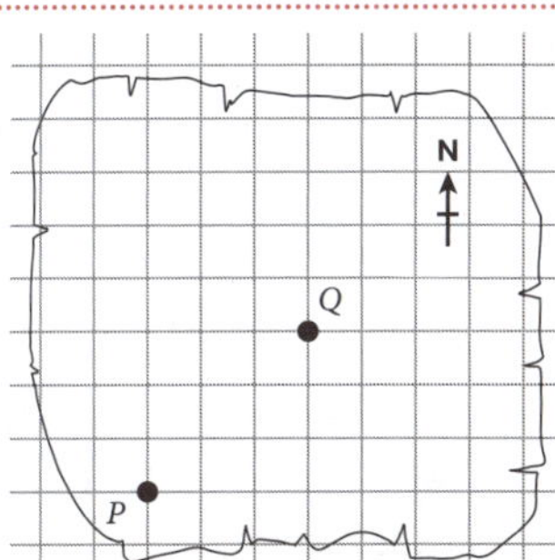

STATISTICS AND PROBABILITY

17 In a bowl there are four apples, two oranges and three bananas. Rory removes two apples from the bowl. Niamh now picks a piece of fruit without looking. What is the most likely fruit she picks?

18 The graph shows the number of after-school activities for a group of friends each week. What was the total number of activities for the four friends?

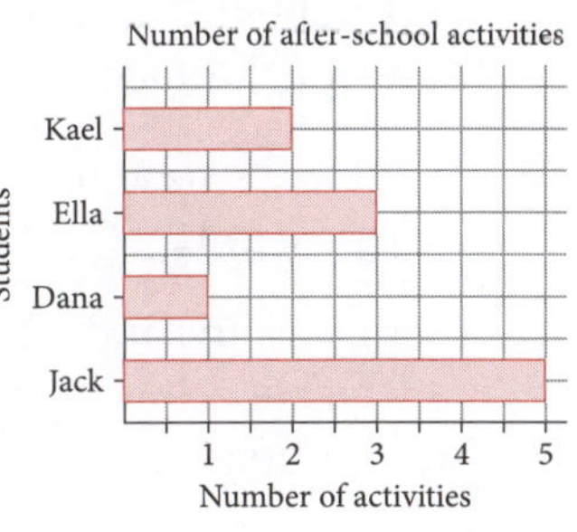

NUMBER AND ALGEBRA

1 Here are five digits: 7, 2, 9, 4, 1. What is the largest even number that can be formed using the digits?

2 There are eight pens in a packet. If Ms Jackson needs 40 pens, how many packets does she need to buy?

3 There are 40 more men than women in a 5-km park run. If there are 136 men, how many women are there?

4 On a small farm there are 12 chickens, six cows and eight sheep. What is the total number of farm animals?

5 There are 10 children at Jerome's birthday party. Each child is to be given three balloons for a game. How many balloons are needed?

6 

Circle the fraction of squares shaded.

$\frac{1}{2}$ $\frac{1}{6}$ $\frac{3}{5}$

7 A stationery supplies shop sells notebooks for $3.20 each. Ethan bought four notebooks. What was the total cost?

8 Eliana wrote a pattern of numbers using the rule 'Start with 10 and add 4'. Circle the two numbers that are in Eliana's sequence.

18 20 24 30

MEASUREMENT AND SPACE

9 The length of one of Sarah's boots is 32 cm. What is the combined length of the pair of boots, in centimetres?

10 Alex buys a 500-mL bottle of tomato sauce. At a party, 200 mL of sauce is used. How much sauce remains?

11 What is the total mass of 200 g, 100 g, 50 g, 10 g?

12 Liam was one and a half minutes late for the bus. How many seconds was he late?

13 Circle the name of the 3D shape which has four faces.

cube sphere triangular pyramid

14 Leighton needs the two dotted lines to be lines of symmetry for the squares on the grid.

Shade the missing squares.

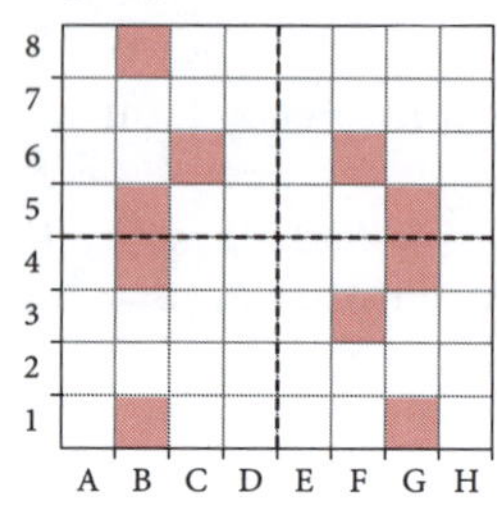

15 Rory located three dots. He drew a line from *A* to *B* and another line from *B* to *C* to form an angle. Is the angle a right angle?

A *B* *C*

16 The school map shows a block of classrooms, the library and the canteen.

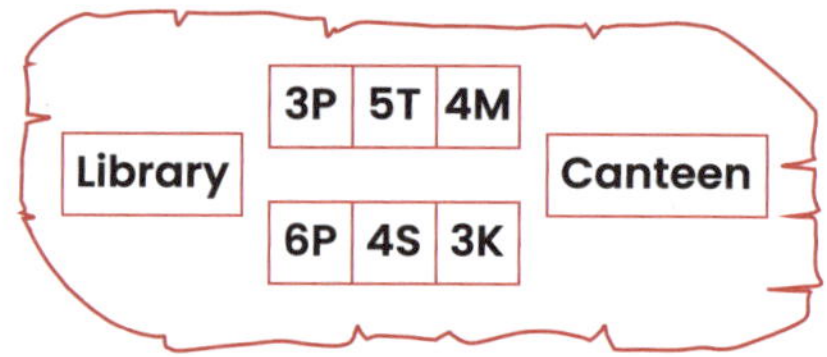

Zayden leaves the canteen and walks into his classroom, which is the second on his left. What class is Zayden in?

STATISTICS AND PROBABILITY

17 Circle the spinner where it is more likely to spin red.

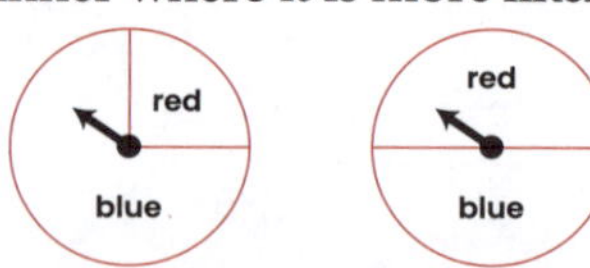

18 The table shows the ages of a family of four.

Age of family members	
Person	**Age**
Daniel	37
Kate	33
Logan	3
Owen	1

How old was Daniel when Logan was born?

NUMBER AND ALGEBRA

1 Maryse used three of the digits 8, 3, 5 and 7 to make the smallest possible number larger than 400. What is Maryse's number?

2 Two teams are competing against each other in a tug-of-war. Lucinda counts 24 legs on the people in the tug-of-war. How many people are on each team?

3 Michael wants to swim two laps of a 50-m pool. He swims the first lap but stops during his second lap with 20 m still to swim. How far did he swim?

4 A bookcase has four shelves. There are 15 books on two of the shelves, 12 books on a third and eight books on the other shelf. What is the total number of books in the bookcase?

5 In a soccer gala a team's win is worth 3 points and a draw is worth 1 point. Lauren's team won four games and had two draws. What is the team's total point-score?

6 How many thirds are in 2?

7 Nicole has $80 to spend at the shops. She spends half the money on a T-shirt. She spends $16 on a book. How much money has she spent?

8 Zach entered 12 into his calculator. He pressed + 5 = four times. What is the last number shown on his calculator?

MEASUREMENT AND SPACE

9 Circle the shortest length.

1001 mm 1 m 102 cm

10 Jenny made this layer of blocks using cubic-centimetre blocks.

She formed a prism by using the same number of blocks in a second and third layer. What is the volume of this new prism?

11 A 3-kg bag of dog food costs $7. How much will Ben pay for 6 kg of dog food?

12 It is 20 to 6 and Owen is hungry. His mother tells him that dinner is in half an hour. What time will Owen's dinner be ready?

13 The area of one face on a cube is 10 cm². What is the total area of all the faces on the cube?

14 Francis needs the dotted line to be a line of symmetry for the squares on the grid. Shade the missing squares.

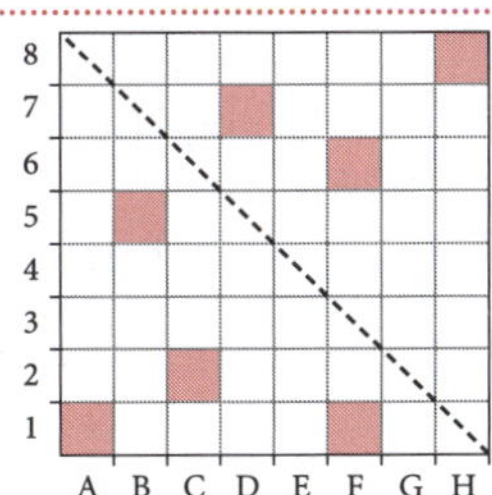

15 Olivia drew these two lines. She looked at the four angles where the lines cross. She has ticked one of the angles.

Tick the other angle that is the same size.

16 The school map shows a block of classrooms, the library and the canteen.

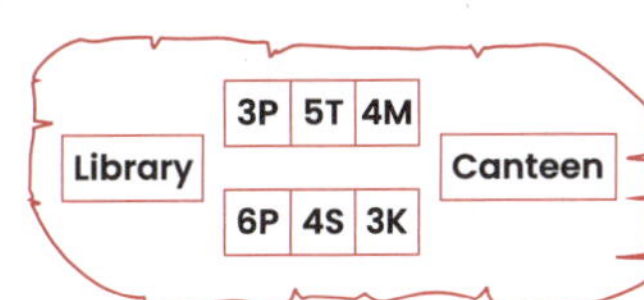

Peyton is in 5T. She leaves her classroom and turns right. She enters the first door on her right. What classroom does she walk into?

STATISTICS AND PROBABILITY

17 Circle the spinner on which it is least likely to spin red.

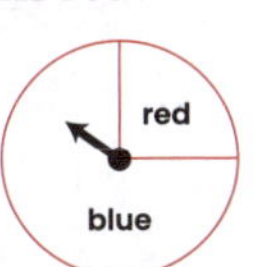

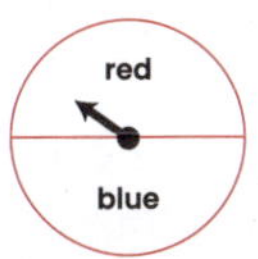

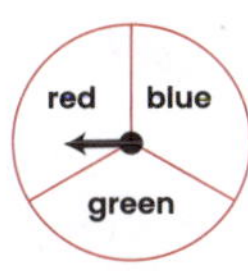

18 The table shows the ages of a family of four. How old will Kate be when Owen is 11 years old?

Age of family members	
Person	**Age**
Daniel	37
Kate	33
Logan	3
Owen	1

NUMBER AND ALGEBRA

1 Bohdi has a four-digit PIN to withdraw cash. The digits are in descending order starting with 3. What is his PIN?

2 What is the total of 30, 40 and 50?

3 In a game of basketball a team scored 76 points. One player scored 36 points. How many points were scored by the rest of the team?

4 How many 3s are in 33?

5 Farmer Bob has five hens. Each hen lays an egg every day. How many eggs has Bob after one week?

6 Here are eight tomatoes.

If half of the tomatoes are used, how many remain?

7 The price of a streaming service was $9.99 per month but it is to increase by $1.50. What will be the new price?

8 Here is a sequence of numbers:

80	71	62	53	44			17	8

What are the two missing numbers?

MEASUREMENT AND SPACE

9 Dean measured the height of a basketball ring as 3 m 5 cm. What is this height in centimetres?

10 Andrew uses his garden hose to water some plants. Water flows out of the hose at 15 L every minute. How much water will he use in 2 minutes?

11 Ken poured four bags of salt into his swimming pool. Each bag had a mass of 20 kg. What was the total mass of salt?

12 What time is 25 minutes after 8:10?

13 Amarli sketched a 3D shape. The shape has one curved surface and no flat surfaces. What shape did Amarli sketch?

14 Harvey drew a regular shape and cut it into two identical shapes. Here is one of the shapes.

What shape did Harvey originally draw?

15 Rod looked at the kitchen clock. The time showed half past 6. If the minute hand moved through a right angle, what will be the time shown on the clock?

16 Here is a street map with 12 shops. Thomas leaves shop *K*, crosses Zeta St and walks down Brown St. What is the fourth shop on the right?

A B | C D | E F
Pye St. | Brown St. | Zeta St.
G H | I J | K L

STATISTICS AND PROBABILITY

17 The table shows the number of different-coloured balls in a box. A ball is chosen without looking.

Colour	Number
green	5
brown	3
yellow	6
orange	7

Which colour is least likely to be chosen?

18 Students recorded the season in which they were born. There were eight students born in spring, six in winter, seven in autumn and five in summer. Complete the table.

Season of birth	
Season	**Number**
summer	
autumn	
winter	
spring	

NUMBER AND ALGEBRA

1 Benji needed to change his four-digit pin. He remembered his PIN as five thousand six hundred and seven. Benji added 2 to each of the digits in the PIN. What is his new PIN?

2 At the school's swimming carnival Booral house finished with 768 points. It was 109 points behind Congewai. How many points had Congewai house scored?

3 Myles has 30 golf balls. He gives eight balls to Phil and six balls to Donald. How many balls does Myles keep?

4 Michaela baked some cakes. She arranged the cakes into four rows of five cakes. Her mother placed the cakes into two containers. How many cakes were in each container?

5 A supermarket sells bags of carrots. Milla buys three bags. If there are 12 carrots in each bag, how many carrots did she buy?

6 Divide this rectangle into quarters and shade $\frac{1}{2}$ of the rectangle.

7 A pizza shop had a 'two pizzas for $30' deal. If Harry bought six pizzas, how much did he pay?

8 The numbers in the boxes form a pattern.

X	39	48	57	66		*Y*

What is the sum of the numbers represented by *X* and *Y*?

MEASUREMENT AND SPACE

9 Millie draws a rectangle on a centimetre grid. The width of the rectangle is 4 cm. The distance around the rectangle is 18 cm. What is the length of the rectangle?

10 The volume of shape *A* is 60 cm³.

Shape *B* has the same length and width as Shape *A*, but only half its height.

What is the volume of Shape *B*?

11 Zen had two rocks with a combined mass of 16 kg. The mass of one rock was 7 kg. What was the difference between the masses of the two rocks?

12 What time is three-quarters of an hour after 20 past 7?

13 Tom had a 150-cm roll of wire. He removed identical lengths of wire from the roll to make the frame of a cube. Each edge of the cube was 10 cm long. What length of wire remained on the roll?

14 Kate drew some quadrilaterals and some octagons. The number of sides on all the quadrilaterals equalled the number of sides on all the octagons. She counted a total of 32 sides on all her shapes. What was the total number of shapes drawn?

15 Anne looked at the kitchen clock. The time showed 10 to 3. If the minute hand moved through a right angle, what will be the time shown on the clock?

16 Here is a street map with 12 shops.

A B | Pye St. | C D | Zeta St. | E F
Brown St.
G H | | I J | | K L

Thomas leaves shop *G* and walks down Brown Street. After crossing two streets, what is the second shop on his right?

STATISTICS AND PROBABILITY

17 A bag contains four red balls and four green balls. A red ball is selected and removed from the bag. Another ball is chosen without looking. Which colour is more likely to be chosen?

18 Twenty students recorded the season in which they were born. There were seven students born in spring, four in winter and five in summer. Write the numbers in the table and work out how many students were born in autumn.

Season of birth	
Season	**Number**
summer	
autumn	
winter	
spring	

NUMBER AND ALGEBRA

1 Taya wrote the number forty-two thousand, three hundred and ninety-seven. What is Taya's number rounded to the nearest thousand?

2 At a dog park Mollie counted 40 legs on the dogs that were running around. How many dogs were in the park?

3 A teacher gives each student in the class three plastic shapes. There are 24 students enrolled in the class but four students are absent. How many shapes are handed out by the teacher?

4 There are 26 players in a soccer squad. One weekend nine of the players are injured and unavailable to play. How many players are available?

5 In a lap-a-thon, Boston completed 13 laps, Kimberley 15 laps and Bethany 9 laps. What was the total number of laps?

6 Here are 12 cupcakes. If two-thirds of the cakes are eaten, how many remain?

7 James saved $10 each week for 5 weeks. How much **more** does he need to buy a basketball for $70?

8 Owen uses matchsticks to form triangles.

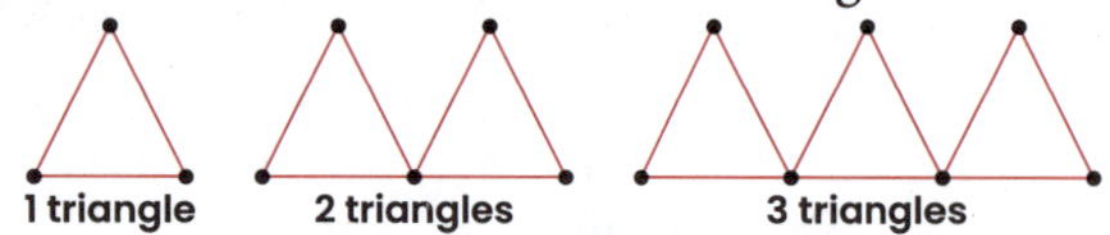

How many matches does Owen use to form five triangles?

MEASUREMENT AND SPACE

9 A rectangle measuring 4 cm by 3 cm is drawn. What is the distance around the outside of the rectangle?

10 Sarah brushes her teeth for 2 minutes every morning and night. She leaves the water running and uses 3 L of water each minute.

How much water has she used each day?

11 Sugar is sold in 2-kg bags. Eden buys a total of 10 kg of sugar. How many bags does she buy?

12 Ella's netball training lasts for an hour and a half. If training starts at 4 o'clock, what time does it finish?

13 This net is folded to form a cube. What is the letter that will be on the opposite face to *C*?

A			
B	C	D	E
			F

14 Abe added the number of lines of symmetry on a square and a regular triangle. What was the total?

15 Here is a kite, which has one line of symmetry. Tick the two angles that are the same size.

16 Tanha left B5 and walked south to B2. He then walked to F2.

What was the total number of units Tanha walked?

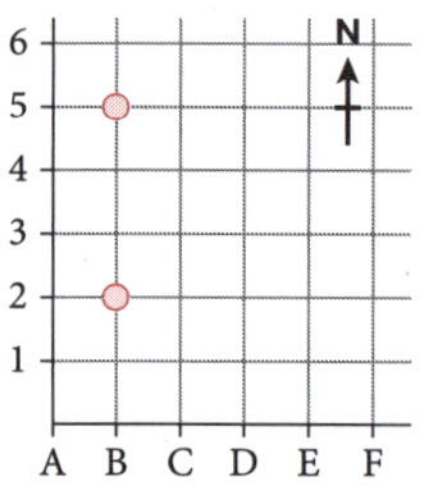

STATISTICS AND PROBABILITY

17 Circle the spinner on which it is impossible to spin yellow.

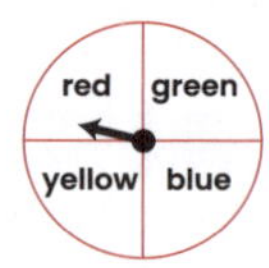

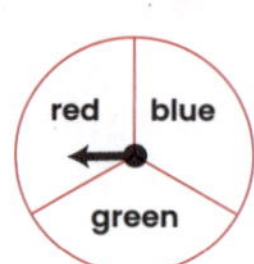

18 The favourite Saturday activity of students in classes 3K and 3P is shown in the graph.

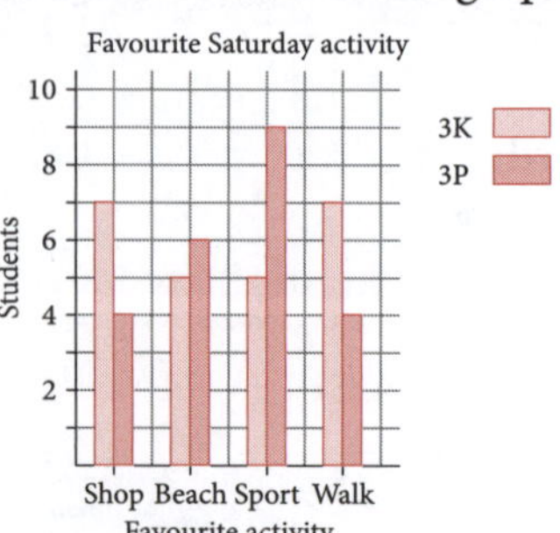

How many students chose playing sport?

NUMBER AND ALGEBRA

1 Mariama writes a four-digit number. There is a 3 in the hundreds place and a 7 in the ones place. The other two digits are fives. She then rounded the number to the nearest hundred. What is the new number?

2 What is the missing number?

$20 \div 10 = 20 \div$ **?** $\div 2$

3 In a shop there are four tricycles and five bicycles for sale. What is the total number of wheels?

4 A high school has 1000 students. Today there are 973 students present. How many students are absent?

5 In a car park there are 68 cars, 23 vans and 11 trucks. What is the total number of vehicles, to the nearest ten?

6 Olive is thinking of a whole number that when expressed as a fraction has a numerator four more than its denominator. Which of these is Olive's number?

2 3 4 6

7 Amy bought a pencil for 99c and an eraser for 89c. How much change did she receive from a $2 coin?

8 Owen uses matchsticks to form squares.

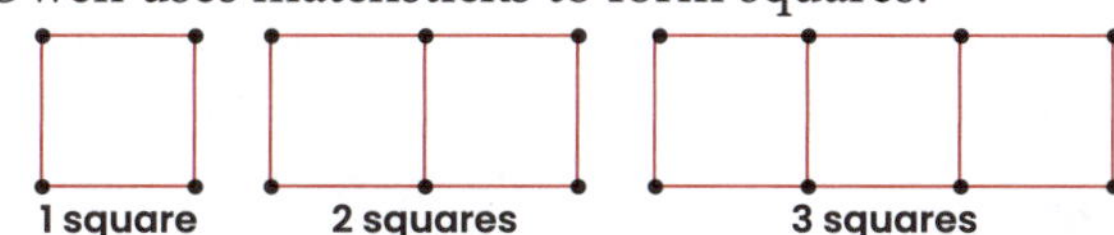

How many matches does Owen use to form six squares?

MEASUREMENT AND SPACE

9 Here are three lengths of straws. Can these straws form a triangle?

10 Evie uses 10 mL of shampoo every time she washes her hair. A bottle of shampoo contains 500 mL.

If Evie washes her hair every day, how many days will the bottle last?

11 The mass of a cylinder is 12 kg. What is the mass of a cube?

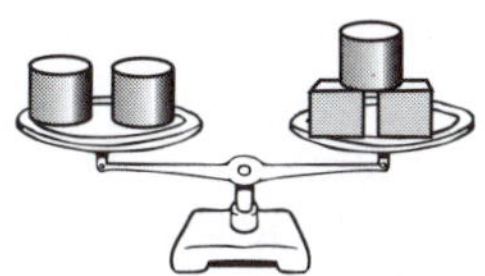

12 Esme arrived at the train station at 7:41. Her train is timetabled to arrive 11 minutes later. If the train was 4 minutes late, what time did the train arrive?

13 Daniel measured the faces of a rectangular prism. There were two rectangles measuring 6 cm by 4 cm and two rectangles measuring 4 cm by 3 cm. What was the length of the other two rectangles?

14 Joachim looked at the angles in a square. What is the sum of the angles in degrees?

15 Lori drew a square. She then drew a line that cut the square in half.

She placed a dot on one of the angles. How many more angles are the same size as the angle marked with a dot?

16 Ritchie left F3 and walked west for 4 units. He turned right and walked 2 units, and then turned right again and walked 2 units.

What is Ritchie's new location?

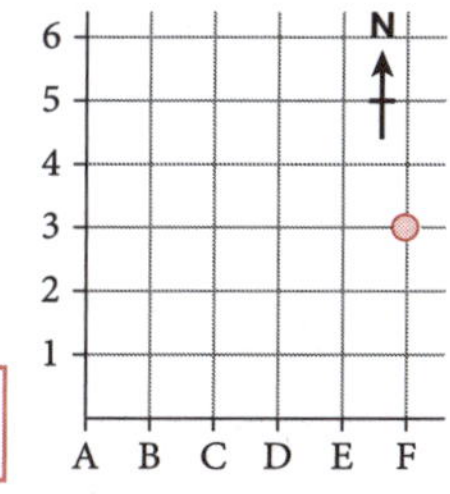

STATISTICS AND PROBABILITY

17 Circle the spinner on which it is more likely to spin red.

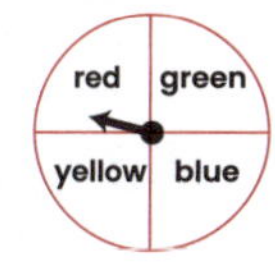

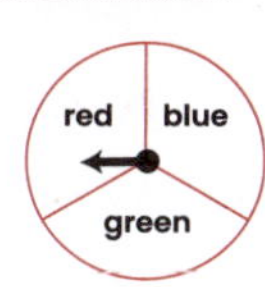

18 The favourite Saturday activity of students in classes 3K and 3P is shown in the graph.

What was the total number of students in 3P?

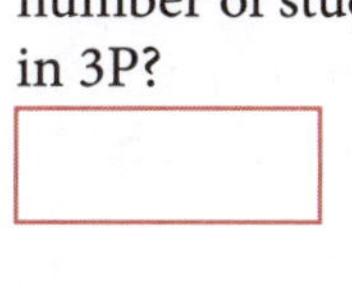

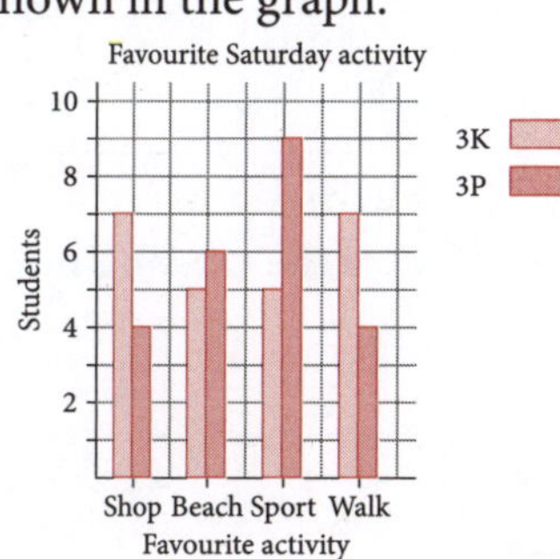

NAPLAN-STYLE TEST 2

1 There are 36 chairs in the library.
The chairs are to be placed in rows of nine chairs for an information evening.
How many rows will there be?

2 Lawrence added two numbers together and the answer was 63.
If the smaller number was 28, what was the larger number?

3 Sung Jae thought of a number. He doubled it and added 5.
His answer is 13. What was Sung Jae's original number?

A 36 **B** 4 **C** 16 **D** 8

4 Mrs Johnston has a new box of 12 pencils. Each pencil is exactly 20 cm in length.
Hope lays all the pencils end to end. Which of these is the length of the line of pencils?

A 32 cm **B** 200 cm **C** 212 cm **D** 240 cm

5 Here are four numbered cards. 8 2 9 5

What is the smallest three-digit even number that can be made?

6 Conor bought a hamburger and a drink. The total cost was $6.75.
If the hamburger cost $4.20, what was the cost of the drink? $

7 A movie started at 7:30 pm. It ran for 135 minutes.
What was the time the movie finished?

A 8:55 pm **B** 9:15 pm **C** 9:45 pm **D** 9:55 pm

8 The map shows where students *A*, *B*, *C*, *D* and *E* live.
Who lives on the corner of Ren Street and Mya Street?

A *A*
B *B*
C *C*
D *D*
E *E*

9 How many 20-cent coins equal the total amount shown below?

A 6 **B** 12 **C** 13 **D** 14

10 Which **two** of these shapes have the same area?

A **B** **C** **D**

11 Corey drew a net of a cube, where opposite faces **multiply** to the same number.
What is the missing number marked with *?

12 Adam is tossing a fair coin nine times. Here is a list of his first eight results.

head, head, tail, head, head, tail, head, head

Which of the following is true for Adam's next toss?

A It is most likely a head. **B** It is most likely a tail.

C Both a head or a tail is equally likely.

13 Abbey counted the vehicles that passed the school during recess. There was a total of 36 vehicles.

Here is the table showing most of the information.

She forgot to write the number of trucks.

What was the missing number?

Vehicles passing school	
Type	**Number**
motorbike	3
car	22
truck	
van	6

A 3 **B** 4

C 5 **D** 6

14 Carolina uses a grid to shade squares.
The dotted line is to be a line of symmetry.

How many more squares should she shade?

A 4 **B** 5

C 6 **D** 7

15 Which of these objects is made from the most cubes?

A **B** **C** **D** **E**

16 Here are 12 oranges.
Elizabeth uses a quarter of the oranges to make juice.

How many oranges remain?

A 8 **B** 6 **C** 10 **D** 9

17 Here is a pattern of numbers.
Tom continues the pattern by writing the next four numbers.

5	7	9	11			*A*	*B*

What is the total of the numbers represented by *A* and *B*?

A 36 **B** 32 **C** 20 **D** 38

18 Pearl drew a quadrilateral with sides of different length.
It has exactly **one** pair of parallel opposite sides. What shape has Pearl drawn?

A kite **B** trapezium **C** square **D** pentagon

19 A grocer is selling two different-sized bags of potatoes.
Small bags contain 10 potatoes and large bags contain 20 potatoes.

The grocer has eight small bags and six large bags available for sale.

What is the total number of potatoes?

20 Isaac buys an orange, a banana and a mango.
The total mass of the orange and the banana is 250 g.

The total mass of the banana and the mango is 350 g.

The total mass of the orange and the mango is 400 g.

What is the total mass of the orange, banana and mango? g

WORKED SOLUTIONS & ANSWERS

Section 1

Unit 1A — PAGE 10

1. 2846
2. 7632
3. 7399
4. 1000
5. 668
6. 87
7. 350
8. 2
9. true
10. 5 hundreds
11. 70
12. 500
13. 7000
14. 5042
15. 4001
16. eight thousand, five hundred and three
17. two thousand and sixty
18. 534
19. 471
20. 468, 508
21. 80
22. 3860
23. 100
24. 8
25. 9
26. 125

Unit 1B — PAGE 11

1. **9247**
   As the number is greater than 8000, the first digit is 9. As the number is odd, the last digit is 7. As $2 < 4$, the 2 is in the hundreds place and the 4 is in the tens place. The number is 9247.
2. **9700**
   Look at the digit in the tens place. As 3 is less than 5, the distance is rounded down to 9700 km, to the nearest 100 km.
3. **1966**
   In order, the years of the coins are 1966, 1971, 1982 and 2001. The smallest number is 1966, which is the oldest coin.
4. **6666**
   You look for 4 identical numbers that add to 24. As $6 + 6 + 6 + 6 = 24$, the number is 6666.
5. **76**
   $7 + 6$ is 13 and 76 is even. Ashley's grandmother is 76.
6. **261**
   You start with 1 in the ones place. This means there is a 2 in the hundreds place and, as $3 \times 2 = 6$, there is a 6 in the hundreds place. The number is 261.
7. **11 000**
   You look for the digit in the hundreds place. As $6 > 5$, the number rounds to 11 000, to the nearest thousand.
8. **1200**
   You look at the digit in the tens place. As it is a 5, the number rounds to 1200, to the nearest 100.
9. **6**
   There are 10 coins. Ignore the first 2 coins and the last 2 coins. This will leave 6 coins.
10. **50**
    As 1 dozen = 12, then 4 dozen is $4 \times 12 = 48$. This means Oliver collected 50 eggs, to the nearest 10.
11. **553**
    Here are Bella's numbers: 523, 533, 543, 553 … Her fourth number is 553.
12. **3113**
    If the digits add to 8, they must be small. If the 2 middle digits are 1s, and the other 2 digits are 3s, the PIN is 3113.
13. **6700**
    You should look at the digit in the tens place. As $2 < 5$, the number rounds down to 6700.
14. **4**
    The largest possible number is formed using the digits in descending order. Lara's number is 9743. The digit in the tens place is 4.
15. **Hannah**
    Hannah calls out 1, then 4, then 7, then 10. This means Hannah will call out the number 10.
16. **6530**
    To form the largest number, arrange the digits in descending order. The number is 6530.
17. **30**
    Cameron's number is 700 and Levi's number is 670. The difference between 670 and 700 is 30.
18. **1387**
    A descending order is from highest to lowest. The order is 1822, 1803, 1387, 1378, 1087. The middle number is 1387.
19. **Saturday**
    You need to continue the pattern of numbers which is Tuesday 26, Wednesday 27, and so on. Lincoln will complete 30 push-ups on Saturday.
20. **1380**
    1380 rounds to 1400, to the nearest 100.
21. **490**
    The smallest even number is 486 and the largest odd number is 497. From the list, the number between 486 and 497 is 490.

Unit 2A — PAGE 12

1. 20
2. 22
3. 80
4. 650
5. 69
6. 458
7. 200
8. 82
9. 98
10. 200
11. 850
12. 4000
13. 3000
14. 4000
15. 4
16. 31
17. 47
18. 320
19. 6
20. 7
21. 8
22. 9

23. 61

24. 90

25. 60

26. 18

27. 10

28. 15

29. 30

30. 70

Unit 2B PAGE 13

1. **51**
The total is 26 + 25 = 26 + 20 + 5. This is 46 + 5 = 51. This means there is a total of 51 students.

2. **65**
You need to add the numbers 16, 21 and 28. First 21 + 28 is easy to add to 49. Then 49 + 16 is 49 + 1 + 15. This is 50 + 15 = 65. Cyril picked a total of 65 tomatoes.

3. **41**
You need to add 12, 16 and 13. First 12 + 16 = 28 and then 28 + 13 = 41. This means Jensen has a total of 41 blocks.

4. **69**
As 23 + 23 = 46 there were 46, fish in the second tank. Now add 46 and 23. This is 69. There was a total of 69 fish in the two tanks.

5. **51**
Adding 23 and 28 is 28 + 23 = 28 + 20 + 3. As 48 + 3 = 51, Charley sold a total of 51 muffins.

6. **46**
First, as 12 + 12 = 24, there are 24 red counters. The total is 10 + 12 + 24 = 22 + 24 = 46. There are 46 counters in the bag.

7. **90**
As 42 + 6 = 48, James has 48 marbles. The total is 48 + 42 = 48 + 40 + 2. This is 88 + 2 = 90. The boys have a total of 90 marbles.

8. **52**
You can add the two bigger numbers first. 24 + 16 = 24 + 10 + 6. This is 34 + 6 = 40. Now add 40 and 12. This is 52. Grace bought 52 balloons for the party.

9. **90**
First you add the two numbers together. 47 + 39 = 47 + 30 + 9. This is 77 + 9 = 86. This is rounded to 90, to the nearest 10.

10. **24**
Ariana's number is 16 less than 40. 40 – 16 = 40 – 10 – 6. This is 30 – 6 = 24. Ariana's original number was 24.

11. **43 km**
You need to find the difference between 80 and 37. 80 – 30 – 7 = 50 – 7 = 43. William needs to ride 43 km.

12. **16**
You can subtract 20 and then add 1. 35 – 19 = 35 – 20 + 1. This is 15 + 1 = 16. Ben has 16 toy cars.

13. **25**
You find the difference between 43 and 18. 43 – 18 = 43 – 20 + 2. This is 23 + 2 = 25. Kate was 25 when Addison was born.

14. **19**
You find the difference between 47 and 28. 47 – 28 = 47 – 30 + 2. This is 17 + 2 = 19. 19 students left the learning centre.

15. **57**
81 – 24 = 81 – 20 – 4. This is 61 – 4 = 57. There are 57 occupied parking spaces.

16. **38**
96 – 58 = 96 – 60 + 2. This is 36 + 2 = 38. There were 38 cookies yet to be sold.

17. **560**
8 hundreds is 800 and 24 tens is 240. 800 – 240 = 800 – 200 – 40. This is 600 – 40 = 560.

18. **18**
Jalailah's numbers are 75 and 57. 75 – 57 = 75 – 50 – 7. This is 25 – 7 = 18. The difference between the two numbers is 18.

19. **1**
First 500 – 320 = 500 – 300 – 20. This is 200 – 20 = 180. There is 1 hundred (also 8 tens and 0 ones) in 180.

20. **83**
Find the difference between 180 and 97. 180 – 97 = 180 – 100 + 3. This is 80 + 3 = 83. There are 83 vacant seats.

21. **270**
Work out the difference between 43 and 16. 43 – 16 = 43 – 10 – 6. This is 33 – 6 = 27. This means 430 – 160 = 270. The driver delivered 270 packages after 10 am.

22. **42**
100 – 29 = 100 – 30 + 1. This is 70 + 1 = 71. The larger number is 71. 71 – 29 = 71 – 30 + 1. This is 41 + 1 = 42. The difference between the two numbers is 42.

Unit 3A PAGE 14

1. 16

2. 20

3. 21

4. 45

5. 24

6. 12, 26

7. 9, 21

8. 10

9. 30

10. 60

11. 24

12. 800

13. 750

14. 130

15. 20

16. 10

17. 5

18. even

19. 0

20. 12

21. 10

22. 50

23. 24

24. 4

25. 4

26. 5

27. 12

28. 10

29. 13

30. 480

Unit 3B PAGE 15

1. **27**
9 × 3 = 27. There are 27 biscuits.

2. **16**
A pair is 2. 8 × 2 = 16. Jake uses 16 pegs.

3. **20**
Each square has 4 sides. 5 × 4 = 20. There are 20 sides.

4. **60**
6 × 10 = 60. Frida reads 60 pages.

5. **40**
$8 \times 5 = 40$. There is a total of 40 cookies.

6. **35**
$7 \times 5 = 35$. There is a total of 35 lemons.

7. **40**
$20 \times 2 = 40$. There were 40 sheets handed out.

8. **20**
$5 \times 4 = 20$. There are 20 competitors.

9. **60**
$6 \times 10 = 60$. The restaurant can seat 60 customers.

10. **24**
$8 \times 3 = 24$. There are 24 slices of pizza.

11. **27**
$9 \times 3 = 27$. Matilda has 27 stuffed animal toys.

12. **30**
$6 \times 5 = 30$. Mia used 30 one-dollar coins.

13. **30**
You multiply the 3 numbers to find the number they all can divide into. $2 \times 5 \times 3 = 10 \times 3$. This is 30. The smallest number of blocks is 30 as 2, 3 and 5 can divide into 30.

14. **8**
$3 \times 8 = 24$. This means $24 \div 3 = 8$. There were 8 friends who received lollies.

15. **12**
$3 \times 12 = 36$. This means $36 \div 3 = 12$. There were 12 oranges in each group.

16. **5**
$3 \times 5 = 15$. This means $15 \div 3 = 5$. This means 5 cars are required.

17. **10**
$6 \times 5 = 30$. James has a total of 30 stickers. If $3 \times 10 = 30$, then $30 \div 3 = 10$. There would be 10 stickers in each box.

18. **4**
$20 \times 2 = 40$. A total of 40 pencils are needed. If $10 \times 4 = 40$, then $40 \div 10 = 4$. This means 4 boxes of pencils are needed.

19. **12**
$10 \times 6 = 60$. There are 60 chairs. If $12 \times 5 = 60$, then $60 \div 5 = 12$. There are 12 rows in Jack's arrangement.

20. **12**
If $4 \times 3 = 12$, then $12 \div 4 = 3$. The two original numbers are 4 and 3.
Half of 4 is 2 and twice 3 is 6.
As $6 \times 2 = 12$, Thomas's answer is 12.

21. **2**
If $6 \times 3 = 18$, then $18 \div 3 = 6$. The number on the card was 6.
If $3 \times 2 = 6$, then $6 \div 3 = 2$. Jasper's answer would be 2.

22. **4**
If $3 \times 8 = 24$, then $24 \div 3 = 8$. There would be 8 groups of 3.
If $2 \times 12 = 24$, then $24 \div 2 = 12$. There would be 12 pairs.
As $12 - 8 = 4$, Ms Turnbull would make 4 more groups.

Unit 4A PAGE 16

For questions 1, 3, 4, 5, 10 and 18 a sample answer has been provided with the correct number of shaded shapes.

1. 

2. 8

3.

4.

5. 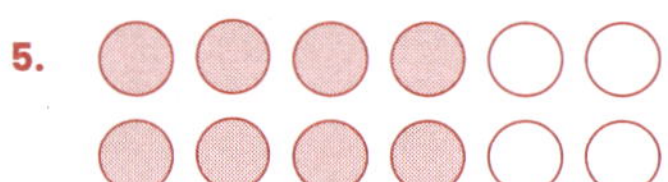

6. $\frac{5}{8}$

7. false

8. $\frac{1}{2}$

9. $\frac{5}{8}$

10. 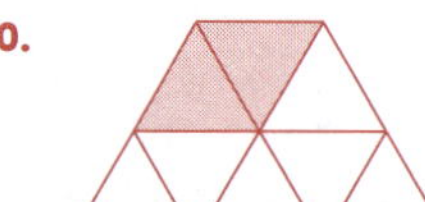

11. $\frac{3}{4}$

12. $\frac{4}{5}$

13. $\frac{2}{8}$

14. 3

15. $\frac{4}{5}$

16. $\frac{7}{8}$

17. $1\frac{1}{5}$

18. 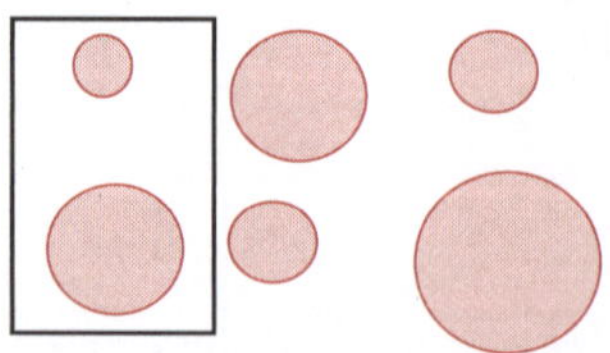

There are other correct answers.

19. $\frac{3}{8}$ $\frac{4}{8}$ $\frac{5}{8}$ $\frac{6}{8}$ $\frac{7}{8}$ 1

20. 6

21. 5

22. $\frac{1}{2}$ (or $\frac{2}{4}$)

23. $\frac{4}{8}, \frac{4}{4}, \frac{4}{3}, \frac{4}{2}$

24. true

Unit 4B PAGE 17

1. $\frac{7}{8}$
7 out of 8 squares are shaded. This is $\frac{7}{8}$ of the shape.

2. **3**
Half of 6 is $6 \div 2 = 3$. There are 3 chocolate cookies.

3. **6**

4. **2**
Half of 8 is 4. There are 4 red and 2 green balls. $8 - 4 - 2 = 4 - 2 = 2$. There are 2 blue balls in the bag.

5. $\frac{1}{5}$
$2 + 2 = 4$. This means 4 squares are shaded and 1 remains unshaded. 1 square out of 5 is unshaded, which is written as $\frac{1}{5}$.
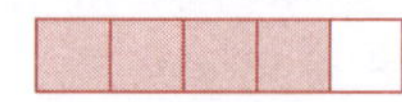

6. $\frac{1}{2}$
6 out of 12 eggs were used. This is half of the eggs.

7. **4**
There are 12 pencils. Finding one-third of 12 is the same as $12 \div 3$. If $3 \times 4 = 12$, then $12 \div 3 = 4$. Asher used 4 pencils.

8. **4**
There are 8 halves. Two halves make a whole. There were originally 4 apples.

9. $\mathbf{\frac{3}{10}}$
There are 10 tenths in one whole. $10 - 5 - 2 = 5 - 2 = 3$. Noah keeps $\frac{3}{10}$ of the balls.

10. $\mathbf{\frac{3}{5}}$
Alice read 3 out of 5 books. This means she had read $\frac{3}{5}$ of her books.

11. $\mathbf{\frac{1}{4}}$
There are 4 people. Caleb ate $\frac{1}{4}$ of the chocolates.

12. $\mathbf{\frac{3}{8}}$
$8 - 3 - 2 = 5 - 2 = 3$. This means 3 students out of 8 had walked to school. This is written as $\frac{3}{8}$.

13. **16**
There are 8 eighths in one whole. There are 2 pizzas. This means there were $8 \times 2 = 16$ slices.

14. $\mathbf{\frac{7}{10}}$
$10 - 3 = 7$. There were 7 circles not coloured in. This is written as $\frac{7}{10}$.

15. **2**
You can think of the 8 cushions arranged into 4 groups of 2 cushions. Blake keeps 1 group of cushions, which is 2 cushions, on her bed.

16. **3**
The bananas can be arranged in 2 groups of 3. As Emma ate 1 group, there was 1 group, or 3 bananas, remaining.

17. **Elias**
Compare $\frac{1}{2}$, $\frac{1}{4}$ and $\frac{1}{3}$. Each of the fractions has a numerator of 1. The smallest fraction has the largest denominator. The smallest fraction is $\frac{1}{4}$, which means Elias ate the smallest amount.

18. **3**
There are 12 squares. Half of 12 is $12 \div 2 = 6$. Ivy will leave 6 unshaded squares. If Audrey shaded half of these 6 squares, there were still 3 squares not shaded.

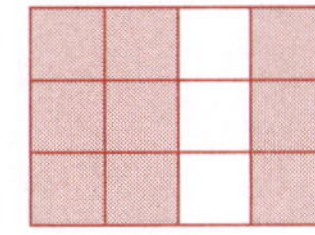

19. $\mathbf{\frac{1}{10}}$
$5 + 3 = 8$ and $10 - 8 = 2$. The total of green and white jelly beans is 2. This means there is only 1 white jelly bean out of 10. This is written as $\frac{1}{10}$.

Unit 5A PAGE 18

1. $1.40
2. $3.45
3. $2.30
4. $11.55
5. 20
6. $3.85
7. 80c
8. $7.05
9. $1.60
10. $4.95
11. $4.40
12. $2.70
13. 10
14. $85
15. $10
16. 6
17. 4
18. 30
19. 11
20. $18
21. $41.30
22. 3

Unit 5B PAGE 19

1. **$1**
$2 + $1 + 50c + 20c + 5c = $3.75. The $1-coin is missing.

2. **$4**
If $3 \times 4 = 12$, then $12 \div 3 = 4$. Each can of dog food costs $4.

3. **$35**
$100 - 65 = 100 - 60 - 5$. This is $40 - 5 = 35$. Josiah has $35 remaining on his gift card.

4. **$24**
$6 \times 4 = 24$. Skylar is paid $24.

5. **$12.20**
$9 + $3 + 20 cents = $12.20. The total cost is $12.20.

6. **$80**
$5 + 2 + 1 = 8$. This means $50 + 20 + 10 = 80$. Stella received $80.

7. **$160**
$8 \times 2 = 16$. This means $80 \times 2 = 160$. Brielle received $160.

8. **$1.25**
$3.00 + 75 cents = $3.75. You now subtract this amount from $5.
Subtract the dollars and then subtract the cents. $5 – $3.75 = $2 – 75 cents = $1.25. Hannah received change of $1.25.

9. **$12**
You need to add $9.20 and $2.80. $9 + $2 + 20c + 80c = $11 + $1. This is $12. Henry spent $12.

10. **$1.60**
As $40 \times 6 = 240$, the apples cost $2.40. As $2 × 2 = $4, Ethan paid $4. Use subtraction to find the change. $4 – $2.40 = $2 – 40 cents. This is $1.60. Ethan received change of $1.60.

11. **$142**
You need to add $130 and $12. As $130 + 12 = 142$, the total cost will be $142.

12. **$10**
As $45 + 45 = 90$, the flowers cost $90. Use subtraction to find the change. As $100 - 90 = 10$, Zoey was given $10 change.

13. **5**
The coins are $2 + $1 + 50c + 10c + 5c = $3.65. Liam could have used 5 coins.

14. **$23**
$11.50 + $11.50 = $11 + $11 + 50c + 50c. This is $23. The cost will be $23.

15. **$5.97**
Multiplying $1.99 by 3 is multiplying $2 by 3 and then subtracting 3 cents. $6 minus 3 cents is $5.97. Mason spent $5.97.

16. **$62**
As $20 + $10 + $5 + $2 + $1 = $38, Kiara had $38 remaining.
$100 - 38 = 100 - 30 - 8$. This is $70 - 8 = 62$. Kiara spent $62.

17. **$1.60**
$3.42 rounds down to $3.40.
$5 – $3.40 = $2 – 40 cents. This is $1.60. Sebastian received change of $1.60.

18. **$60**
You can work out $240 \div 4$ by thinking about $24 \div 4$. If $4 \times 6 = 24$, then $24 \div 4 = 6$. This means $240 \div 4 = 60$. Each person will receive $60.

19. **$16.40**

$10 – $3.60 = $10 – $3 – 60c. This is $7 – 60c = $6.40. Mia has $6.40. $10 + $6.40 = $16.40. The girls have a total of $16.40.

20. **$94**

42 + 10 = 52. Levi has saved $52. 42 + 52 = 42 + 50 + 2. This equals 94. The boys have saved a total of $94.

21. **$4**

90 + 60 + 50 is 200. The cost of one of each fruit is $2. As 2 × 2 = 4, Lyla spent $4.

22. **$20.70**

10 × 2 = 20, 10 × 5 = 50 and 4 × 5 = 20. Noah has $20 + 50c + 20c. This is $20.70.

Unit 6A — PAGE 20

1. 20
2. 35
3. 21, 24
4. 3
5. 54
6. 31, 25
7. 24
8. 483, 67
9. 98
10. 31
11. 67, 76
12. 76
13. 90
14. 6, 11, 16, 21
15. 6
16. 9
17. 10
18. 45
19. 1066
20. 75
21. 8, 24
22. 97
23. 48, 60
24. 1080
25. 18
26. 281, 302
27. 100

Unit 6B — PAGE 21

1. **19**

The list of numbers is 7, 13, 19, 25 … The number on Charlotte's list is 19.

2. **26**

The list of numbers is 43, 34, 25, 16, 7. The number not on Lincoln's list is 26.

3. **Saturday**

The pattern is 2, 4, 6, 8 ,10, 12 … He rode 12 km on the sixth day, which was Saturday.

4. **even**

Four more than an odd number is still odd. Harper's number is also odd. When two odd numbers are added, the result is always even.

5. **3**

The two numbers are 101 and 98. 101 – 98 = 3. The difference is 3.

6. **$4800**

5400 – 200 – 200 – 200 = 5000 – 200. This is 4800. The price is $4800.

7. **40**

The rule is to add 5. The list of numbers is 15, 20, 25, 30, 35, 40 … The sixth number is 40.

8. **21**

The pattern is 6, 9, 12, 15, 18, 21 … As 21 is the sixth number, there are 21 students in Group 6.

9. **16**

Here is Adrian's pattern: 28, 24, 20, 16 … The fourth number is 16.

10. **120**

As 320 – 200 is 120, the rule is 'Start with 440 and subtract 120'.

11. **70**

Ryan's numbers are 100, 90, 80, 70 … The fourth number is 70.

12. **15**

Maya's number pattern is **20**, 25, 30, **35** … As 35 – 20 is 15, the difference is 15.

13.

The rectangle is in the 4th, 8th, 12th and 16th positions.

14. **36 cm**

As 12 + 8 = 20, the plant is 20 cm tall after 1 week. The pattern of heights at the end of each week, in cm, is 20, 28, 36. The plant is 36 cm tall after 3 weeks.

15. **6**

Isla counts 1, 3, 5, 7, 9, 11, 13, 15, 17, 19 … Willow counts 1, 4, 7, 10, 13, 16, 19 … Lucy counts 1, 5, 9, 13, 17 … The numbers 2, 6, 8, 12, 14, 18 are not counted.

16. **5**

The pattern is 12, 10, 8, 6, 4. There are 5 numbers in this pattern. This means there are 5 rows of tissue boxes in the display.

17. **28**

The rule is to add 4. The pattern is 4, 8, 12, 16, 20, 24. As 24 + 4 = 28, the total is 28.

18. **28**

In Eliana's pattern, the numbers are getting smaller. As 20 + 4 + 4 = 28, the pattern will be 28, 24, 20 … The first number is 28.

19. **$36**

The pattern is 12, 10, 8, 6 … As 12 + 10 + 8 + 6 is 36, Gianna charges $36.

20. **11**

Ava lights the 2nd, 5th, 8th and 11th candles. The smallest number is 11 candles.

21. **24**

Here is Dylan's list: 4, 9, 14, 19, **24**, 29 … Here is Miles's list: 30, **24**, 18, 12, 6 … The number on both lists is 24.

Unit 7A — PAGE 22

1. 13 cm
2. 11 cm
3. 2 cm
4. 13 cm
5. 12 cm
6. 3 m
7. 4 cm
8. 200
9. 1 m 25 cm
10. 10 cm
11. 53
12. 5 cm
13. 42
14. 27 cm
15. 42 mm
16. 100
17. 5 m
18. 5 cm
19. 200 mm
20. 2003
21. <
22. 8 cm^2
23. 10 cm^2

Unit 7B PAGE 23

1. **180 cm (1 m 80 cm)**
As 1 m is 100 cm, then 1 m 45 cm is 145 cm. As 145 + 35 = 180, Jo's father is 180 cm tall.

2. **20 cm**
A square has 4 equal sides.
$5 \times 4 = 20$. The distance is 20 cm.

3. **30 km**
15 + 15 is 30. Jack drives a total distance of 30 km.

4. **5 cm**
If $3 \times 5 = 15$, then $15 \div 3 = 5$. The rectangle is 5 cm wide.

5. **7 cm**
A square has 4 equal sides.
If $4 \times 7 = 28$, then $28 \div 4 = 7$. Each side of the square is 7 cm.

6. **5 cm**
25×2 is 25 + 25 = 50. Jack's line is 50 mm long. As 10 mm is 1 cm, then Jack's line is 5 cm.

7. **7 cm**
19 – 12 = 7. The scarf is 7 cm longer.

8. **185 m**
155 + 30 = 185. Symon hit the ball 185 m.

9. **9 cm**
The USB is 6 cm long and the pen is 15 cm. As 15 – 6 = 9, the difference in lengths is 9 cm.

10. **28 km**
As $7 \times 4 = 28$, Scott walked a total of 28 km.

11. **180 cm**
As $9 \times 2 = 18$, then $90 \times 2 = 180$. Sophia will eventually be 180 cm tall.

12. **2 cm**
The dimensions of the rectangle are 6 cm by 4 cm. As 6 – 4 = 2, the rectangle is 2 cm longer than it is wide.

13. **55 cm**
100 cm is 1 m. 100 – 45 = 100 – 40 – 5. This is 60 – 5 = 55. The longer length is 55 cm.

14. **20 m**
$5 \times 4 = 20$. The length is 20 m.

15. **142 cm**
139 + 3 = 139 + 1 + 2. This is 142. Grace is 142 cm tall.

16. **160 m**
As $8 \times 2 = 16$, then $8 \times 20 = 160$. Alice swims 160 metres.

17. **10 months**
As 1 cm = 10 mm, then 2 cm is 20 mm. If $2 \times 10 = 20$, then $20 \div 2 = 10$. It will take 10 months for her fingernails to grow 2 cm.

18. **10**
If 100 cm is 1 m, then 200 cm is 2 m. If $20 \times 10 = 200$, then $200 \div 20 = 10$. Sebastian has used 10 pencils.

19. **2 cm**
As half of 20 is 10, the total of the length and width of the rectangle is 10 cm. As 10 – 8 = 2, the width is 2 cm.

20. **480 m**
If 24 + 24 is 48, then 240 + 240 = 480. Mateo walks a total of 480 m.

21. **5**
There is 100 cm in 1 m.
As $2 \times 5 = 10$, then $20 \times 5 = 100$. This means $100 \div 20 = 5$. Allison can cut 5 lengths.

22. **3 cm**
The rectangle covers 15 squares. As $15 \div 5 = 3$, the width is 3 cm.

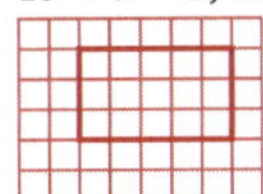

Unit 8A PAGE 24

1. 7
2. bottle of hand sanitiser
3. 16 cm^3
4. 16
5. 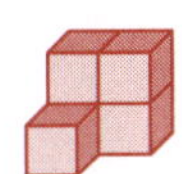
6. 500 mL
7. 10 L
8. $\frac{1}{2}$ L
9. 12
10. $\frac{1}{4}$
11. 960 g
12. 4 kg
13. 1
14. 6
15. 30 kg
16. 

17. 12 kg
18. 3 kg
19. <
20. 1:45
21. 25, 8
22. 

Unit 8B PAGE 25

1. **5 cm^3**
The solid contains 9 cubes.
If $9 \times 5 = 45$, then $45 \div 9 = 5$. The volume of each cube is 5 cm^3.

2. **6**
Half of 12 buckets is 6 buckets. Khloe would use 6 buckets.

3. **1550 L**
As 9 + 6 = 15, then 900 + 50 + 600 is 1550. The tank contains 1550 L.

4. **25 L**
First, $10 \times 2 = 20$ and half of 10 is 5. As 20 + 5 = 25, Cameron has used 25 L.

5. **16 L**
As 6 – 4 = 2, there are 2 bottles that contain 2 L each. $4 \times 3 = 12$ and $2 \times 2 = 4$. As 12 + 4 = 16, a total of 16 L of olive oil was purchased.

6. **3**
Half of 48 is 24. If $8 \times 3 = 24$, then $24 \div 8 = 3$. Monty needs 3 small containers.

7. **10 L**
As 26 – 6 = 20, Mo has poured 20 L of water into Cylinder A.
If $2 \times 10 = 20$, then $20 \div 2 = 10$. Cylinder B has a capacity of 10 L.

8. **26 L**
50 – 24 = 50 – 20 – 4. This is 30 – 4 = 26. Teagan buys 26 L of petrol.

9. **6 kg**
As 3 + 2 + 1 = 6, the total mass is 6 kg.

10. **24 kg**
As $6 \times 2 = 12$, there is a total of 12 boxes. As $12 \times 2 = 24$, the total mass is 24 kg.

11. **66 kg**
There are 11 cubes in the shape. As $11 \times 6 = 66$, the mass of Mark's solid is 66 kg.

12. **60 kg**
15 + 15 + 15 + 15 = 30 + 30. This is 60. The mass is 60 kg.

13. **10 kg**
7 + 7 = 14 and 24 – 14 = 10. The third box has a mass of 10 kg.

14. **2 kg**
If 2 × 3 = 6, then 6 ÷ 2 = 3. The mass of each ball is 3 kg. As 5 – 3 = 2, the mass of the cube is 2 kg.

15. **120 kg**
As 6 × 2 = 12, then 6 × 20 = 120. The total mass was 120 kg.

16. **12 kg**
As 10 × 2 = 20, the total mass of 5 blocks is also 20 kg. If 5 × 4 = 20, then 20 ÷ 5 = 4. The mass of each block is 4 kg. As 3 × 4 = 12, the total mass of 3 blocks is 12 kg.

17. **89 kg**
47 + 47 = 47 + 40 + 7. This is 87 + 7 = 94. As 94 – 5 = 89, the mass of Nadia's father is 89 kg.

18. **17 minutes**
The clock shows 13 minutes past 9, or 9:13. Half past 9 is 9:30.
30 – 13 = 20 – 3 = 17. The bus is 17 minutes late.

19. **45 minutes**
The two clocks are showing 9:30 and 10:15. From 9:30 there are 30 minutes until 10:00 and another 15 minutes until 10:15. 30 + 15 = 45. The test takes 45 minutes.

20. **35 minutes**
A quarter to 11 to 11 o'clock is 15 minutes. From 11 o'clock to 20 past 11 is 20 minutes. As 20 + 15 is 35, the appointment lasted 35 minutes.

Unit 9A — PAGE 26

1. cone
2. 
3. 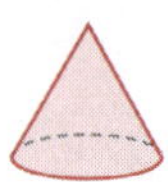
4. 2
5. 1
6.  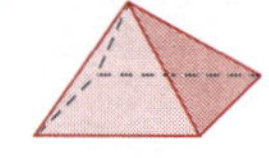
7. ball
8. 5
9. cube
10. circle
11. 8
12. triangular pyramid
13. 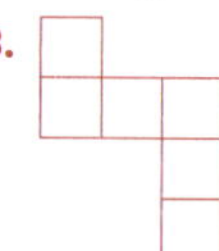
14. circle
15. 12
16. 2
17. 6

Unit 9B — PAGE 27

1. **square**
The cube has 6 identical square faces. The shape is a square.

2. **rectangle**
The cylinder rolls on its curved surface. From above, Paul saw a rectangle.

3. **sphere**
Cones, spheres and cylinders have curved surfaces. Only a sphere has no flat surfaces.

4. **rectangle**
The curved surface of the cylinder could be flattened into a rectangle. The label is in the shape of a rectangle.

5. **4**
The shape is a square pyramid. There are 4 triangular faces.

6. **6**
There are 6 faces. Camilla used the numbers 1 to 6.

7. **6**
The shape is a prism. There are 6 faces.

8. **sphere**
A sphere has no flat surfaces and one curved surface.

9. **5**
3 and 4 are on opposite faces.
As 3 + 4 = 7, opposite faces add to 7.
The * is opposite 2. As 7 – 2 = 5, the missing number is 5.

10 **40 cm²**
In a cylinder, the circles on the ends are identical. The area is 40 cm².

11. **12**
The net forms a cube. A cube has 12 edges.

12. **7**
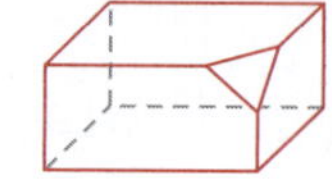

13. **1**
A square prism has 6 faces and a square pyramid has 5 faces.
As 6 – 5 = 1, there is 1 more face.

14. **30 cm²**
In a cube, all 6 faces are identical. As 6 × 5 = 30, the total area is 30 cm².

15. **rectangle**
Alissa has made a rectangular prism. This means the base is in the shape of a rectangle.
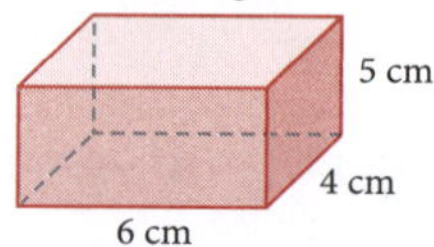

The base of the prism is a rectangle.

16. **24 cm²**
By counting, there are 24 small squares. The area is 24 cm².

17. **cube**
6 squares with sides 2 cm are in the net. The net forms a cube.

18. **4 cm²**
If 6 × 4 = 24, then 24 ÷ 6 = 4. The area of each face is 4 cm².

19. **24 cm**
In a cube there are 12 edges, all of equal length. From the net, each edge is 2 cm. As 12 × 2 = 24, the total length is 24 cm.

20. **1**
An octagon has 8 sides and a hexagon has 6 sides. An octagonal pyramid has 9 faces and a hexagonal prism has 8 faces. As 9 – 8 = 1, the difference is 1.

21. **44 cm²**
There are 4 identical triangles. As 8 × 4 = 32, the total area of the triangles is 32 cm². As 32 + 12 = 44, the area of all the faces is 44 cm².

22. **12**
As 3 + 2 = 5 and 4 + 2 = 6, the rule is 'Adding 2 to the number of sides gives the number of faces'. A decagon has 10 sides. 10 + 2 = 12.
A decagonal prism has 12 faces.

Unit 10A — PAGE 28

1. 
2. 2
3. 1
4. square

5. true
6. square
7. octagon
8. 5
9. equal
10. 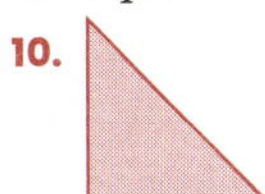
11. C
12. 4
13. 
14. 3
15. 2
16. 2
17. 8

Unit 10B PAGE 29

1. 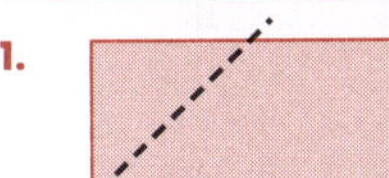
2. 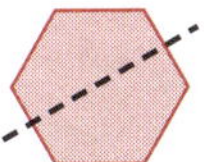
3. 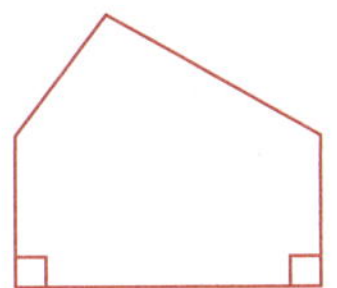

   A pentagon has 5 sides.
4. **6**

   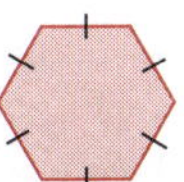

   A regular hexagon has 6 equal sides and 6 equal angles. All the angles are larger than a right angle.
5. 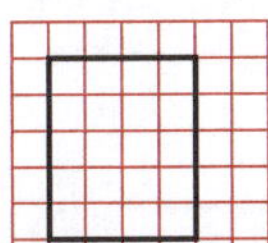
6. **20 cm²**

   There are 5 rows of 4 squares. As $5 \times 4 = 20$, the area is 20 cm².
7. **18 cm**

   Opposite sides of the rectangle are equal. As $5 + 5 + 4 + 4 = 18$, the distance is 18 cm.
8. 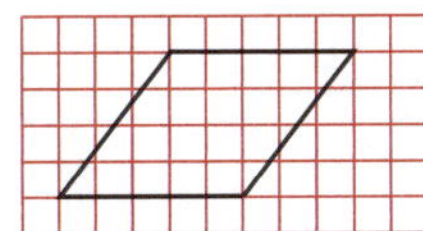
9. **20 cm**

   All sides of a rhombus are equal. The side on the bottom of the rhombus is 5 cm. As $4 \times 5 = 20$, the distance is 20 cm.
10. **triangle**

    The number of sides on the shapes is decreasing. The next shape will have 3 sides and is a triangle.
11. 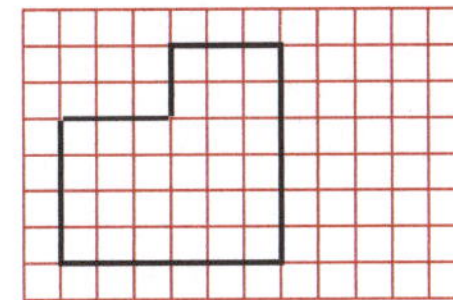
12. **30 cm²**

    There are 2 rows of 3 squares and 4 rows of 6. 2×3 plus 4×6 is $6 + 24 = 30$. The area is 30 cm².
13. **24 cm**

    As $3 + 2 + 3 + 6 + 6 + 4 = 24$, the distance is 24 cm.
14. **5**

    Here are the five right angles inside the hexagon.

    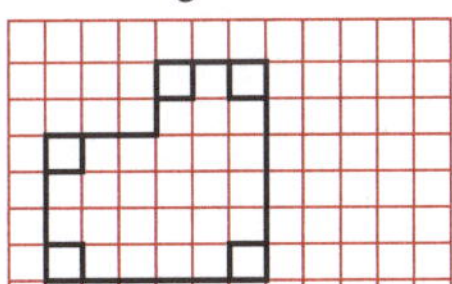
15. **3**

    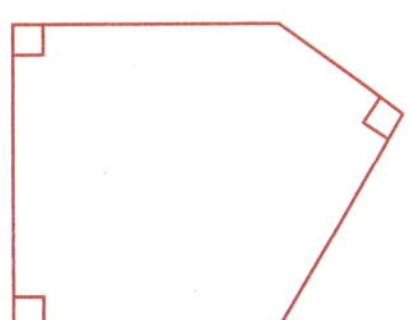

    The pentagon can have up to 3 right angles.
16. **90°**

    The hands form a right angle which is 90°. (The angle could also be expressed as 270°.)
17. **4**

    A regular octagon has 8 equal sides. There are 4 pairs of sides that are parallel.

    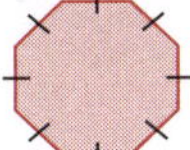
18. **10 o'clock**

    A quarter turn on the clock is 3 hours. The time will be 10 o'clock.

19. **360°**

    There are 4 right angles inside a rectangle. As $9 \times 4 = 36$, then $90 \times 4 = 360$. There is a total of 360°.
20. **Those sides are equal and parallel as well.**

    Kristie has drawn a parallelogram (or rectangle, rhombus or square). The other two sides are also equal and parallel.
21. 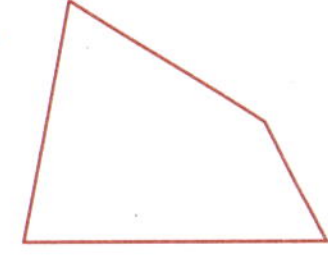

    A quadrilateral has 4 sides and 4 angles. There is only one angle larger than a right angle.
22. **7:25**

    A rotation of 90° is a quarter-turn. This is 15 minutes. The time will be 25 past 7, or 7:25.

Unit 11A PAGE 30

1. 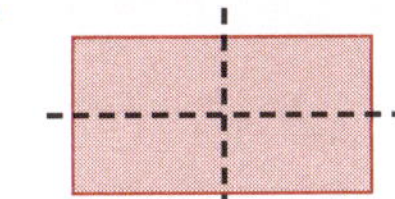
2. 4
3. A, E and U
4. 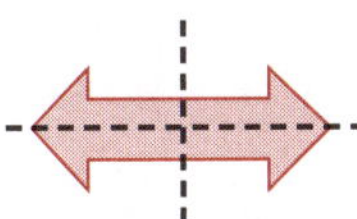
5. circle
6. 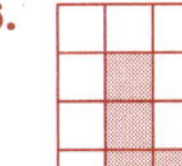 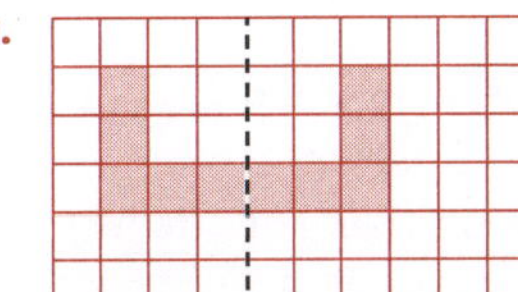
7. 
8.

9. F5

10.

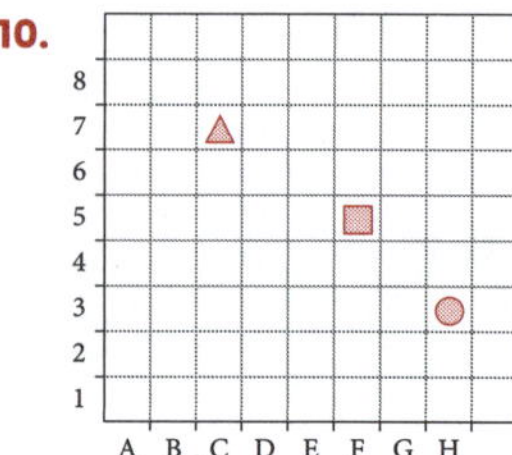

11. A6

12. C2

13. 4

Unit 11B PAGES 31–32

1. **5**

He writes his name as CEDRIC. All the letters have at least one line of symmetry except for R. This means 5 letters have at least a line of symmetry.

2. **6**

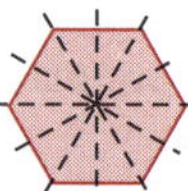

There are 6 lines of symmetry.

3. **7**

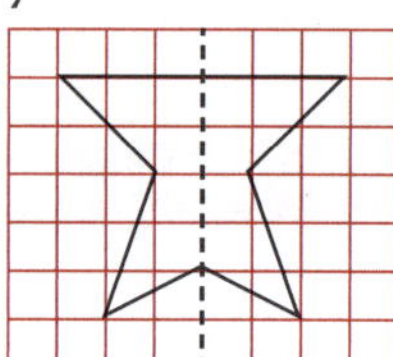

There will be 7 sides.

4. **3**

A regular triangle is an equilateral triangle, with 3 equal sides.

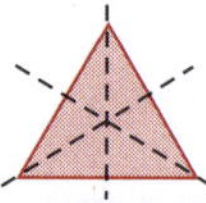

There are 3 lines of symmetry.

5. **rhombus**

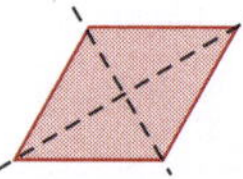

The shape is a rhombus. (Remember that a square has 4 lines of symmetry.)

6. **4**

Look at each row of the grid and count the new squares to be shaded. There will be 4 squares.

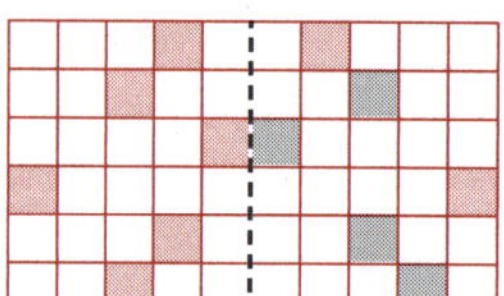

7. **2**

The circle has an infinite number of lines of symmetry, the octagon has 8 and the rectangle has 2. This means the logo has only 2 lines of symmetry.

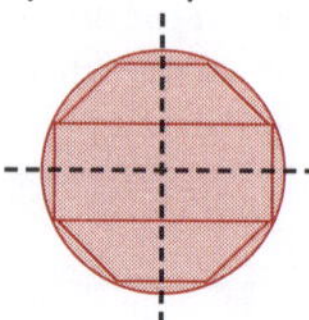

8. **5**

A regular octagon has 8 lines of symmetry. As $8 - 3 = 5$, Freya has 5 more lines to draw.

9.

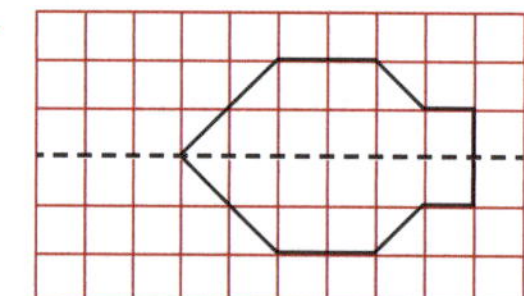

The top shape is repeated under the horizontal line.

10. **3**

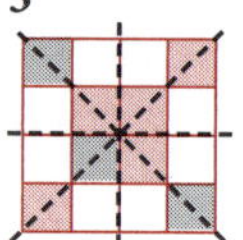

Larry needs to shade 3 more squares.

11. **1**

Here is the completed diagram.

   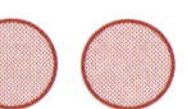

Haydn can add 1 shaded circle.

12. **7**

Damon needs to shade 7 more squares.

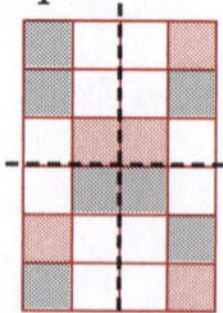

13.

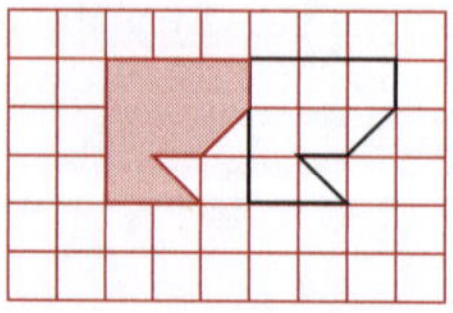

14. **G6**

From C2, forward to C6, left to B6, then back to G6.

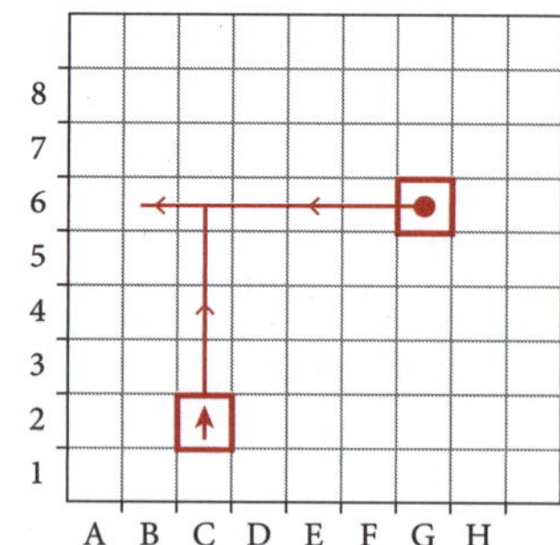

15. **cinemas**

Tom turns left out of school and, after turning left at the second street, walks past the shopping centre. At the end of this street, he turns right and the cinemas are on his left.

16. **4 units**

A rectangle has opposite sides equal. As *R* is 4 units from *Q*, then *S* is 4 units from *P*.

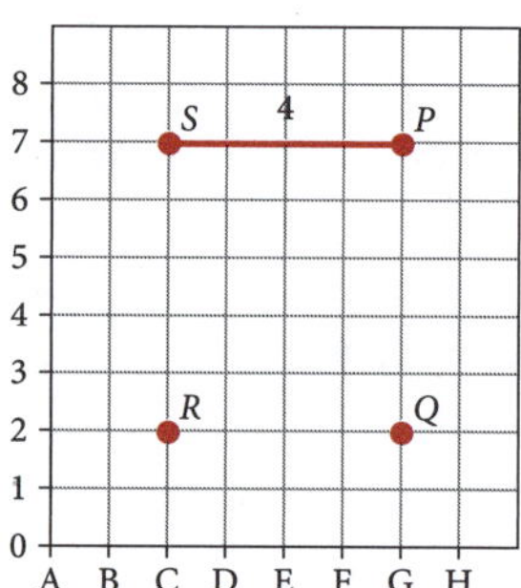

17.

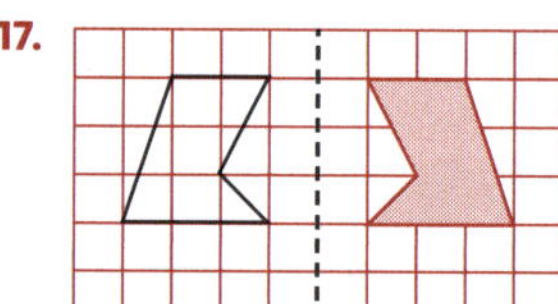

18. **21**

As there are 3 students on Toby's right, each row has 7 students. There must be 3 rows, as $7 \times 3 = 21$. (If there were five or more rows, there would be more than 30 students.) There are 21 students in the photo.

19. **George Street**

The bank and the church are both on George Street.

20. **Ada Street**

The first street he passes is Bell Street and the second is Ada Street.

21. **hotel**

Chelsea walks along Margaret Street into Bell Street. She then turns into George Street and passes the hotel.

22. **police station**

Zane walked left down Margaret Street, right into Angel Street, right into George Street, left into Ada Street and then left into Hunter

Street where the police station was on his left.

Unit 12A — PAGE 33

1. 2
2. 2
3. 2
4. 1, 7
5. 2
6. fruit
7. 16
8. 3
9. blue
10. yellow
11. 4
12. 6
13. 4
14. 3
15. Saturday
16. 3

Unit 12B — PAGES 34–35

1. **rolling a 5**
   There are two numbers less than 3, three numbers that are even and only one 5. The least likely outcome is rolling a 5.
2. **15**
   Half the numbers on the dice are odd. As half of 30 is 15, he would expect about 15 odd numbers.
3. **16**
   As white and green balls are equally likely, there must also be 4 green balls. There are twice as many blue balls as green balls. This means there are 8 blue balls. As $4 + 4 + 8 = 16$, there is a total of 16 balls.
4. **purple**
   As $12 - 6 - 4 = 2$, there are 2 purple balls in the bag. This means the least likely colour is purple.
5. **1**
   The result of the third spin is not dependent on the previous results. The number 1 covers the largest area and so is the most likely.
6. **blue**
   There are 3 red, 4 blue and 3 green balls. The highest number is 4. The most likely ball chosen is blue.
7. **red**
   There are then 3 red, 2 blue and 2 green balls. This means now the most likely ball chosen is red.
8. **cricket**
   Six students nominated soccer and 4 nominated cricket. This means cricket is the second most popular.
9. **4**
   $6 - 2 = 4$. There were 4 more students who liked soccer than hockey.
10. **21**
    $3 + 2 + 4 + 6 + 3 + 3 = 21$. There were 21 students surveyed.
11. **20**
    $5 + 6 + 4 + 2 + 3 = 20$. There were 20 students surveyed.
12. **4**
    $5 + 6 = 11$. A total of 11 students liked purple or pink. $4 + 3 = 7$. A total of 7 students liked red or blue. As $11 - 7 = 4$, the difference is 4 students.
13. **yes**
    $5 + 6 = 11$. As half of 20 is 10, and 11 is larger than 10, Jake is correct.
14. **4**
    10 students travelled by car and 6 students walked. As $10 - 6 = 4$, the difference is 4 students.
15. **bus**
    $8 + 4 + 10 + 6 + 2 = 30$. There were 30 students surveyed. As $30 - 22 = 8$, the column representing 8 students is bus travellers.
16. **13**
    $10 - 3 = 7$. There were 7 students who travelled in a car on Wednesday. As $7 + 6 = 13$, there were 13 students who walked or travelled by car.
17. **14**
    As half of 8 is 4, there were 4 bus travellers who walked.
    As $4 + 4 + 6 = 14$, there were 14 students who walked to school on Friday.
18. **15**
    There are 15 dots on the graph.
19. **12**
    $4 + 4 + 3 + 1 = 12$. There were 12 students who swam at least 2 laps.
20. **300 m**
    Jake swam 6 laps. As 50×6 is 300, he swam 300 m.
21. **40**
    1 student swam 0 laps, 2 swam 1, 4 swam 2, 4 swam 3, 3 swam 4 and 1 swam 6.
    $0 + 2 + 8 + 12 + 12 + 6 = 40$. A total of 40 laps were swum.
22. **18**
    $10 + 8 = 18$. There were 18 passengers.
23. **Friday**
    On Friday there were 2 adults and 4 children.
24. **3**
    On Monday there were 6 children, on Wednesday 8 children and on Thursday 6 children. There were more than 4 children on 3 days.
25. **32**
    $8 + 6 + 10 + 6 + 2 = 32$. There was a total of 32 adult passengers.
26. **Thursday**
    On Thursday there were 6 adults and 6 children. As $6 + 6 = 12$, there were 12 passengers on Thursday.

Section 2

Unit 1A — PAGE 36

1. **9**
   The smallest number is 9. The youngest cousin is 9 years old.
2. **17**
   You can pair the numbers to make the addition easier. $3 + 7 = 10$ and $5 + 2 = 7$. Finally $10 + 7$ is 17.
3. **8**
   $12 - 4 = 8$. Mo is 8 years old.
4. **12**
   As 4×3 is 12, Lucy had a total of 12 cakes.
5. **4**
   As $2 \times 4 = 8$, then $8 \div 2 = 4$. There are 4 buttons in each row.
6. There are other correct answers.
7. **70 cents**
   3 lots of 20 is 60. As $60 + 10 = 70$, Matilda has 70 cents.
8. **26**
   The pattern is adding 4.
   As $22 + 4 = 26$, the next number is 26.
9. **16 cm**

One end of the pencil is at 0 cm and the other end is at 16 cm. The length is 16 cm.

10. **20 L**

   2 × 10 = 20. Marin has 20 L of water.

11. **peach, apple, grape**

   A watermelon has a mass of more than 1 kg. A peach, an apple and a grape each have a mass of less than 200 g, which is less than 1 kg.

12. **20**

   The time is 20 past 9.

13. **6**

   A cube has 6 faces and so does a rectangular prism.

14. **quadrilateral**

   A four-sided shape is called a quadrilateral. A triangle has three sides and a hexagon has six sides.

15. 

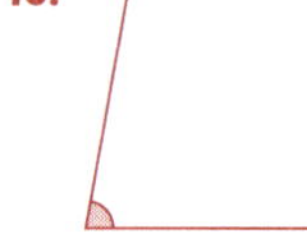

16. **4**

   Shape A has been moved 4 units to the right.

17. **Tomorrow the sun will rise.**

   Macy's netball team **might** win but it is **certain** that the sun will rise tomorrow.

18. **7**

   As 5 + 2 = 7, there were 7 goals scored.

Unit 1B — PAGE 37

1. **1760**

   All four numbers start with 1 thousand. There are two numbers with 7 in the hundreds place. There is a 6 in the tens place in 1760. The largest number is 1760.

2. **30**

   The total is 12 + 18. You could write the larger number first and then add 10 then 2. 18 + 10 + 2 = 28 + 2. This is 30. Carol has 30 cards.

3. **16**

   38 – 22 = 38 – 20 – 2. This is 18 – 2 = 16. Chloe used 16 more beads.

4. **20**

   There are four 5s. As 4 × 5 = 20, the total is 20.

5. **10**

   As 3 × 10 = 30, then 30 ÷ 3 = 10. There are 10 balls in each row.

6. 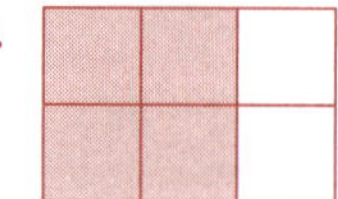

   There are other correct answers.

7. **35 cents**

   To $2.65, add 5c to give $2.70 and then 30c to give $3. This is a total of 35 cents.

8. **4**

   The pattern is adding 6. The first number will be 6 less than 10. As 10 – 6 = 4, the missing number is 4.

9. **16 cm**

   One end of the pen is at 2 cm and the other end is at 18 cm. As 18 – 2 = 16, the length is 16 cm.

10. **20**

   To find half you can divide by 2. As 4 ÷ 2 = 2, so 40 ÷ 2 = 20. The container has 20 L of water.

11. **2000**

   There is 1000 g in 1 kg. This means there is 2000 g in 2 kg.

12. **40**

   There are 60 minutes in an hour. The time is 20 past 9, so there is another 40 minutes to 10 o'clock.

13. **8**

   There are 2 hexagonal faces and 6 rectangular faces. As 2 + 6 = 8, there is a total of 8 faces.

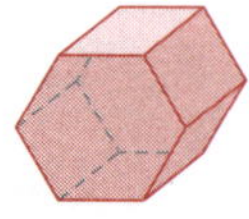

14. **21**

   A triangle has 3 sides, a quadrilateral has 4, a hexagon has 6 and an octagon has 8.
   As 3 + 4 + 6 + 8 = 21, Isaac drew a total of 21 sides.

15. **true**

   The length of the arms of the angle does not affect the size of the angle. Both angles are the same size.

16. **3**

   The unshaded shape was translated 3 units to the right.

17. **The traffic light will be green.**

   The traffic could be green, amber or red. It is not certain that it will be green.

18. **24**

   First 4 × 5 = 20. Now add 4: 20 + 4 = 24. There were 24 goals scored.

Unit 2A — PAGE 38

1. **7**

   The number is six thousand, seven hundred and twenty-nine. The number has a 7 in the hundreds place.

2. **24**

   13 + 11 = 13 + 10 + 1. This is 23 + 1 = 24. There are 24 passengers on the bus.

3. **19**

   23 – 4 = 23 – 3 – 1. This is 20 – 1 = 19. There are 19 students present.

4. **24 km**

   As 6 × 4 = 24, Liz has walked 24 km.

5. **5**

   As 3 × 5 = 15, then 15 ÷ 3 = 5. There are 5 cows in each paddock.

6. $\frac{5}{6}$

   There are 6 circles. 5 out of 6 circles are shaded. This means $\frac{5}{6}$ of the circles are shaded.

7. **60 cents**

   As 10 × 6 = 60, Liam has 60 cents.

8. **36**

   The pattern is adding 8. 28 + 8 = 28 + 2 + 6. This is 30 + 6 = 36. The next number is 36.

9. **5 cm**

   This is called a centimetre grid because the grid is made up of small squares each with a side of 1 cm. By counting, the line is 5 cm long.

10. **drinking glass**

   A drinking glass usually has a capacity of about 200 mL. The capacity of a kitchen sink is around 15 litres and a medicine cup 30 mL.

11. **4 kg**

   As 4 × 1 = 4, the total mass is 4 kg.

12. **25**

   The time is 25 to 6.

13. **5**

   There are 4 triangular faces and another face on the base. This means there are 5 faces.

14. **rectangle, square**

   A rectangle and a square have parallel opposite sides.

15. 

16.
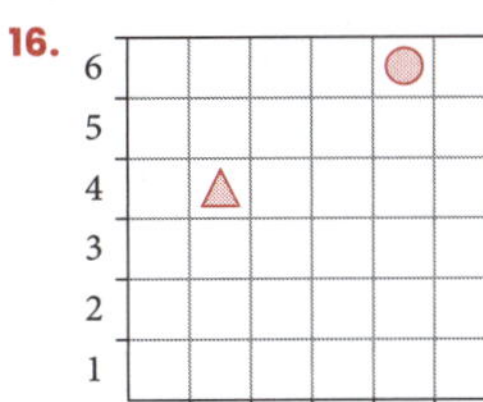

17. **heads, tails**

When the coin is tossed, the two possible outcomes are heads and tails.

18.

Pages read each day		
Day	**Tally**	**Number**
Monday	|||	3
Tuesday	||	2
Wednesday	~~||||~~	5

Unit 2B PAGE 39

1. **9063**

The number 9063 has a 9 in the thousands place, 0 in the hundreds place and 6 in the tens place. 3 is in the ones place.

2. **28 km**

$6 + 6 + 8 + 8 = 12 + 16$. This is 28. William ran 28 km.

3. **12**

$28 - 16 = 28 - 10 - 6$. This is $18 - 6 = 12$. There are 12 apartments not sold.

4. **20**

$5 \times 4 = 20$. Bailey gave 20 balls to his friends.

5. **8**

A pair means 2 items. As $2 \times 8 = 16$, then $16 \div 2 = 8$. James has 8 pairs of shoes.

6. $\mathbf{\frac{1}{6}}$

There are 6 circles. 1 out of 6 circles is not shaded. This means $\frac{1}{6}$ of the circles is not shaded.

7. **13**

There are 130 cents in \$1.30. You need to work out $130 \div 10$. This is the same as $13 \div 1 = 13$. There are 13 10-cent coins.

8. **27**

The pattern is adding 9. The first number will be 9 less than 36. As $36 - 9 = 27$, the missing number is 27.

9. **15 mm**

$80 - 65 = 80 - 60 - 5$. This is $20 - 5 = 15$. The index finger is 15 mm longer than the little finger.

10. **6 L**

$3 \times 2 = 6$. Ezra has 6 L of milk.

11. **40 kg**

$8 \times 5 = 40$. The total mass of ice was 40 kg.

12. **35**

There are 60 minutes in an hour and 30 minutes in half an hour.
As $30 + 5 = 35$, there have been 35 minutes since 5 o'clock.

13. **4**

A square has 4 sides. This means there are four triangular faces on the pyramid.

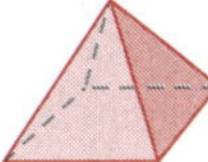

14. **square**

A regular shape has all sides and angles equal. A square has all sides equal and all angles equal.

15.

16. **D4**

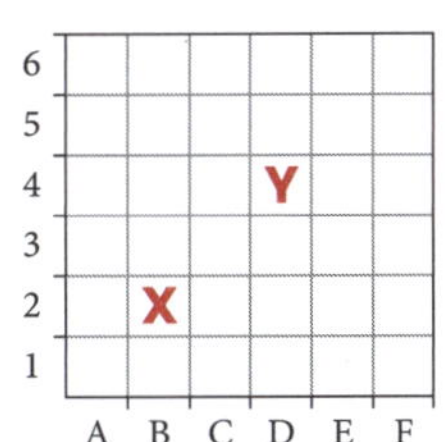

17. **heads, tails**

It does not matter that Sophia tossed a head and then another head. When the coin is tossed next, the two possible outcomes are heads and tails.

18.

Pages read each day		
Day	**Tally**	**Number**
Monday	|||	3
Tuesday	||	2
Wednesday	~~||||~~	5
Thursday	||	2
Friday	||||	4

Unit 3A PAGE 40

1. **3601**

Three thousand six hundred is 3600. One more than this number is 3601.

2. **9**

$2 + 2 + 3 + 1 + 1 = 9$. Peta had 9 coffees.

3. **68 cm**

$78 - 10 = 68$. The shorter piece is 68 cm long.

4. **24 m**

$8 \times 3 = 24$. Chelsea swam 24 m.

5. **4**

As $3 \times 4 = 12$, then $12 \div 3 = 4$. Each friend was given 4 fish.

6. $\mathbf{\frac{2}{4}}$ **or** $\mathbf{\frac{1}{2}}$

Two out of 4 rectangles are shaded. This is $\frac{2}{4}$ or $\frac{1}{2}$ of the shape.

7. **\$1**

Half a dozen is 6. $6 \div 6 = 1$. Each donut costs \$1.

8. **22**

The pattern is adding 3. As $19 + 3 = 22$, the next number is 22.

9. **4 cm**

The rectangle is 4 cm long and 3 cm wide. The length is 4 cm.

10. **3**

There are 3 layers of 4 blocks.

11. **6**

$3 \times 2 = 6$. This means 3 blocks have the same mass as 6 balls.

12.

The minute hand is pointing to 4.

13. **2**

A cylinder has 2 flat surfaces on the ends.

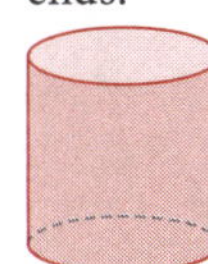

14.

There are many correct shapes with 4 sides of different lengths. Above is one answer.

15.
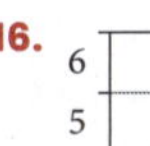

16.
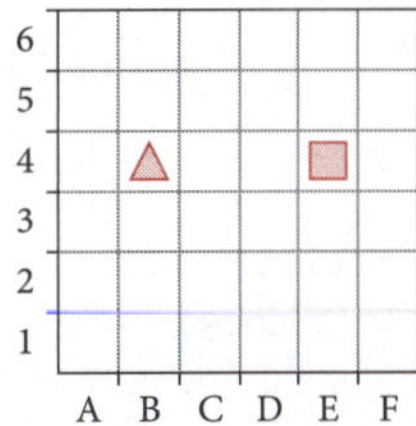

The triangle is at B4.

17. 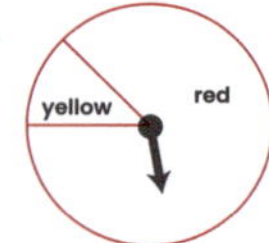

Look for the spinner with an area that is coloured yellow.

18. **6**

There are 6 stars in the row for week 2.

Unit 3B PAGE 41

1. **26 029**

Peter's number is 26 009. Twenty more than this number is 26 029.

2. **158**

86 + 72 = 86 + 70 + 2. This is 156 + 2 = 158. The team scored a total of 158 points.

3. **14**

40 – 26 = 40 – 20 – 6. This is 20 – 6 = 14. There are 14 balloons remaining.

4. **40**

10 × 4 = 40. There are 40 legs on the desks.

5. **5**

As 4 × 5 = 20, then 20 ÷ 4 = 5. There were 5 students in the group.

6. $\frac{3}{4}$

Two out of 4 rectangles were originally shaded. After a third rectangle is shaded, there will be $\frac{3}{4}$ of the shape shaded.

7. **10**

You need to work out 50 ÷ 5. As 5 × 10 = 50, then 50 ÷ 5 = 10. There are 10 5-cent coins.

8. **5**

The odd numbers are 101, 103, 105, 107 and 109. There are 5 odd numbers.

9. **3 cm**

The length is 6 cm and the width is 3 cm. As 6 – 3 = 3, the length is 3 cm longer.

10. **14 cm^3**

The bottom layer has 8 blocks and the top layer has 6 blocks.
As 8 + 6 = 14, the volume is 14 cm^3.

11. **4 kg**

You need to work out 8 ÷ 2. As 2 × 4 = 8, then 8 ÷ 2 = 4. Each ball has a mass of 4 kg.

12. 

The minute hand is pointing to 5.

13. **circle**

The two flat surfaces are in the shape of a circle.

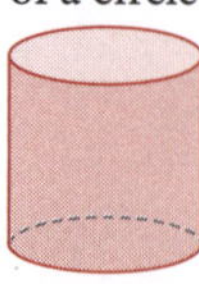

14. **6 cm, 4 cm**

Opposite sides of a parallelogram are equal. The other two sides are 6 cm and 4 cm.

15. 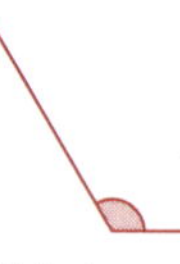

This is one example of an angle larger than a right angle.

16. 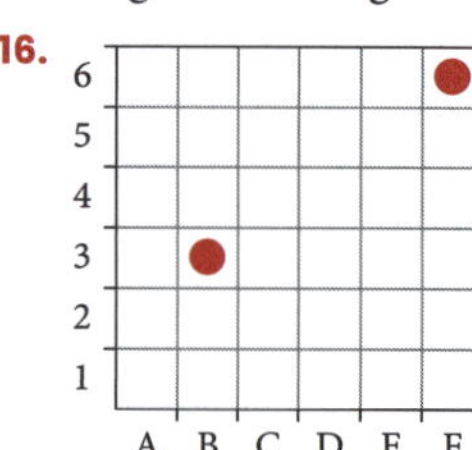

17.

Look for the spinner with a larger area coloured yellow.

18. **10**

There were 4 stars in week 1 and 6 stars in week 2. As 4 + 6 = 10, Bella received a total of 10 stars.

Unit 4A PAGE 42

1. **2458**

The smallest number is formed by writing the digits in ascending order. The number is 2458.

2. **20**

8 + 7 + 5 = 15 + 5. This is 20. Patrick has 20 marbles.

3. **14**

23 – 9 = 23 – 10 + 1. This is 13 + 1 = 14. Sienna has 14 peas left on her plate.

4. **50**

25 × 2 = 25 + 25 which is 50.

5. **6**

As 3 × 6 = 18, then 18 ÷ 3 = 6. There are 6 teams in the competition.

6. $\frac{4}{5}$

3 + 1 = 4. There will be 4 out of 5 squares shaded. This is written as $\frac{4}{5}$.

7. **$3.55**

Add the coins with the higher value first. $2 + $1 + 50c + 5c is $3.55.

8. **22**

The pattern is adding 4. As 18 + 4 = 22, the missing number is 22.

9. **3 cm**

The square has a side length of 3 cm.

10.  

11. **6 kg**

As 6 × 1 = 6, the mass would be about 6 kg.

12. 

The minute hand is pointing to the 10.

13. 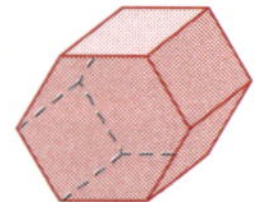

The easiest shape to stack is the prism.

14. **square, rhombus**

A square and a rhombus both have 4 equal sides.

15. 

16. ◇

The diamond is at D3.

17. **Aldo will eat dinner tonight**

There is a greater chance that Aldo will eat dinner tonight than Lena winning the lottery.

18. 卌 |||

By counting, there are 8 runs. This is represented as 卌 |||.

Unit 4B PAGE 43

1. 863
The digits are arranged in descending order. The number is 863.

2. 60
20 + 30 + 10 = 50 + 10. This is 60. The students baked a total of 60 cupcakes.

3. 8
24 – 16 = 24 – 10 – 6. This is 14 – 6 = 8. There are 8 chocolates left.

4. 40 km
8 × 5 = 40. Ruben cycled a total distance of 40 km.

5. 12
As 2 × 12 = 24, then 24 ÷ 2 = 12. Margot washed 12 jerseys.

6. $\frac{5}{5}$ **or 1 whole**
3 + 2 = 5. There will be 5 out of 5 squares shaded. This is $\frac{5}{5}$, which is 1 whole.

7. $2.50
Add the coins with the higher value first. $2 + 20c + 10c + 10c + 10c is $2.50.

8. 34
The rule is to subtract 3.
As 40 – 3 – 3 = 37 – 3 = 34, the sixth number is 34.

9. 40 cm
There is 100 cm in 1 m. You need to subtract 60 from 100.
As 10 – 6 = 4, then 100 – 60 = 40.
There is 40 cm of ribbon remaining on the roll.

10. 240 mL
As 12 + 12 = 24, then 120 + 120 = 240. There is 240 mL in the two mugs.

11. 2 kg
3 – 1 = 2. The mass would be about 2 kg.

12.

The minute hand is pointing to the 10.

13.

14. pentagon
The shape has 5 sides. It is a pentagon.

15.

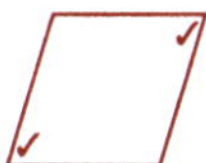

Note that a square is a rhombus and has no angles less than a right angle.

16. E5
E5 is 3 squares from B5. Rosie could be at E5.

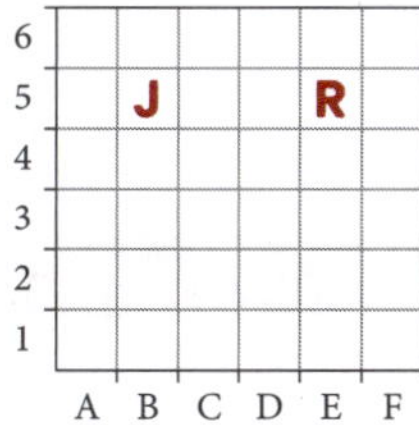

17. William chose a red ball.
There are more red balls than green balls in the bag. It is more likely that William chose a red ball.

18. Wildcats by 4 goals
The difference in the scores is 12 – 8. Wildcats are winning by 4 goals.

Unit 5A PAGE 44

1. 400
Even numbers end in an even digit. Counting on 2 from 398 is 400.

2. 23
Reorder the numbers.
12 + 8 + 3 = 20 + 3. The total is 23.

3. 17
24 – 7 = 24 – 4 – 3. This is 20 – 3 = 17. This means 17 biscuits were eaten.

4. 30
6 × 5 = 30. Isaiha's answer is 30.

5. 10
As 10 × 10 = 100, then 100 ÷ 10 = 10. Chelsea swam 10 laps of the pool.

6.

7. no
$2 + 50c + 50c + 10c + 5c is $3.15, which is less than $3.90. No, Caitlin does not have enough money.

8. 6
As 5 + 6 = 11, 11 + 6 = 17, and so on, the rule is 'Start with 5 and add 6'.

9. 120 cm
As 120 is more than 87, the longer length is 120 cm.

10. 400 mL
The level of juice is a little less than 500 mL. The best estimate is 400 mL.

11. 41 kg
37 + 4 = 37 + 3 + 1. This is 40 + 1 = 41. Brad's mass is 41 kg.

12.

13. faces
Two faces meet at an edge.

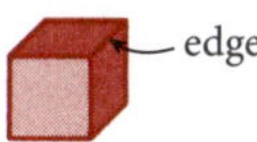

14. rectangle
A rectangle has 4 right angles.

15. 9 o'clock, 3 o'clock
The times are 9 o'clock and 3 o'clock.

16. 2
The shape has been translated 2 units down the grid.

17. 6
The faces on the dice are numbered 1, 2, 3, 4 ,5 and 6. This means there are 6 possible outcomes.

18.

Favourite fruit		
Fruit	**Tally**	**Number**
apple	|||	3
grapes	||||	4
banana	𝍸 |	6
mandarin	𝍸 |||	8

Unit 5B PAGE 45

1. 2
Between 105 and 110 there are two odd numbers: 107 and 109.

2. 59
36 + 14 = 46 + 4. This is 50. Now add 9. 50 + 9 is 59. The total is 59.

3. 4
9 – 4 – 1 = 5 – 1. This is 4. There are 4 biscuits left in the packet.

4. 40
8 × 5 = 40. There are 40 cans in the boxes.

5. 5
As 10 × 5 = 50, then 50 ÷ 10 = 5. This means 5 of Brandan's friends received marbles.

6. 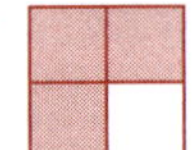 or

There are other correct answers.

7. **4**

50c + 50c = $1. As 2 coins equals $1, then 4 coins will equal $2. Declan used 4 50-cent coins.

8. **23, 9**

As 23 + 9 = 32, 32 + 9 = 41, and so on, the rule is 'Start with 23 and add 9'.

9. **120 cm**

Use 1 m = 100 cm. The three lengths are 120 cm, 100 cm and 86 cm. As 120 is the largest number, the longest length is 120 cm.

10. **700 mL**

The level of juice is more than 500 mL but less than 750 mL. The best estimate is 700 mL.

11. **$12**

4 × 3 = 12. The cost of the tomatoes is $12.

12. **20 to 4 or 3:40**

When the minute hand is pointing to 8 you say '20 to'. The hour hand is moving towards the 4. The time is 20 to 4, or 3:40.

13. **faces**

Three faces meet at a vertex.

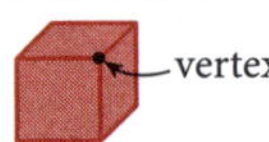

14. **rectangle**

Helen's original quadrilateral was a rectangle.

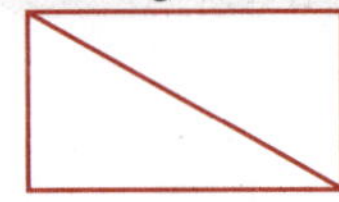

15. **10 o'clock, 2 o'clock**

The times are 10 o'clock and 2 o'clock. The angle between the hands at a time of 7 o'clock is more than a right angle.

16. **4**

The image is shaded and has been translated 4 units from the original shape.

17. **4**

The faces on the dice are numbered 1, 2, 3, 4, 5 and 6. Four faces have numbers less than 5 so there are four different outcomes less than 5.

18.

Favourite fruit		
Fruit	**Tally**	**Number**
apple	||||	4
grapes	卌 ||||	9
banana	卌 |||	8
mandarin	卌 卌 ||	12

Unit 6A PAGE 46

1. **6**

Bryan counts 2, 4, 6 … The third number is 6.

2. **20**

12 + 6 + 2 = 18 + 2. This is 20. Holly received 20 eggs.

3. **21**

28 – 7 = 21. Scotty has 21 cards.

4. **60**

6 × 10 = 60. There are 60 buns.

5. **6**

As 4 × 6 = 24, then 24 ÷ 4 = 6. There are 6 students at each table.

6.

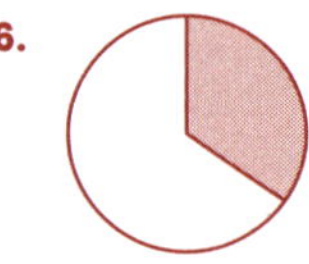

7. **$6.90**

1c (and 2c) rounds down. $6.91 rounds down to $6.90.

8. **8**

The pattern is subtracting 4. As 12 – 4 = 8, the missing number is 8.

9. **53 mm**

As 1 cm = 10 mm, then 6 cm = 60 mm. The two lengths are 53 mm and 60 mm. The shorter length is 53 mm.

10. **4 L**

As 2 × 2 = 4, Jackson has 4 L of juice.

11. **10 kg**

You need to work out half of 20. As 2 × 10 = 20, then 20 ÷ 2 = 10. The mass of a bag of potting mix is 10 kg.

12. **25**

The times are 2 o'clock and 25 past 2. The time difference is 25 minutes.

13.

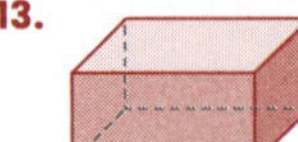

14. **2**

A rectangle has 2 pairs of parallel sides.

15.

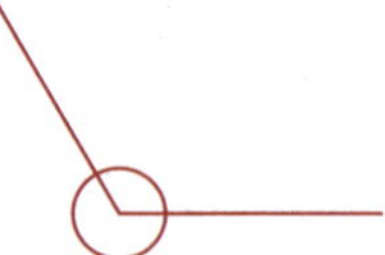

16. **false**

The rectangle has been translated to the right. The statement is false.

17. **true**

It is possible but very unlikely. The statement is true.

18.

Favourite season		
Season	**Tally**	**Number**
summer	卌	5
autumn	||	2
winter	|||	3
spring	卌 ||	7

Unit 6B PAGE 47

1. **999**

The number before 1000 is 999.

2. **79**

47 + 32 = 47 + 30 + 2. This is 77 + 2 = 79. There were 79 points scored in the match.

3. **7**

26 – 19 = 26 – 20 + 1. This is 6 + 1 = 7. There were 7 more birds in the first tree.

4. **60**

As 3 × 2 = 6, then 30 × 2 = 60. The seagulls have 60 legs.

5. **8**

As 3 × 8 = 24, then 24 ÷ 3 = 8. Carla can make 8 bunches of balloons.

6.

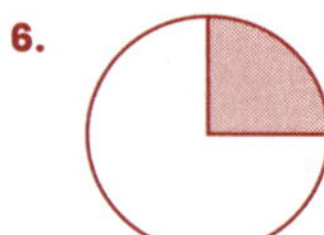

7. **$3.00**

8c (and 9c) rounds up. $2.98 rounds up to $3.00.

8. **98**

The pattern is subtracting 3. As 101 – 3 = 98, the missing number is 98.

9. **60 mm**

Use 1 cm = 10 mm and 1 m = 1000 mm. First, 8 cm = 80 mm and 1 m = 1000 mm. The three lengths are 80 mm, 1000 mm and 60 mm. As 60 is the smallest number, the shortest length is 60 mm.

10. **1000**

Milli- means a thousand and there is 1000 mm in 1 m. There is 1000 mL in 1 L.

11. **500**

There is 1000 g in 1 kg. As half of 1000 is 500, there is 500 g in half a kg.

12. **25**

The times are 20 past 6 and quarter to 7. It takes 10 minutes for the minute hand to move from 4 to 6. Then it takes 15 minutes to move to 9. As 10 + 15 = 25, the time difference is 25 minutes.

13. 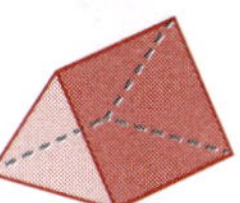

14. **1**

A trapezium has 1 pair of parallel sides.

15. **2**

There are 2 arms forming the angle.

16. **false**

The triangle has been translated 3 units to the left. The statement is false.

17. **A**

There are 2 As and 1 of each other letter. This means the most likely letter is A.

18. **6**

9 students prefer spring and 3 students prefer autumn. As 9 – 3 = 6, there were 6 more students.

Unit 7A PAGE 48

1. **2**

Elijah can form the numbers 5210 and 2051. As there is no 3, he cannot form the number 3501.

2. **16**

6 + 5 + 3 + 2 = 16. The total is 16.

3. **13**

24 – 11 = 24 – 10 – 1. This is 14 – 1 = 13. Emily has 13 cupcakes remaining.

4. **18**

9 × 2 = 18. There are 18 socks in the drawer.

5. **5**

As 5 × 6 = 30, then 30 ÷ 6 = 5. Each child ate 5 cherries.

6. $\frac{3}{5}$

Look at the top numbers (numerators). The numbers are 1, 2, [?], 4. The missing number is 3 and so the missing fraction is $\frac{3}{5}$.

7. **$59.45**

3c (and 4c) rounds up. $59.43 rounds up to $59.45.

8. **26**

The pattern is subtracting 6. The missing number is 6 more than 20. As 20 + 6 = 26, the missing number is 26.

9. **138 cm**

There is 100 cm in 1 m. As 100 + 38 = 138, Danielle is 138 cm tall.

10. **2 L**

As 8 – 6 = 2, Grace needs another 2 L of water.

11. **12 kg**

6 × 2 = 12. The total mass is 12 kg.

12. **20**

The times are 10 past 8 and half past 8. The time difference is 20 minutes.

13. 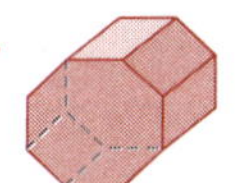

The only prism is an octagonal prism.

14. **rectangle**

Each angle in a rectangle is a right angle. This means all the angles are equal.

15. 

16. **no**

For a translation, a shape is moved left/right or up/down. The image will be identical to the original. In the diagram the image triangle is larger.

17. **3**

There are 3 Bs, which means there are 3 blue marbles.

18. **3**

Daphne tidied her bedroom 3 times.

Unit 7B PAGE 49

1. **0**

Jordan's number is 3530. This means the number 0 is missing.

2. **40**

26 + 14 = 26 + 10 + 4. This is 36 + 4 = 40. Mrs Rhys has 40 coloured pencils.

3. **22**

35 – 13 = 35 – 10 – 3. This is 25 – 3 = 22. Ben has 22 marbles.

4. **30**

6 × 5 = 30. Noah scored 30 points.

5. **9**

As 10 × 9 = 90, then 90 ÷ 10 = 9. There are 9 buckets of plums.

6. $1\frac{1}{2}$

The pattern is adding halves. The missing number is $1\frac{1}{2}$.

7. **$14.25**

7c (and 6c) rounds down. $14.27 rounds down to $14.25.

8. **51**

The pattern is subtracting 6. The missing number is 6 more than 45. As 45 + 6 = 51, the missing number is 51.

9. **63**

There is 10 mm in 1 cm. This means there is 60 mm in 6 cm. As 60 + 3 = 63, Keira's hair is 63 mm long.

10. **180 mL**

You need to find 40 + 60 + 80. This is 100 + 80, which is 180. The total capacity is 180 mL.

11. **20 kg**

4 × 5 = 20. The total mass is 20 kg.

12. **45**

The times are 20 to 11 and 25 past 11. As 20 + 25 = 45, the time difference is 45 minutes.

13. **3**

There are 3 shapes that are not prisms.

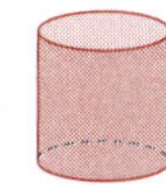 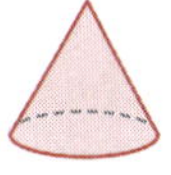 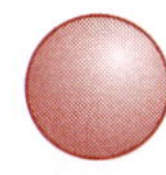

14. **kite**

A regular shape has equal sides and equal angles. A kite is not regular so it is said to be irregular.

15. 

16. **no**

For a translation a shape is moved left/right or up/down. The image will have the same orientation. In the diagram the triangle has been flipped as well.

17. red

There are 7 red balls and 3 blue balls. As 7 is more than 3, she is more likely to choose a red ball.

18. 2

As $4 - 2 = 2$, Eloise tidied her bedroom 2 more times than Sebastian.

Unit 8A PAGE 50

1. 1400

In 1429, there is a 2 in the tens place. This means the number rounds down to 1400.

2. 15 hours

$6 + 4 + 5 = 15$. George worked 15 hours.

3. 8

$18 - 10 = 8$. There are 8 horses remaining.

4. 12

$4 \times 3 = 12$. Eleanor babysits for a total of 12 hours.

5. 2

A dozen is 12. As $6 \times 2 = 12$, then $12 \div 6 = 2$. Each child receives 2 doughnuts.

6.

0 $\frac{1}{5}$ $\frac{2}{5}$ $\frac{3}{5}$ $\frac{4}{5}$ 1

7. $85

$50 + 20 + 10 + 5 = 70 + 10 + 5$ which is 85. The total amount of money is $85.

8. 33

The pattern is adding 5.
As $28 + 5 = 33$, the missing number is 33.

9. 45 mm

There is 10 mm in 1 cm. This means there is 40 mm in 4 cm. Another 5 mm means the length is 45 mm.

10. 7 cm³

As $4 + 3 = 7$, the volume is 7 cm³.

11. 9 kg

You need to find half of 18. As $9 \times 2 = 18$, then $18 \div 2 = 9$. Andrew uses 9 kg of fertiliser.

12. 07:20

20 past 7 is 20 minutes after 7:00. The time on the digital clock is 7:20.

13. rectangular prism

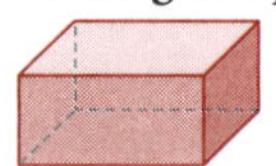

14.

15. 5

There are 5 right angles inside the shape.

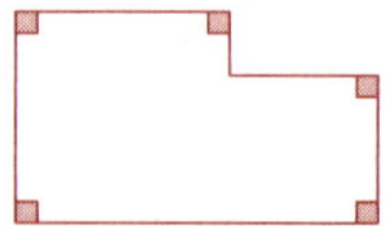

16. 4

By counting, the missing number is 4.

17. true

There are 3 blue balls and 2 yellow balls. The statement is true.

18. 11

There were 11 students who liked orange juice.

Unit 8B PAGE 51

1. 13 000

Look at the 8 in the hundreds place. As this number is more than 5, the number rounds to 13 000.

2. 62

$38 + 12 = 48 + 2$. This is 50. Shane's father is 50 years old. As $50 + 12 = 62$, the total is 62 years.

3. 24

$61 - 37 = 61 - 30 - 7$. This is $31 - 7 = 24$. Jenny has read 24 more pages than Michael.

4. 30

$10 \times 3 = 30$. There are 30 under-9 players.

5. 10

As $3 \times 10 = 30$, then $30 \div 3 = 10$. There are 10 crayons in each box.

6.

0 $\frac{1}{4}$ $\frac{2}{4}$ $\frac{3}{4}$ 1 $1\frac{1}{4}$

7. $45

$20 + 10 + 5 + 5 + 5 = 30 + 15$ which is 45. The total amount of money is $45.

8. 71

Look at 77 and 83. As $83 - 77 = 6$, the pattern is adding 6. The missing number is 6 more than 65. As $65 + 6 = 71$, the missing number is 71.

9. 4 m 60 cm

$2 + 2 = 4$. $30 + 30 = 60$. The total length is 4 m 60 cm.

10. 18 cm³

$6 \times 3 = 18$. The volume is 18 cm³.

11. 2 kg

You need to work out $6 \div 3$. As $3 \times 2 = 6$, then $6 \div 3 = 2$. Each cube has a mass of 2 kg.

12. 04:50

10 to 5 is 10 minutes to 5. There are 60 minutes in 1 hour. $60 - 10 = 50$. This means the time is 4:50.

13. triangular prism

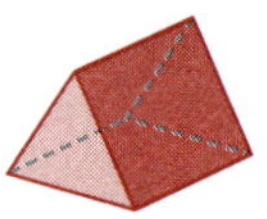

14. unequal

The diagonals are different lengths.

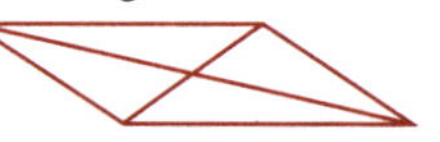

15. 4

A quadrilateral has 4 sides and 4 angles. A square and a rectangle have 4 right angles each.

16. 9

The coin was moved 4 spaces down and 5 spaces to the right. As $4 + 5 = 9$, the coin was moved 9 spaces.

17. blue

There are 3 blue balls and 2 yellow balls. A blue ball is more likely to be chosen.

18. 13

$6 + 7 = 13$. A total of 13 students said apple juice or pineapple juice.

Unit 9A PAGE 52

1. 6

The numbers are 738, 783, 378, 387, 873 and 837. There are 6 different numbers.

2. 900 m

$500 + 400 = 900$. Stewart swam 900 m.

3. 12

$18 - 4 - 2 = 14 - 2$. 12 children attended the party.

4. 24

$8 \times 3 = 24$. The 3 spiders have a total of 24 legs.

5. **2**

As 10 × 2 = 20, then 20 ÷ 10 = 2. Sara can make 2 dresses each day.

6. **4**

As $\frac{4}{4}$ = 1, then 4 quarters is 1 whole.

7. **$120**

3 lots of 20 is 60. 50 + 60 + 10 = 120. The total amount of money is $120.

8. **4**

As 45 – 41 = 4, 41 – 4 = 37, and so on, the rule is 'Start with 45 and subtract 4'.

9. **6**

By counting, there are 6 squares.

10. **600 mL**

A recyclable plastic water bottle is 600 mL. The bottle Alma takes to school would be about the same size.

11. **9 kg**

14 – 5 = 14 – 4 – 1. This is 10 – 1 = 9. The mass of the rock was 9 kg.

12. **10 to 4**

The minute hand is pointing to 10. This means the time is '10 to … '. A possible time is 10 to 4.

13. **3**

There are 6 faces on a rectangular prism. On the diagram, 3 faces can be seen. As 6 – 3 = 3, there are 3 hidden faces.

14. **square**

Each side of a square has the same length. Each angle is a right angle.

15.

16. **9, right**

C is 9 spaces to the right of *A*.

17. **12**

As 2 × 5 = 10 and 10 + 2 is 12, Millie recorded 12 tails.

18. **4**

Count the number of days shown in the left-hand column of the table. The pizza shop is open for 4 days.

Unit 9B PAGE 53

1. **264**

From smallest to largest, the numbers are 246, 264, 426, and so on. The second smallest is 264.

2. **2800**

16 + 12 = 28. This means 1600 + 1200 = 2800. There were 2800 passengers.

3. **13**

40 – 27 = 40 – 20 – 7. This is 20 – 7 = 13. There are 13 more students in the second line.

4. **18**

6 × 3 = 18. Brendan planted 18 bean plants.

5. **10**

As 7 × 10 = 70, then 70 ÷ 7 = 10. There were 10 players in each team.

6. **100**

As $\frac{100}{100}$ = 1, then 100 hundredths is 1 whole.

7. **$155**

2 lots of 50 is 100. 3 lots of 10 is 30. 100 + 30 + 20 + 5 is 155. The total amount of money is $155.

8. **47, 11**

As 47 + 11 = 58, 58 + 11 = 69, and so on, the rule is 'Start with 47 and add 11'.

9. **12**

There are 4 rows of 3 squares. As 4 × 3 = 12, there are 12 squares.

10. **9 L**

2 lots of 4 is 8. As 8 + 1 = 9, Brooklyn bought 9 L of paint.

11. **$15**

$4.99 is very close to $5. As 5 × 3 = 15, the cost is about $15.

12. **quarter past 8**

The hour hand is closer to 8 than 9 but is not exactly on the 8. The time is likely to be quarter past 8.

13. **6**

An octagonal prism has 2 octagon-shaped faces and 8 rectangle-shaped faces. As 2 + 8 = 10, there is a total of 10 faces. The diagram shows 4 faces. As 10 – 4 = 6, there are 6 hidden faces.

14. **rhombus**

A square and a rhombus have equal side lengths.

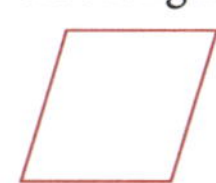

15. ***A*, *C*, *B***

The smallest angle is *A* which is less than a right angle. *C* looks like a right angle and angle *B* measures more than a right angle. The order is *A*, *C*, *B*.

16. ***X***

Callum moves 5 spaces up and 3 to the right. As 5 + 3 = 8, the coin finishes on *X*.

17. **30**

There are 5 groups of 5. This is 25. Now add another 4 and 1. 25 + 4 + 1 = 30. Chloe tossed the coin 30 times.

18. **56**

The weekend is Saturday and Sunday. 36 + 20 = 56. There were 56 pizzas sold.

Unit 10A PAGE 54

1. **3470 km**

Look at the digit in the ones place. The digit is 9 so the number in the tens place increases by 1. The distance is 3470 km.

2. **14**

8 + 3 + 2 + 1 = 11 + 3. This is 14. There are 14 pets.

3. **40**

67 and 27 are the odd numbers. 67 – 27 = 40. The difference is 40.

4. **40**

10 × 4 = 40. There are 40 cards in the packets.

5. **10 kg**

As 4 × 10 = 40, then 40 ÷ 4 = 10. Each bag has a mass of 10 kg.

6.

7. **$600**

There are 6 $100 notes. As 6 × 100 is 600, Brodie was given $600.

8. **27**

The pattern is adding 3. From 24, the next numbers are 27, 30 … This means Callum will write 27.

9. **9**

By counting, 2 + 2 + 5 = 9. There are 9 small squares not shaded.

10. **5 L**

Half of 10 is 10 ÷ 2 = 5. There is 5 L of water remaining in the bucket.

11. **5 kg**

The ball is heavier than the cube. This means the mass of the cube is less than 8 kg. From the choices, a possible mass is 5 kg.

12. **11:10**

The time is 10 past 11. This is written as 11:10.

13. **1**

A cone has 1 flat surface (and 1 curved surface).

14. **1**

The trapezium has 1 pair of parallel sides.

15. **E, F**

The letters E and F have perpendicular lines.

16. 

17. **possible**

There may be a student having a birthday today. This means that it is possible.

18. **dog**

The highest number is 12. Most students said that a dog was their favourite pet.

Unit 10B PAGE 55

1. **375**

The number 375 rounds to 380 because the 5 in the ones place means that the 7 in the tens places rounds up to 8.

2. **107**

62 + 45 = 62 + 40 + 5. This is 102 + 5 = 107. Donald picked 107 cucumbers.

3. **29 years old**

41 – 12 = 41 – 11 – 1. This is 30 – 1 = 29. Kenrick is 29 years old.

4. **30**

5 × 6 = 30. The total is 30.

5. **9**

When a number is doubled, it is multiplied by 2. As 2 × 9 = 18, then 18 ÷ 2 = 9. Jazlyn's original number was 9.

6. $\mathbf{\frac{3}{4}}$

Each of the fractions has a numerator of 3. Look at the denominators. The largest fraction has the smallest denominator. This means $\frac{3}{4}$ is the largest fraction.

7. **$275**

2 lots of 100 is 200. 2 lots of 10 is 20. As 200 + 50 + 20 + 5 is 275, Filip was given a total of $275.

8. **105**

The pattern is adding 7. From 91, the next numbers are 98, 105 … This means Bianca will write 105.

9. **4**

The rectangle has an area of 16 cm^2. You need to find how many 4s are in 16. As 4 × 4 = 16, then 16 ÷ 4 = 4. This means 4 squares will fit.

10. **B**

Container A has between 300 and 400 mL. Container B has more than 500 mL. This means Container B has more water.

11. **170 g**

8 + 9 = 17. This means 80 + 90 = 170. The total mass is 170 g.

12. **4:45**

The time is quarter to 5. This is 45 minutes after 4:00 which is written as 4:45.

13. **7**

A pentagon has 5 sides. On the pentagonal prism there are 2 pentagonal faces and 5 rectangular faces. As 2 + 5 = 7, Beka counted 7 faces.

14. **13 cm**

As 6 + 6 = 12, the length of the third side must be less than 12 cm. This means it is impossible for the length to be 13 cm.

15. **2**

Only H and T have perpendicular lines.

16. **16**

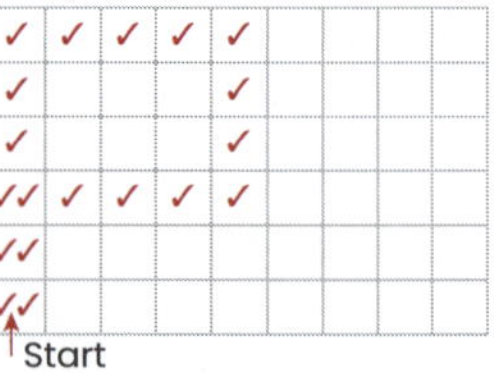

There are 16 squares with at least one tick.

17. **certain**

The faces on the dice are numbered 1 to 6. As all the numbers are less than 7, then it is certain.

18. **20**

8 + 12 = 20. There were 20 students who said a dog or a cat.

Unit 11A PAGE 56

1. **6789**

The digits are written in ascending order. The number is 6789.

2. **36**

20 + 16 = 20 + 10 + 6. This is 30 + 6 = 36. Evan sold a total of 36 cups.

3. **31**

18 + 13 = 18 + 10 + 3. This is 28 + 3 which is 31. There was a total of 31 people.

4. **40**

10 × 4 = 40. There were 40 coloured pencils in the boxes.

5. **6**

As 5 × 6 = 30, then 30 ÷ 5 = 6. There are 6 counters in each group.

6. **7**

The numerator is the top number in a fraction. 7 is the numerator in $\frac{7}{10}$.

7. **35c**

There are 100 cents in $1. 100 – 65 = 100 – 60 – 5. This is 40 – 5 which is 35. Romeo receives 35c change.

8. **3**

The even numbers end in an even digit (0, 2, 4, 6 or 8). The even numbers are 380, 118 and 572. He wrote 3 even numbers.

9. **4**

Another four squares can be drawn.

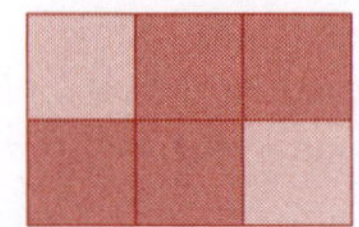

10. **8 cm^3**
The bottom layer has 5 blocks and the top layer has 3 blocks. As $5 + 3 = 8$, the volume is 8 cm^3.

11. **12 kg**
$4 \times 3 = 12$. The total mass is 12 kg.

12. **2:25**
The time is 25 minutes past 2. This is written as 2:25.

13. **2**
A triangular prism has 2 triangular faces.

14. **2**
A square has 2 pairs of parallel sides.

15.
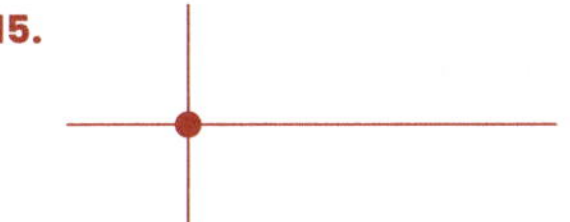

16. **H7**
From D2 move 4 spaces to H2 and then 5 spaces to H7.

17. **4**
There are six 4s in the bag which means that a 4 is most likely to be chosen.

18. **purple**
The highest number is 12. The most popular colour was purple.

Unit 11B PAGE 57

1. **3579**
The odd digits are 1, 3, 5, 7 and 9. The smallest 4-digit number larger than 2000 will start with a 3. Francis will use 3, 5, 7 and 9 in that order. The number is 3579.

2. **42**
$23 + 19 = 23 + 20 - 1$. This is $43 - 1 = 42$. Jarrod spotted 42 species of birds.

3. **30**
$60 - 10 - 20 = 50 - 20$. This is 30. Megan kept 30 beads.

4. **20**
A square has 4 sides. As $5 \times 4 = 20$, there are 20 sides on the squares.

5. **6 m**
As $5 \times 6 = 30$, then $30 \div 5 = 6$. Each piece of rope is 6 m long.

6. $\mathbf{\frac{3}{5}, \frac{1}{3}}$
For $\frac{3}{5}$, 3 is 2 less than 5. Also, in $\frac{1}{3}$, 1 is 2 less than 3.

7. **$1.15**
$100 - 85$ is 15. Also, $2 - 1 = 1$. Juliet receives $1.15 change.

8. **92**
The smallest odd 3-digit number is 101. $101 - 1 - 8 = 100 - 8 = 92$. Her new number was 92.

9. **7 cm**
The two lengths are 16 cm and 9 cm. As $16 - 9 = 7$, the difference is 7 cm.

10. **16 cm^3**
The bottom layer has 10 blocks and the top layer has 6 blocks. As $10 + 6 = 16$, the volume is 16 cm^3.

11. **7**
You need to work out the number of 5s in 35. This is $35 \div 5$. As $5 \times 7 = 35$, then $35 \div 5 = 7$. The baker ordered 7 bags.

12. **11:22**
The time is 22 minutes past 11. This is written as 11:22.

13. **8**
An octagonal prism has 8 rectangular faces.

14. **triangle**
The square was cut into a quadrilateral and a triangle.

15.

16. **C2**
Reverse the directions. From G7 move left 4 squares and then down 5 squares. The coin started on C2.

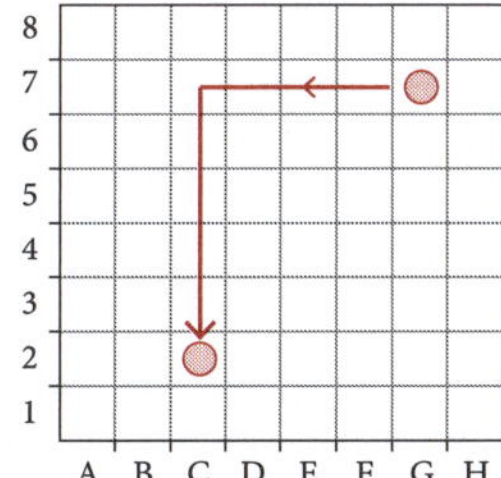

17. **6**
There is only one 6. This means a 6 is the least likely number to be chosen.

18. **22**
12 students said purple and 10 students said red. As $12 + 10 = 22$, a total of 22 students said purple or red.

Unit 12A PAGE 58

1. **7654**
The digits Holly used were 7, 6, 5 and 4. Using them in descending order gives the largest possible number which is 7654.

2. **32**
Re-order the numbers to make it easier to add. $11 + 9 + 12 = 20 + 12$. This is 32. Leo scored 32 points.

3. **6**
$24 - 18 = 24 - 10 - 8$. This is $14 - 8$ which is 6. There were 6 sausages remaining.

4. **35**
$7 \times 5 = 35$. There are 35 books.

5. **5**
As $4 \times 5 = 20$, then $20 \div 4 = 5$. There were 5 cars in the car park.

6. $\mathbf{\frac{1}{10}}$
Each of the fractions have the same numerator of 1. The smallest fraction has the largest denominator. The smallest fraction is $\frac{1}{10}$.

7. **4**
$2, $1, 20c, 20c. The machine would give 4 coins as change.

8. **35**
The sequence of numbers uses the rule 'Adding 7'. As $28 + 7 = 35$, the next number is 35.

9. **3 cm**
$18 - 15 = 3$. The difference is 3 cm.

10. **21 L**
As $3 \times 7 = 21$, the tap wastes 21 L in a week.

11. **12 kg**
$7 + 5 = 12$. The total mass is 12 kg.

12.

The time is 20 past 8.

13. **1**
There is 1 square and 4 triangles. Annalise drew 1 square.

14.

A regular shape has all sides and angles equal. A quadrilateral has 4 sides. The shape is a square.

15. 

16. **2, 6**

From the triangle, move 2 squares left and 6 squares down.

17. **The number is less than 6.**

All the numbers are less than 6. This means it is certain that the number is less than 6.

18. **3**

The table shows 3 motorbikes.

Unit 12B PAGE 59

1. **40 596**

Isaac's number was 49 806. Swapping the digits gives 40 896. There is an 8 in the hundreds place. As 8 – 3 = 5, the final number is 40 596.

2. **4**

2 + 1 + 1 = 4. Tahlia scored 4 goals.

3. **17**

24 – 7 = 24 – 4 – 3. This is 20 – 3 = 17. There were 17 chocolates remaining.

4. **24**

8 × 3 = 24. Jacob needs 24 lemons.

5. **5**

As 8 × 5 = 40, then 40 ÷ 8 = 5. Taj drew 5 circles on the chart.

6. **4**

There are 2 halves in one container. This means there are 4 halves in 2 containers. The milk will last 4 days.

7. **6**

$2, $2, 50c, 20c, 20c, 5c. The machine would give 6 coins as change.

8. **19**

1, 3, 5, 7, 9, 11, 13, 15, 17, 19 … The tenth number in the sequence is 19.

9. **180 cm**

18 × 10 = 180. The length of the desk is 180 cm.

10. **24 L**

A dozen is 12.
As 12 × 2 = 12 + 12 = 24, Ava orders 24 L of milk.

11. **5000**

There is 1000 g in 1 kg. As 5 × 1000 = 5000, there is 5000 g in 5 kg.

12. 

The time is 48 minutes past 6. There are 60 minutes in 1 hour.
60 – 48 = 20 – 8 = 12. The time is 12 to 7.

13. **4**

There are 4 triangles.

14. **parallelogram, octagon**

A parallelogram has 4 sides and an octagon has 8 sides.

15. 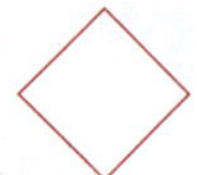

16. ***S***

Student *S* lives at H2 which is on the corner of Tye Street and Ned Street.

17. **The number is odd.**

1, 3 and 5 are odd and 2 and 4 are even. There are more odd numbers than even. This means it is more likely that the number will be odd.

18. **4**

The table shows 1 bus and 3 trucks. As 1 + 3 = 4, a total of 4 buses and trucks went past the school.

Unit 13A PAGE 60

1. **7083**

There are 0 hundreds so there is a 0 in the hundred place. Her number is 7083.

2. **49**

26 + 23 = 20 + 20 + 3 + 6. This is 40 + 9 = 49. There are 49 cars.

3. **22**

27 – 2 – 3 = 25 – 3. This is 22. There are 22 students in class.

4. **24**

12 × 2 = 24. Wesley bought 24 eggs.

5. **9**

A pair is 2 items. As 2 × 9 = 18, then 18 ÷ 2 = 9. There are 9 pairs of dolls.

6. $\mathbf{\frac{4}{5}}$

The number line is marked in fifths.
A represents $\frac{4}{5}$.

7. **$4.40**

$2.20 + $2.20 is $4 plus 40c. This is $4.40.

8. **even**

Adding 2 odd numbers like 3 and 5 always gives an even result.

9. **40 cm**

As 180 – 140 = 40, then 188 – 148 is also 40. The bed is 40 cm longer than Rohan.

10. **100 mL**

As half of 2 is 1, then half of 200 is 100. There is still 100 mL of soy sauce remaining in the bottle.

11. **9 kg**

5 + 3 + 1 = 9. The total mass was 9 kg.

12. 

The time is quarter past 10.

13. **2**

A sphere and a cylinder have curved surfaces and so can roll.

14. **3**

A regular hexagon has 6 equal sides. There are 3 pairs of parallel sides.

15. **no**

A horizontal line and a vertical line are perpendicular. The second line is not vertical.

16. 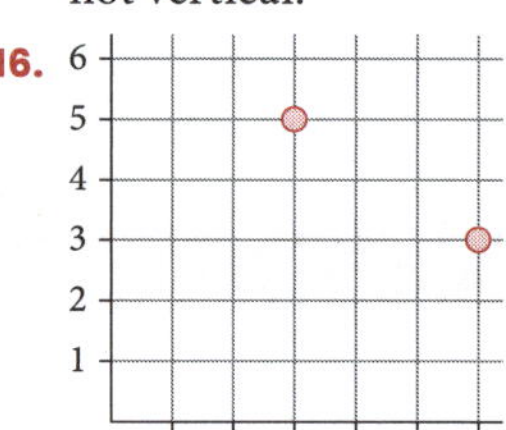

17. **red**

There are 8 red and 4 black jelly beans. This means it is more likely that the jelly bean was red.

18. **4**

From the table, 4 students wore green T-shirts.

Unit 13B PAGE 61

1. **14**

Kristin needed 10 tens to represent 100 and 4 tens to represent 40. As 10 + 4 = 14, Kristin used 14 tens and 8 ones.

2. **31**

16 + 15 = 16 + 10 + 5. This is 26 + 5 = 31. There is a total of 31 girls.

3. **11**

26 – 15 = 26 – 10 – 5. This is 16 – 5 = 11. This means 11 T-shirts had been sold.

4. **27**

$9 \times 3 = 27$. This means 27 people can ride the roller-coaster.

5. **12**

As $3 \times 12 = 36$, then $36 \div 3 = 12$. There are 12 cards in each row.

6. $\mathbf{\frac{3}{10}}$

The number line is marked in tenths. As 3 is between 2 and 4, *A* represents $\frac{3}{10}$.

7. **$3.90**

2 lots of $1.50 is $3. Another 90c is $3.90.

8. **odd**

Think of a list of an odd number of odd numbers. Here are three odd numbers: 3, 5 and 7. Adding 3 and 5 gives the even number 8. But then adding an odd number will give an odd result of 15. Isla's result must be odd.

9. **1005**

There is 1000 mm in 1 m. As $1000 + 5 = 1005$, there is 1005 mm.

10. **6 L**

$9 - 3 = 6$. Another 6 L of water will fill the bucket.

11. **16 kg**

$5 + 5 + 3 + 1 + 1 + 1 = 16$. The total mass was 16 kg.

12. 

The time is 43 minutes past 3. There are 60 minutes in 1 hour.
$60 - 43 = 20 - 3 = 17$. The time is 17 to 4.

13. **cone**

A cone has an apex, a curved surface and a flat surface.

14. **4**

A regular octagon has 8 equal sides. There are 4 pairs of parallel sides.

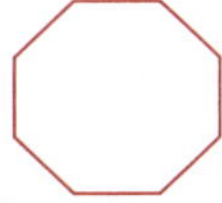

15. **10**

The shape is a decagon. It has 10 sides and 10 angles.

16. **5**

As $6 - 1 = 5$, there are 5 units between D1 and D6.

17. **black**

As $20 - 9 = 11$, there are 11 black jelly beans. This means it is more likely that the jelly bean was black.

18. **10**

6 students wore red T-shirts and 4 students wore green. As $6 + 4 = 10$, there are 10 students who wore red or green T-shirts.

Unit 14A PAGE 62

1. **399**

20 is 2 tens. The number 379 has 7 tens. As $2 + 7$ is 9, the new number will be 399.

2. **68**

$42 + 26 = 42 + 20 + 6$. This is $62 + 6 = 68$. Indie's grandmother is 68.

3. **27**

$50 - 23 = 50 - 20 - 3$. This is $30 - 3 = 27$. The group planted 27 trees on Sunday.

4. **30**

$6 \times 5 = 30$. Stuart had 30 cookies.

5. **3**

As $5 \times 3 = 15$, then $15 \div 5 = 3$. Each child receives 3 cards.

6. $\mathbf{\frac{3}{8}}$

There is a total of 8 balls. There are 3 balls out of 8 inside the rectangle. This is written as $\frac{3}{8}$.

7. **$19**

$15 + 4 = 19$. The total cost is $19.

8. **95**

$105 - 10 = 105 - 5 - 5$. This is $100 - 5 = 95$. Erika's next number is 95.

9. **12 cm**

The square has side lengths 3 cm. $3 + 3 + 3 + 3 = 12$. The distance around the outside is 12 cm.

10. **510 mL**

Look for a number more than 300 but less than 550. The number is 510. It is possible the jug has 510 mL of water.

11. **30 kg**

$15 + 15 = 10 + 5 + 10 + 5$. This is 30 so the mass is 30 kg.

12. **60**

There are 60 seconds in 1 minute.

13. **false**

A cylinder does not have any vertices.

14. **4**

A square has 4 lines of symmetry.

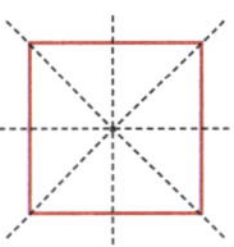

15.

16. 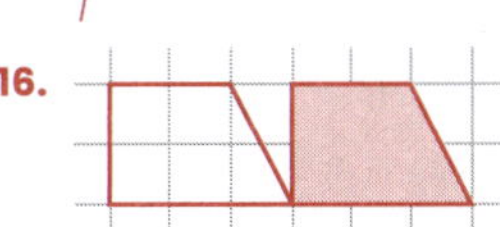

17. **unlikely**

There is only 1 triangle out of the 3 shapes. This means it is unlikely.

18. **6**

From the table, Donald had 6 cows on his farm.

Unit 14B PAGE 63

1. **000789**

The car was showing 3 hundred and 89. Another 4 hundred means it will show 7 hundred and 89, or 000789 km.

2. **46 minutes**

$29 + 17 = 30 + 16$. This is 46. Anthony spent 46 minutes reading and watching TV.

3. **40**

As $80 - 40 = 40$, then $85 - 45 = 40$. There are 40 cows to be milked.

4. **70**

$10 \times 7 = 70$. There are 70 oranges in the bags.

5. **9**

As $10 \times 9 = 90$, then $90 \div 10 = 9$. Bryan's original number was 9.

6. $\mathbf{\frac{5}{8}}$

There is a total of 8 balls. There are 3 balls out of 8 inside the rectangle. As $8 - 3 = 5$, the fraction outside the rectangle is $\frac{5}{8}$.

7. **$38**

$19 + 19$ is $20 + 20 - 2$. This is $40 - 2 = 38$. The cost is $38.

8. **101**

The largest 2-digit number is 98. $98 + 3 = 98 + 2 + 1$. This is $100 + 1 = 101$.

9. **2 cm**

The length is 5 cm and the width is 3 cm. As $5 - 3 = 2$, the difference is 2 cm.

10. **470 mL**

As $25 + 22 = 47$, then $250 + 220 = 470$. Ethan has 470 mL of iced tea.

11. **12 kg**

$5 + 5 + 2 = 12$. The total mass is 12 kg.

12. **300**

There are 60 seconds in 1 minute. As $6 \times 5 = 30$, then $60 \times 5 = 300$. There are 300 seconds.

13. **cube**

All faces on the prism are squares. The shape is a cube.

14. **0**

A parallelogram has no lines of symmetry.

15. ***P*, *Q*, *R***

The largest angle is *P* which looks like a right angle. *Q* is a little less than a right angle and angle *R* is smaller than *Q*. The order is *P*, *Q*, *R*.

16.

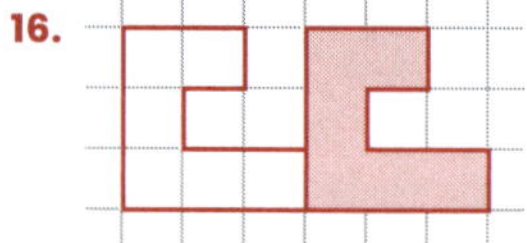

17. **unlikely**

Only 1 in 10 shoppers receive a voucher. This means it is unlikely that Harry will receive a voucher.

18. **4**

There were 6 cows and 10 sheep. As $10 - 6 = 4$, Donald had 4 more sheep than cows.

Unit 15A PAGE 64

1. **10**

Both 47 and 37 have 7 in the ones place. 4 tens minus 3 tens is 1 ten. There were 10 cars that left the car park.

2. **56**

$30 + 26 = 30 + 20 + 6$. This is $50 + 6 = 56$. Ethan has 56 cards.

3. **14**

$46 - 32 = 46 - 30 - 2$. This is $16 - 2$ which is 14. The smaller number was 14.

4. **30**

$10 \times 3 = 30$. Tayla used 30 balloons.

5. **3**

As $8 \times 3 = 24$, then $24 \div 8 = 3$. There are 3 full trays.

6.

There are other correct answers.

7. **Archer**

For one 20-cent coin there needs to be four 5-cent coins. Archer has 4 times as many coins as Lane.

8. **101**

The pattern is adding 10. As $90 + 10 = 100$, then $91 + 10 = 101$. The next number is 101.

9. **14 cm**

The rectangle is 4 cm long and 3 cm wide. $4 + 3 + 4 + 3 = 14$. The distance around the outside is 14 cm.

10. **15 mL**

$5 \times 3 = 15$. Peyton will take 15 mL of medicine.

11. **9 kg**

$4 + 3 + 2 = 9$. The total mass is 9 kg.

12. **4**

The 2 clocks are half past 1 and half past 5. As $5 - 1 = 4$, the time difference is 4 hours.

13. **cylinder**

The base of her shape is a circle. Eva has made a cylinder.

14. **kite**

A kite does not have parallel sides.

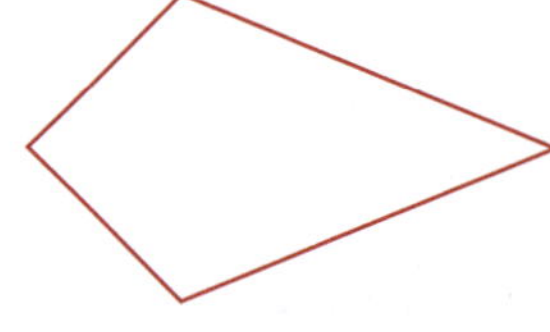

15.

16. **10 units**

From *A* to *B* is 5 units. From *B* to *C* is 5 units. As $5 + 5 = 10$, Alison moved 10 units.

17. **certain**

All the cards have odd numbers. This means it is certain that an odd number is chosen.

18. **16**

From the table, there were 16 students who travelled by bus.

Unit 15B PAGE 65

1. **3297**

3000 and 297 gives a total of 3 thousands, 2 hundreds, 9 tens and 7 ones. This is written as 3297.

2. **198**

$120 + 78 = 120 + 70 + 8$. This is $190 + 8 = 198$. There is a total of 198 stamps.

3. **80**

$20 - 12 = 8$. This means $200 - 120$ is 80. There are 80 sheep remaining.

4. **40**

$8 \times 5 = 40$. Hannah drew a total of 40 hearts.

5. **3**

There are 7 days in a week. As $7 \times 3 = 21$, then $21 \div 7 = 3$. There are 3 weeks until Abby's birthday.

6. **4**

There are 3 rows. One-third of the triangles is one row. This means $\frac{1}{3}$ of 12 is 4.

7. **$35**

$2 \times 50 = 100$. Caitlin paid $100. $100 - 65 = 100 - 60 - 5$. This is $40 - 5 = 35$. She received change of $35.

8. **69, 109**

The sequence is formed by adding 10. $79 - 10 = 69$ and $99 + 10 = 109$. The two numbers are 69 and 99.

9. **12 cm**

As $6 \times 2 = 12$, the length was 12 cm.

10. **no**

The level of the water is halfway between 200 and 400. It is likely to have about 300 mL of water.

11. **60 g**

Half of 12 is 6. This means half of 120 is 60. The mass is 60 g.

12. **9**

The 2 clocks are 11 minutes to 3 and 11 minutes to 12. As $12 - 3 = 9$, the time difference is 9 hours.

13. **cone**

In a cone, the area of the cross-section is smaller than the area of the base. (The area of the cross-section of a cylinder is identical to the area of its circular base.)

14. **rhombus**

A square and a rhombus have 4 equal sides. A square has 4 lines of symmetry but a rhombus only has 2 lines of symmetry.

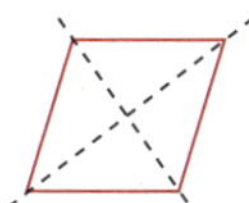

15. 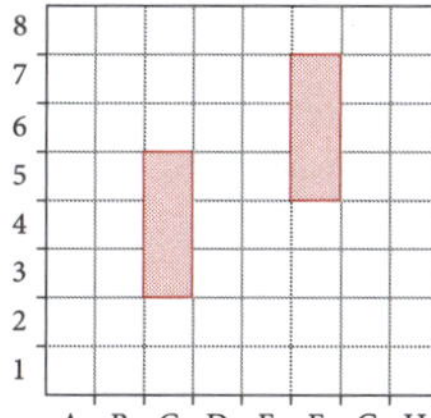

You could also draw a rectangle.

16. **A5**

Up 2 units from E3 is E5. Moving 5 units to the left is A5.

17. **very unlikely**

As 6 + 6 + 6 = 18, Tommi must have rolled three sixes. This is very unlikely.

18. **16**

4 students walked to school and 12 students travelled by car. As 12 + 4 = 16, there were 16 students.

NAPLAN-style Test 1 PAGES 66–67

1. **378, 387, 738, 783, 873**

Look at the digit in the hundreds place first and then the tens place. The order is 378, 387, 738, 783, 873.

2. **B**

The missing number is the answer to 50 − 17. This is 50 − 10 − 7 = 40 − 7 = 33. The missing number is 33.

3. **B**

The pattern is adding 4. As 29 + 4 = 33, the missing number is 33.

4. **B and D**

2 + 2 + 2 + 2 + 2 + 2 + 2 has 7 2s. 7 × 2 = 14, not 12. Also, 6 + 2 = 8, which is not 12. The two number sentences that do not equal 12 are 2 + 2 + 2 + 2 + 2 + 2 + 2 and 6 + 2.

5. **C**

The shape has 3 layers. The bottom layer has 8 cubes. The middle layer has 3 cubes. The top layer has 1 cube. As 8 + 3 + 1 = 12, the solid is made of 12 cubes.

6. **B**

A quadrilateral has 4 sides. An octagon has 8 sides and so is not a quadrilateral.

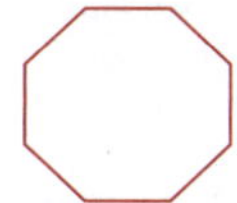

7. **C**

Here is a grid showing the shaded image. The new rectangle covers F5.

8. **C**

In three-quarters of an hour the minute hand travels around three-quarters of a rotation. The minute hand moves from the 9 around to the 6. This time is half past 8, which is 8:30.

9. **D**

As 3 + 3 + 3 = 9, a shopper can buy 3 bags of lemons and receive $1 in change. As 5 × 3 = 15, Jannah can buy 15 lemons.

10. **D**

As 17 − 2 = 15, the pen is 15 cm long. As 11 − 5 = 6, the USB is 6 cm long. As 15 − 6 = 9, the pen is 9 cm longer than the USB.

11. **6100**

Six thousand and ninety-eight is written as 6098. As 98 + 2 = 100, then 6098 + 2 = 6100.

12. **A**

Half of $40 is $20. Theo has $5 more than $20 and Agnes has $5 less than $20. This means Agnes has $15.

13. **A, B, E**

The dice has the numbers 1 to 6 on its faces. This means there are no 9s. Also, Daisy is only rolling once which means she cannot get two numbers like 3 and 4. Daisy can roll a 6 or a number less than 4 or an even number.

14. **C**

The solid has a square face and 4 identical triangular faces. This means the solid is a square pyramid, which has 8 edges.

15. **A**

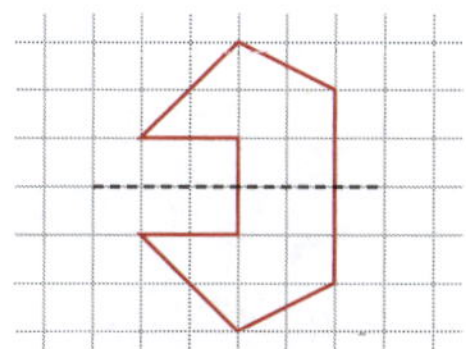

There will be 8 sides in the completed shape.

16. **C**

The fraction he scores plus the fraction he does not score adds to one whole. You need to subtract $\frac{2}{5}$ from one whole. There are $\frac{5}{5}$ in one whole. As 5 − 2 = 3, the fraction is $\frac{3}{5}$.

17. **8**

As 3 × 8 = 24, then 24 ÷ 3 = 8. There are 8 coloured pencils in each box.

18. **B**

The temperature on Monday was 14 °C. Two degrees warmer is a temperature of 16 °C. This was the temperature on Thursday.

19. **A**

As 4 × 2 = 8, there is 8 L of water in the container. As 9 − 8 = 1, another 1 L of water is needed to fill the container.

20. **A**

4 = 2 + 2, 7 = 2 + 5, 9 = 3 + 6, 11 = 6 + 5. It is not possible to get a total of 3.

Unit 16A PAGE 68

1. **206 < 340**

Two hundred and six is 206 and three hundred and forty is 340. The symbol for less than is <.

2. **17**

40 − 23 = 40 − 20 − 3. This is 20 − 3 = 17. The number is 17.

3. **100**

65 + 35 = 65 + 30 + 5. This is 95 + 5 = 100. The girls scored a total of 100 runs.

4. **11**

As 5 × 11 = 55, then 55 ÷ 5 = 11. There are 11 plants in each row.

5. **80**

20 × 4 = 80. Katja swam for 80 minutes.

6. $\frac{3}{4}$

Three out of four small rectangles are not shaded. This is written as $\frac{3}{4}$.

7. **$27**

Half of 18 is 9. As 18 + 9 = 27, the cost is $27.

8. **12**

Here are Alex's numbers: 20, 16, 12, 8 … This means 12 is on his list.

9. **3 cm**

A rectangle has opposite sides equal in length. The other side will be 3 cm long.

10. **5**

As $2 \times 5 = 10$, then $10 \div 2 = 5$. This means 5 containers can be filled.

11. **4**

You need to work out how many 3s are in 12. As $3 \times 4 = 12$, then $12 \div 3 = 4$. Lena should buy 4 bags.

12. **120**

$20 - 18 = 2$. There are 2 minutes between the 2 times. There are 60 seconds in 1 minute. As $6 + 6 = 12$, then $60 + 60 = 120$. There are 120 seconds.

13. **12**

There are 12 edges on a cube.

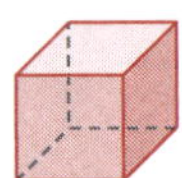

14.

15. ***b***

The smallest angle is *b*.

16. **west**

If Shane is driving north, he is looking north. On his left is west.

17. **unlikely**

The chance that Jack is correct is only 1 out of 3. This means it is unlikely he is correct.

18. **9**

There were 4 kangaroos and 5 koalas. As $5 + 4 = 9$, there was a total of 9 kangaroos and koalas.

Unit 16B PAGE 69

1. **7009**

Theodore's number is 7050. A number less than his number is 7009.

2. **3000**

$11 - 8 = 3$. This means $11\,000 - 8000$ is 3000. George needs to walk another 3000 steps.

3. **35**

$16 + 19 = 16 + 20 - 1$. This is $36 - 1 = 35$. The family ate 35 apples.

4. **10**

As $3 \times 10 = 30$, then $30 \div 3 = 10$. The light will flash another 10 times.

5. **60**

There are 6 items in half a dozen. As $10 \times 6 = 60$, Jemima bought 60 rolls.

6. **10**

There are 4 lots of 5 goals. As half of 4 is 2, Ava scored 2 lots of 5 goals. This means she scored 10 goals.

7. **$1.35**

From 65 cents to $1 is 35 cents. Adding $1 gives $2. Isaac is given $1.35 in change.

8. **Start with 74 and subtract 7**

$74 - 67 = 7$. The rule is 'Start with 74 and subtract 7'.

9. **2 cm**

The longer crayon is 7 cm long. The second crayon starts at 9 cm and ends at 14 cm. As $14 - 9 = 5$, the length of the second crayon is 5 cm. As $7 - 5 = 2$, the difference is 2 cm.

10. **Shape B**

There are 6 blocks in Shape A and 7 blocks in Shape B. This means Shape B has the greater volume.

11. **20 kg**

$23 - 13 = 10$. The mass of 1 cube is 10 kg. As $2 \times 10 = 20$, the mass of 2 cubes is 20 kg.

12. **600**

The 2 times are 5 to 5 and 5 past 5. As $5 + 5 = 10$, there are 10 minutes between the 2 times. There are 60 seconds in 1 minute. As $60 \times 10 = 600$, there are 600 seconds.

13. **18**

There are 18 edges on a hexagonal prism.

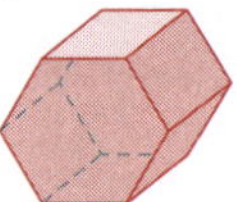

14.

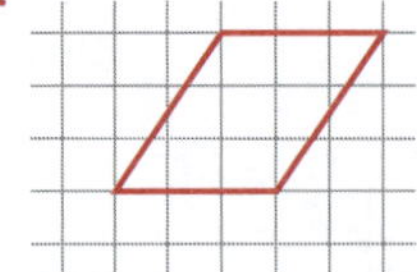

15. ***b*, *d***

The two smaller angles are less than right angles. The angles are *b* and *d*.

16. **east**

If Olivia is driving south, she is looking south. On her left is east.

17. **blue, yellow**

There are 2 blue balls and 2 yellow balls. This means that choosing a blue or yellow ball is equally likely.

18. **14**

There were 4 kangaroos, 2 emus, 3 echidnas and 5 koalas. As $4 + 2 + 3 + 5 = 14$, there was a total of 14 animals counted.

Unit 17A PAGE 70

1 **3000**

There is a 9 in the hundreds place, which is more than 5. This means the 2 in the thousands place rounds up and the number is 3000.

2. **4**

As $5 \times 4 = 20$, then $20 \div 5 = 4$. The team scored 4 goals in every game. This means they scored 4 goals in the final game.

3. **30 °C**

$14 + 13 + 3 = 27 + 3$. This is 30. The temperature was 30 °C.

4. **15**

$24 - 9 = 24 - 10 + 1$. This is $14 + 1 = 15$. There were 15 cans purchased.

5. **50**

$5 \times 10 = 50$. There are 50 seats in the first 5 rows.

6.

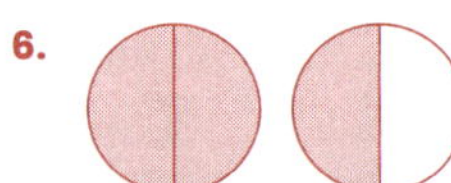

7. **$30**

2 lots of $10 is $20. As $50 - 20 = 30$, Illiana received $30 change.

8. **52**

The pattern is formed by adding 6. The missing numbers are 40, 46, 52. This means *X* is 52.

9. **24 cm**

There are 4 equal sides on a square. $6 \times 4 = 24$. The distance around the outside of the square is 24 cm.

10. **500 mL**

As $6 - 1 = 5$, then $600 - 100 = 500$. There is 500 mL of water remaining.

11. **27 kg**

$10 + 10 + 5 + 2 = 27$. The total mass is 27 kg.

12. **11:45 or quarter to 12**

The clock is showing quarter past 11, or 11:15. Another 30 minutes is quarter to 12, or 11:45.

13. 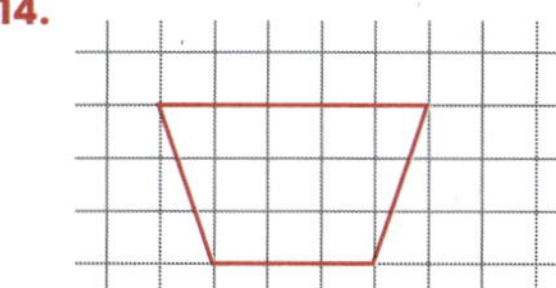

14.

15. **6**

There are six right angles.

16. **F3**

Using the compass, Troy is at F3.

17. **true**

The only colours are green and blue. There is no purple on the spinner. The statement is true.

18. **9**

There were 6 beef and 3 chicken pies sold. As 6 + 3 = 9, a total of 9 pies were sold.

Unit 17B PAGE 71

1. **3000**

There is a 0 in the tens place. This means the number rounds to 3000 to the nearest hundred.

2. **10**

27 + 13 = 40. There are 40 chairs. As 4 × 10 = 40, then 40 ÷ 4 = 10. This means there are 10 tables in the restaurant.

3. **62**

38 + 24 = 38 + 20 + 4. This is 58 + 4 = 62. There are 62 rooms in the hotel.

4. **37 km**

100 – 63 = 100 – 60 – 3. This is 40 – 3 = 37. Theo has 37 km remaining.

5. **48**

12 × 4 = 48. There are 48 chair legs.

6. 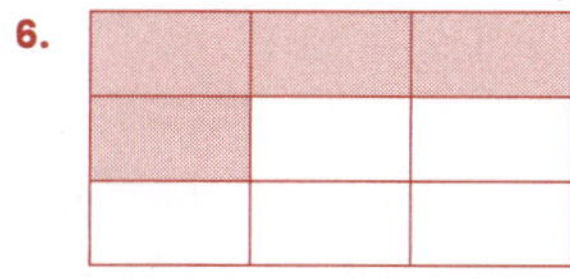

7. **45c**

$2 + $1 + $1 + 50c + 5c = $4.55. From 55 to 100 is 5 + 40 = 45. The total of the coins is 45c short of $5.

8. **56**

Reading the number from right to left, the pattern is formed by subtracting 4. The missing numbers are 68 – 4 = 64, then 64 – 4 = 60 and 60 – 4 = 56. The value of *X* is 56.

9. **150**

There is 100 cm in 1 m and so there is 50 cm in half a metre. As 100 + 50 = 150, the length is 150 cm.

10. **40 L**

As 10 × 2 = 20, each girl needs 20 L. As 20 × 2 = 40, they should take a total of 40 L.

11. **1 kg**

As 5 + 5 = 10, then 5 hundred + 5 hundred is 10 hundred. This is written as 1000. The mass is 1000 g, which is 1 kg.

12. **7:55 or 5 to 8**

The clock is showing 25 past 7, or 7:25. Half an hour is 30 minutes. 25 + 30 = 55. The time will be 7:55, or 5 to 8.

13. **triangular pyramid**

There are 4 triangles. This is the net of a triangular pyramid.

14. 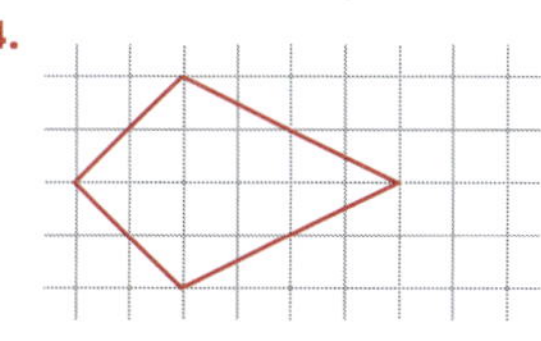

15. 

16. **C1**

Jessica is at C3 and faces towards east. This means C1 is on her right.

17. **false**

The spinner has been divided into 3 equal areas. There are 2 greens and 1 blue. It is more likely the arrow will point to green. The statement is false.

18. **5**

There were 2 mushroom and 3 meat-free pies sold. As 2 + 3 = 5, a total of 5 pies were sold.

Unit 18A PAGE 72

1. **9876**

The number 9876 has a 9 in the thousands and 7 in the tens place. It also has 8 in the hundreds place and 6 in the ones place.

2. **8**

You need to find 80 ÷ 10. As 10 × 8 = 80, then 80 ÷ 10 = 8. This means 8 gifts had been handed out.

3. **55**

68 – 13 = 68 – 10 – 3. This is 58 – 3 = 55. There were 55 koalas in 2023.

4. **40**

8 × 5 = 40. Ellie bought 40 screws.

5. **17**

3 + 5 + 4 + 5 = 5 + 5 + 4 + 3. This is 10 + 7 = 17. She babysits a total of 17 hours.

6. $\frac{1}{3}$

The number line is marked in thirds. As 1 is before 2, *A* represents $\frac{1}{3}$.

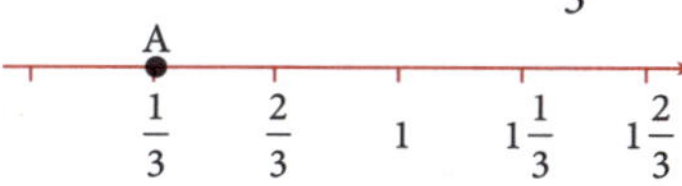

7. **$21.50**

18 + 3 = 21. $21 plus 50c is $21.50. The total cost was $21.50.

8. **15, 16**

The rule is to add 8. As 7 + 8 = 15 and 8 + 8 = 16, the missing numbers are 15 and 16.

9. **12 cm²**

There are 3 rows of 4 squares. As 3 × 4 = 12, the area is 12 square centimetres, or 12 cm^2.

10. **$80**

As 4 × 2 = 8, then 40 × 2 = 80. The petrol costs $80.

11. **7 kg**

20 – 13 = 20 – 10 – 3. This is 10 – 3 = 7. The mass is 7 kg.

12. 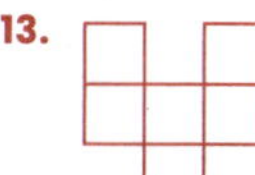

10 past 12 is 10 minutes after 12:00. The time on the digital clock is 12:10.

13.

14.

15. **4**

There are four right angles at the centre of the circle.

16. **B6**

Ariana moves 4 units to D6 and then 2 units to B6.

17. 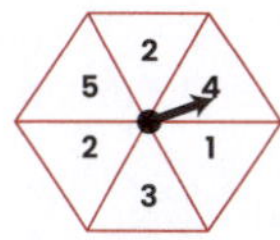

Only the spinner on the left has a number 5.

18. Cam

The tallest column is $40. Cam saved $40.

Unit 18B PAGE 73

1. 2221

2 + 2 + 2 + 2 = 8. You need to find the number one less than 2222. This means the number is 2221.

2. 6

As 1 dozen is 12, then 2 dozen is 24. You need to divide 24 by 4.
As 4 × 6 = 24, then 24 ÷ 4 = 6. Each person receives 6 mangoes.

3. 17 km

53 – 36 = 53 – 30 – 6. This is 23 – 6 = 17. He has 17 km remaining.

4. 120

12 × 10 = 120. There was a total of 120 students.

5. 235

170 + 65 = 170 + 30 + 35. This is 200 + 35 = 235. There are 235 balls.

6. $\mathbf{\frac{5}{4}}$ **or** $\mathbf{1\frac{1}{4}}$

The number line is marked in quarters. *A* represents $\frac{5}{4}$, which can be rewritten as $1\frac{1}{4}$.

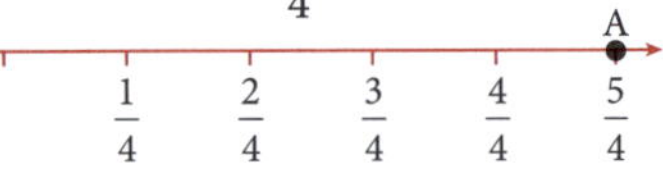

7. 10c

8c (and 9c) rounds up. The salami will cost $3.90. Violet will receive 10c change.

8. 19, 32

The bottom number is 5 more than the top number. 14 + 5 = 19. Also, 37 – 5 = 32. The two numbers are 19 and 32.

9. 46 cm

The length of a rectangle is the longer side and the width is the shorter side. The widths of the mattresses are 138 cm and 92 cm. 138 – 92 = 138 – 90 – 2. This is 48 – 2 = 46. The double mattress is 46 cm wider than the single.

10. 225 mL

600 – 375 = 600 – 300 – 75. This is 300 – 75 which is 225. The difference is 225 mL.

11. 500 g

There is 1000 g in 1 kg. At the start the mass of the water was 1000 g. As half of 1000 is 500, the mass of the remaining water will be about 500 g.

12. 10 past 3

Half an hour is 30 minutes. Start at 20 to 3. Adding 20 minutes is 3 o'clock. Another 10 minutes is 10 past 3.

13. circles, rectangle

The net of a cylinder has 2 circles and 1 rectangle.

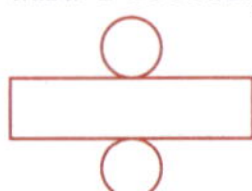

14.

15. ***b*, *c*, *a***

Angle *b* is the smallest and angle *a* is the largest. The order is *b*, *c*, *a*.

16. 3

From X, Katie moves 4 units to F2. From F2 to F5 is 3 units. Katie moved 3 units north.

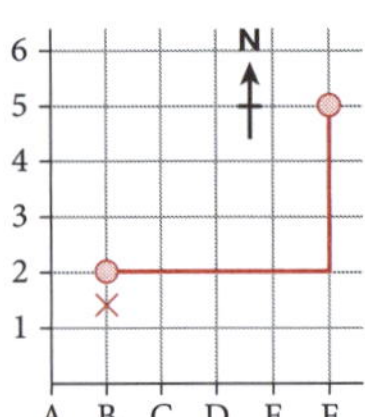

17.

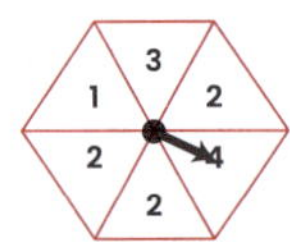

The spinner on the left has two 2s and the spinner on the right has three 2s. This means the spinner on the right has a greater chance.

18. $60

Cam saved $40 and Abe saved $20. As 40 + 20 = 60, the total amount is $60.

Unit 19A PAGE 74

1. 187

The numbers Cameron counts all end in 7. This means he will count 187.

2. 40

8 × 5 = 40. Silas used 40 coins.

3. 5 laps

As 4 × 5 = 20, then 20 ÷ 4 = 5. Each athlete runs 5 laps.

4. 1600

9 + 7 = 16. This means 900 + 700 = 1600. The supermarket sold 1600 packets.

5. 21

60 – 39 = 60 – 30 – 9. This is 30 – 9 = 21. There are still 21 pages to read.

6.

There are other correct answers.

7. $30

As 15 – 12 = 3, then 150 – 120 = 30. Finn still has $30 value on the card.

8. even

Adding 6 and then subtracting 5 is the same as adding 1. Adding 1 to any odd number always gives an even number.

9. ***B***

Rectangle *A* has an area of 5 cm^2.
Rectangle *B* has an area of 6 cm^2.
Rectangle *B* covers the greater area.

10. 4

You need to find 40 ÷ 10. As 10 × 4 = 40, then 40 ÷ 10 = 4. Levi can fill 4 containers.

11. 51 kg

47 + 4 = 47 + 3 + 1. This is 50 + 1 = 51. Kale's mass was 51 kg.

12. 8:52

40 + 12 = 52. Her bus arrives at 8:52.

13.

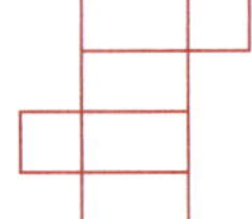

14. 28

A hexagon has 6 sides and a pentagon 5 sides.
As 6 + 6 + 6 + 5 + 5 = 18 + 10 = 28, Marcus drew a total of 28 sides.

15. ***c***

The largest angle is *c*.

16. south

Think of a compass. While looking at the west direction, south is on the left.

17. green and blue

The other possible pair would be for Kristy to select a green ball and a blue ball. The missing pair is green and blue.

18. 16

2 + 3 + 5 + 6 = 16. A total of 16 bikes were sold.

Unit 19B PAGE 75

1. **113**
   All of Erin's numbers have 3 in the ones place. The digit in the tens place is odd. This means 113 will be counted.
2. **36**
   $12 \times 3 = 36$. Monique bought 36 bananas.
3. **16**
   There are 24 chocolates shared between 3 girls. As $3 \times 8 = 24$, then $24 \div 3 = 8$. Each girl receives 8 chocolates. As $8 + 8 = 16$, the two girls receive a total of 16 chocolates.
4. **32**
   $8 + 3 = 11$. Saraya is 11 years old. $11 + 2 = 13$. Harrison is 13 years old. $13 + 11 + 8 = 24 + 8$. This is 32. The sum of their ages is 32.
5. **32**
   $84 - 52 = 84 - 50 - 2$. This is $34 - 2 = 32$. There are 32 people waiting for the next bus.
6. 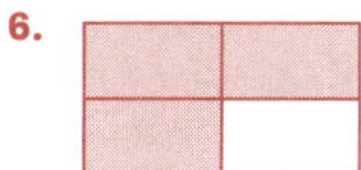
   There are other correct answers.
7. **$6**
   If she makes 50c for 1 bag, she makes $1 for every 2 bags. Multiplying by 6 means she makes $6 for selling 12 bags.
8. **72, 56**
   The pattern is subtracting 8. From 88, the next numbers are 80, 72, 64, 56 … This means Mandy will write 72 and 56.
9. 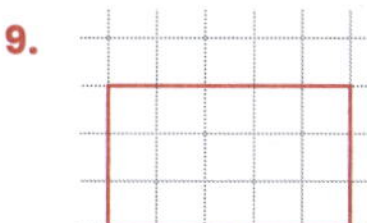
   The side already drawn is 5 cm. As $15 \div 5 = 3$, the width will be 3 cm.
10. **840 mL**
    As 42 + 42 is 84, then $420 + 420 = 840$. There is a total of 840 mL.
11. **13**
    There is 1000 g in 1 kg. As 13 000 is 13×1000, there is 13 kg in 13 000 g.
12. **8:00**
    $36 + 24 = 36 + 20 + 4$. This is $56 + 4 = 60$. The game starts at 8:00.
13. **8**
    A rectangular prism has 6 faces. There are 2 extra faces on this shape. As $6 + 2 = 8$, there are 8 faces.
14. **3**
    The triangle has 3 lines of symmetry.
    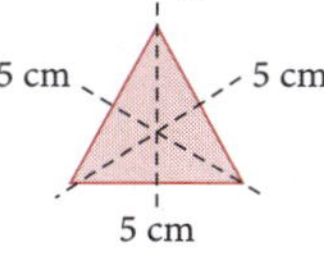

15. Suggested answer:
    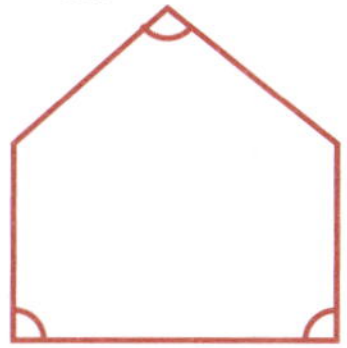
16. **west**
    Think of a compass. From south, a quarter turn is facing west.
17. **6**
    Each of the 3 T-shirts can be worn with each of the 2 pairs of shorts. This means you multiply the numbers. As $3 \times 2 = 6$, there are 6 outfits.
18. **6**
    As $5 + 6 = 11$, a total of 11 bikes were sold on Friday and Saturday. As $2 + 3 = 5$, a total of 5 bikes were sold on Monday and Wednesday. As $11 - 5 = 6$, the difference was 6 bikes.

Unit 20A PAGE 76

1. **16**
   Jason's numbers are 20, 18, 16 … His third number is 16.
2. **930**
   $500 + 430 = 900 + 30$. This is 930. There is a total of 930 books.
3. **6**
   As $5 \times 6 = 30$, then $30 \div 5 = 6$. Each player receives 6 cards.
4. **9**
   $26 - 17 = 26 - 16 - 1$. This is $10 - 1 = 9$. Ruby has 9 balloons remaining.
5. **45**
   $9 \times 5 = 45$. There are 45 lemons in the bags.
6. **10**
   Finding half of a number is dividing it by 2. As $2 \times 10 = 20$, then $20 \div 2 = 10$. There are 10 girls on the bus.
7. **$2.50**
   From $33.50 to $34 is 50c. Another $2 is $36. Adding $2 and 50c is $2.50. The hose is $2.50 cheaper.
8. **11**
   An even number plus an odd number is always odd. From the list the only odd number is 11.
9. **8 mm**
   There is 10 mm in 1 cm. This means there is 20 mm in 2 cm. You need to find the difference between 20 and 12. As $20 - 12 = 8$, the difference is 8 mm.
10. **500 mL**
    As $6 - 1 = 5$, then $600 - 100 = 500$. There is 500 mL remaining in the bottle.
11. **15 kg**
    $5 \times 3 = 15$. The mass is 15 kg.
12. **4:50**
    Half an hour is 30 minutes. As $2 + 3 = 5$, then $20 + 30 = 50$. The lesson finished at 4:50.
13. **square pyramid**
    There is 1 square and 4 triangles. This is the net of a square pyramid.
14.
15. **less than**
    Each angle is less than a right angle.
    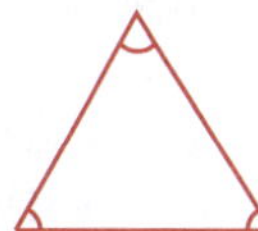
16. **F6**
    Marley walks 5 units from D1 to D6. She then turns right and walks 2 units to F6.
    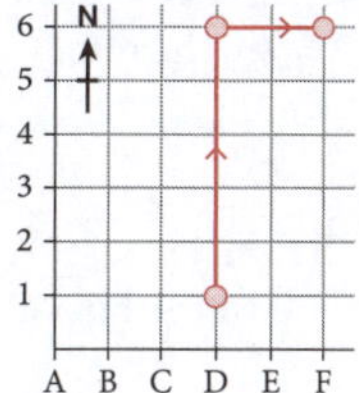

17. **red**

There are 3 red balls, 2 blue balls and 2 yellow balls. The most likely colour is red.

18. **3**

Halfway between 2 and 4 is 3. Dee attended 3 times.

Unit 20B PAGE 77

1. **35**

Here are Aaron's numbers: 20, 25, 30, **35**, 40, 45, 50. The middle number is 35.

2. **67**

38 + 29 = 38 + 30 – 1. This is 68 – 1 = 67. There were 67 customers.

3. **6**

There are 60 minutes in one hour. As 10 × 6 = 60, then 60 ÷ 10 = 6. This means 6 games can be played in one hour.

4. **27**

46 – 19 = 46 – 20 + 1. This is 26 + 1 = 27. Jordan has 27 trading cards.

5. **200**

As 5 × 4 = 20, then 50 × 4 = 200. This means 200 students are on the buses.

6. **4**

Finding one-third of a number is dividing it by 3. As 3 × 4 = 12, then 12 ÷ 3 = 4. There are 4 students who walked to school.

7. **$1.80**

The cost of the fruit is apple = 60c, banana = 70c and mandarin = 50c. Add 60 + 70 + 50. As 6 + 7 + 5 is 18, the total cost is 180c or $1.80.

8. **8**

Here is the sequence of Kathleen's numbers: __, __, 12, __, 16, 18. The numbers are increasing by 2. As 12 – 2 – 2 = 8, the first number was 8.

9. **7 cm**

The length of one paper clip is about 35 mm. As 35 × 2 = 70, the total length is 70 mm, which is 7 cm.

10. **6 L**

The bucket leaks 2 L in 2 hours. As 8 – 2 = 6, there is 6 L in the bucket.

11. **4 kg**

10 + 2 = 12. The total mass of the 3 steel balls is 12 kg. As 12 ÷ 3 = 4, the mass of each ball is 4 kg.

12. **8:15**

40 – 25 = 40 – 20 – 5. This is 20 – 5 = 15. Hudson had left home at 8:15.

13. **7**

There are 6 vertices on the base, and 1 vertex at the apex of the cone. This means there is a total of 7 vertices.

14.

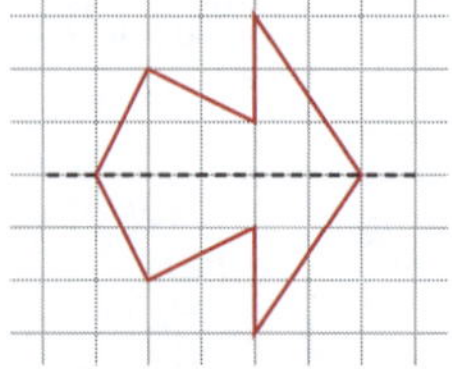

15. **7**

There are 7 angles that measure less than a right angle. Here are the angles:

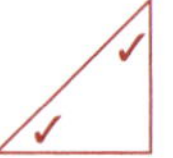

16. **E2**

Charlyze walks 3 units from C5 to C2. She is facing south and so when she turns left she is facing east. She walks 2 units to E2.

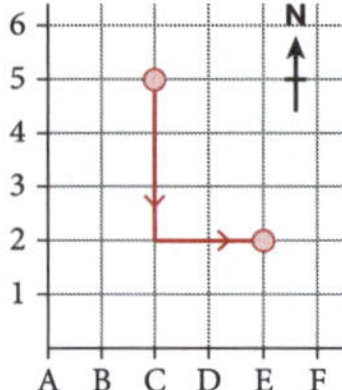

17. **3**

Counting the tally marks:
3 + 2 + 4 + 5 + 3 = 17. As 20 – 17 = 3, the number 5 was rolled 3 times.

18. **3**

Ava attended 9 nights and Cas 6. As 9 – 6 = 3, Ava attended 3 more nights.

Unit 21A PAGE 78

1. **372**

In the number 372, the 7 in the tens place means that the 3 in the hundreds place rounds up.
372 rounds to 400, to the nearest hundred.

2. **9**

As 3 × 9 = 27, then 27 ÷ 3 = 9. There are 9.

3. **20**

There are 5 schooldays in a week. As 4 × 5 = 20, there are 20 more schooldays.

4. **11**

76 – 65 = 76 – 60 – 5. This is 16 – 5 = 11. This means 11 students did not catch the bus in the afternoon.

5. **480 km**

240 + 240 = 480. Buddy drove a total of 480 km.

6.

There are other correct answers.

7. **$5**

80 – 30 – 20 – 25 is 50 – 20 – 25 = 30 – 25. This answer is 5, which means Mia has $5 remaining.

8. **18, 40**

After 14, the numbers on Tom's list are the even numbers greater than 14. The numbers 18 and 40 are on Tom's list.

9. **11 cm**

23 – 12 = 23 – 10 – 2. This is 13 – 2 = 11. The second pencil was 11 cm long.

10. **300 mL**

You need to find half of 600. As half of 6 is 3, then half of 600 is 300. There is 300 mL in each glass.

11. **40 g**

50 – 10 = 40. There are 40 paperclips in the box. These have a mass of about 40 g.

12. **4 minutes**

The times are 3:05 and 3:09. As 9 – 5 = 4, the difference in time is 4 minutes.

13. **cube**

A cube has 12 edges and all the faces are identical squares.

14.

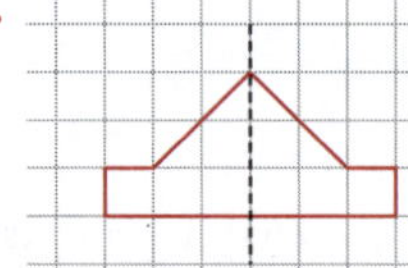

15. **quarter**

A right angle is a quarter turn.

16. ***C***

Two rows in front of *J* is *B*. One desk to the right of *B* is desk *C*.

17.

Equal areas of red and yellow mean there is an equal chance of landing on red or yellow.

18. **18**

Halfway between 16 and 20 is 18. This means Olivia read 18 pages on Thursday.

Unit 21B PAGE 79

1. **2040 hectares**

2040 is only 40 more than 2000. 1930 is 70 less and 3000 is 1000 more. The closest is 2040 hectares.

2. **20**

You need to find $60 \div 3$. As $3 \times 2 = 6$, then $6 \div 3 = 2$. This means $60 \div 3 = 20$ and so 20 cylinders of balls need to be purchased.

3. **18**

A person has 2 legs and their dog has 4 legs. $3 \times 2 = 6$ and $3 \times 4 = 12$. As $6 + 12 = 18$, there is a total of 18 legs.

4. **28**

$96 - 68 = 96 - 60 - 8$. This is $36 - 8 = 28$. Ben still had 28 emails.

5. **476**

$246 + 230 = 246 + 200 + 30$. This is $446 + 30 = 476$. There were 476 passengers.

6.

7. **$7.80**

$3.90 + $3.90 is the same as $4 + $4 – 20c. $8 minus 20c is $7.80.

8. **55, 11**

After 75, the numbers on Andrew's list are the odd numbers less than 75. The numbers 55 and 11 are on Andrew's list.

9. **5**

There are 5 columns of 4 squares. As $5 \times 4 = 20$, the area of the rectangle is 20 cm². As $20 \div 4 = 5$, Benedict can fit 5 shapes on the rectangle. Here is an example of 5 shapes, each with an area of 4 cm².

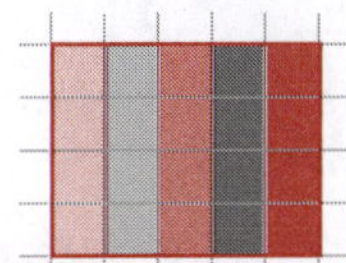

10. **4**

You need to find $20 \div 4$. As $4 \times 5 = 20$, then $20 \div 4 = 5$. A total of 4 teaspoons can be filled.

11. **4400 g or 44 kg**

As 44×10 is 440, then 440×10 is 4400. The mass is 4400 g, or 4.4 kg.

12. **16 minutes**

The time on the clock is 10:10. As $26 - 10 = 16$, the difference in time is 16 minutes.

13. **36**

There are 6 faces on a cube. Use the 6 smallest odd numbers. $1 + 3 + 5 + 7 + 9 + 11 = 36$. The smallest possible total is 36.

14.

15.

16. ***E***

The desk behind *C* is *G*. Two desks to the left of desk *G* is desk *E*.

17. **3**

1 out of the 2 possible outcomes is heads. This means you would expect 3 heads out of the 6 tosses.

18. **6**

On Wednesday Olivia read 10 pages. On Friday she read 4 pages. As $10 - 4 = 6$, Olivia read 6 more pages on Wednesday.

Unit 22A PAGE 80

1. **2009**

The years in ascending order are 2009, 2011, 2016 and 2018. The daughter born in 2009 is the oldest.

2. **41**

$28 + 13 = 28 + 10 + 3$. This is $38 + 3 = 41$. Aisha's mother is 41 years old.

3. **28**

$40 - 12 = 40 - 10 - 2$. This is $30 - 2 = 28$. There are 28 stars not coloured in.

4. **21**

$7 \times 3 = 21$. There are 21 squares.

5. **3**

As $8 \times 3 = 24$, then $24 \div 8 = 3$. This means $24 \div 8 = 3$. There were 3 guides allocated.

6. 

As $3 \times 2 = 6$, one-third is 2 apples. There are other correct answers.

7. **$50**

$25 + 25 = 25 + 20 + 5$. This is $45 + 5 = 50$. Albert is paid $50.

8. **30**

These are the multiples of 3. The tenth multiple of 3 is $10 \times 3 = 30$.

9. **17 cm**

There is 100 cm in 1 m. You need to work out $100 - 83$. $100 - 80 - 3 = 20 - 3$. This is 17, and so Fleur needs to grow 17 cm.

10. **17 cm³**

$8 + 6 + 3 = 14 + 3$. This is 17. The volume is 17 cm³.

11. **9 g, 65 g, 532 g**

Look at the numbers 65, 9, 532. Rearrange these numbers from smallest to largest. The order is 9 g, 65 g, 532 g.

12. **9:35**

Quarter of an hour is 15 minutes. $20 + 15 = 35$. Grace left at 9:35

13. **pentagonal prism**

There are 2 pentagons and 5 rectangles. This is the net of a pentagonal prism.

14.

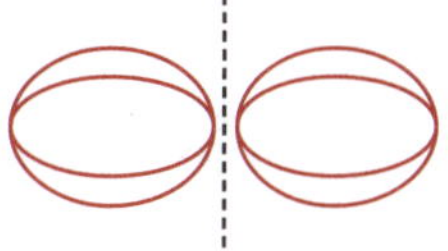

15.

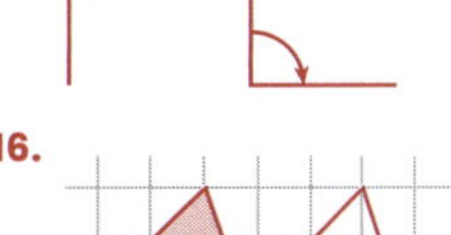

16.

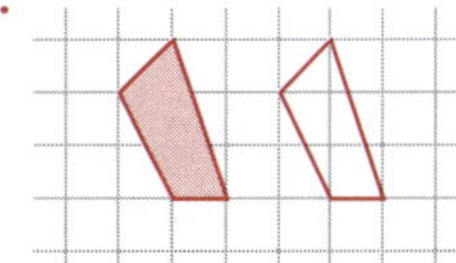

17. **3**

Cameron can choose strawberry and chocolate or strawberry and caramel or chocolate and caramel. This means there are 3 different combinations.

18. **Tuesday**

The shortest column is on Tuesday.

Unit 22B PAGE 81

1. **Olivia**

The heights from shortest to tallest are 142 cm, 147 cm, 155 cm and 158 cm. Jessica is the tallest person at

158 cm. The second tallest person is Olivia at 155 cm tall.

2. **30**

$12 + 9 = 21$. Keeley has 21 balls. $21 + 9 = 30$. Amy now has 30 balls.

3. **2**

$12 - 7 - 3 = 5 - 3$. This equals 2. There are 2 green balls in the bag.

4. **24**

There are 8 shoes in 4 pairs on each shelf. As $8 \times 3 = 24$, Bethany has 24 shoes.

5. **9**

$25 + 20 = 45$. There are 45 students to be organised into groups of 5. As $5 \times 9 = 45$, then $45 \div 5 = 9$. There will be 9 groups formed.

6. $\mathbf{\frac{1}{2}}$

$4 - 2 = 2$. There are 2 quarters that remained which is $\frac{1}{2}$ of the orange.

7. **$10.50**

7 lots of $1 is $7. As $7 \times 5 = 35$, then 7 lots of 50c is 350c or $3.50. Adding $7 and $3.50 gives $10.50.

8. **200**

These are the multiples of 2. The hundredth multiple of 2 is $100 \times 2 = 200$.

9. **7 m**

There are 100 cm in 1 m. 670 is between 600 and 700. It is closer to 700. This means it rounds to 7 m.

10. **6**

You need to find $12 \div 2$. As $2 \times 6 = 12$, then $12 \div 2 = 6$. This means 6 jugs of water are needed.

11. **1 kg, 250 g, 27 g**

There are 1000 g in 1 kg. The masses are 250 g, 27 g, 1000 g. Look at the numbers 250, 27, 1000. Rearrange these numbers from largest to smallest. The order is 1000, 250, 27. The masses are 1 kg, 250 g, 27 g.

12. **2:05**

You need to find the number of minutes between 1:53 and 2:00. There are 60 minutes in an hour. As $60 - 53 = 7$, there are 7 minutes until 2:00. As $12 - 7 = 5$, there is another 5 minutes after 2:00. The movie starts at 2:05.

13. **12**

The number of sides on the base tells you the number of rectangular faces. There are 10 rectangular faces plus the top and bottom. This means there are 12 faces.

14.

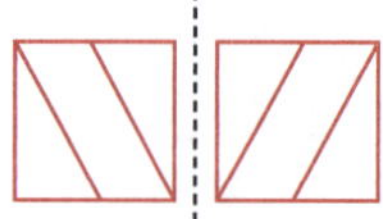

15.

16.

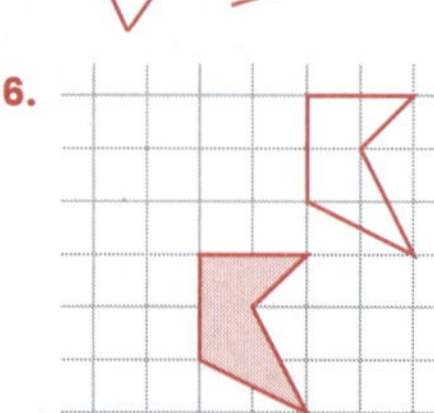

17. **red**

It does not matter where the arrow landed on the first 2 spins. There are more red sections than blue so it is likely the arrow will stop on red.

18. **19**

10 dogs were washed on Wednesday and 9 on Friday. As $10 + 9 = 19$, there was a total of 19 dogs washed.

Unit 23A PAGE 82

1. **5720**

$14 - 5 - 2 - 0$ is $9 - 2$. This is 7. The number is 5720.

2. **14**

A dozen is 12. Two dozen is 24. $24 - 10 = 14$. Charlize has 14 eggs left.

3. **35**

$7 \times 5 = 35$. Ryan reads a total of 35 pages.

4. **39**

$23 + 16 = 23 + 10 + 6$. This is $33 + 6 = 39$. Halle picked 39 strawberries.

5. **6**

Each student was holding up 10 fingers. As $10 \times 6 = 60$, then $60 \div 10 = 6$. There were 6 students in the group.

6. **4**

Half of 8 is found by using $8 \div 2$. As $2 \times 4 = 8$, then $8 \div 2 = 4$. There are 4 white cars.

7. **$10.05**

From $39.95 to $40 is 5c. Another $10 is $50. As $10 + 5c is $10.05, Jackson received change of $10.05.

8. **24**

The rule is to add 8. As $16 + 8 = 24$, the missing number is 24.

9. **60 cm**

You need to find $120 \div 2$. Think about $12 \div 2$. As $2 \times 6 = 12$, then $12 \div 2 = 6$. This means $120 \div 2 = 60$. Each new piece is 60 cm.

10. **2 L**

As $8 \div 4 = 2$, the capacity of each jug is 2 L.

11. **400 g**

As $2 + 2 = 4$, then $200 + 200 = 400$. The mass is 400 g.

12. **Jen**

Arrange the times from earliest to latest: 3:10, 3:35, 4:00 and 4:55. The doctor's first patient is Jen at 3:10.

13. **triangular prism**

There are 2 triangles and 3 rectangles. This is the net of a triangular prism.

14.

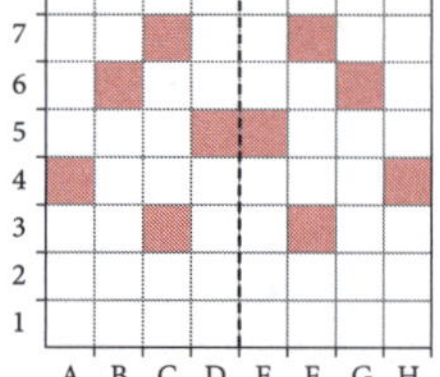

A4 and G6 need to be shaded.

15. **16**

There are 4 groups of 4 right angles. As $4 \times 4 = 16$, there is a total of 16 right angles.

16. **F4**

X is at E3. Up 5 is E8, left 2 is C8, down 4 is C4 and right 3 is F4.

17. **green**

There are now 2 green cards and 1 pink card. This means it is more likely Rosie will select a green card.

18. **5**

Counting the dots for black hair, there are 5 students.

Unit 23B PAGE 83

1. **631**

$6 - 5 = 1$. There is a 1 in the ones place. As $10 - 6 - 1$ is 3, there is a 3 in the tens place. The number is 631.

2. **20**
$36 - 6 - 6 - 4 = 30 - 6 - 4$. This is $24 - 4 = 20$. Aunt Sharon kept 20 cakes.

3. **27**
$9 \times 3 = 27$. Ariarne is 27 years old.

4. **9100**
$87 + 4 = 91$. This means $8700 + 400$ is 9100. Jordan has 9100 points.

5. **3**
As $6 \times 2 = 12$, there is a total of 12 strawberries. $3 + 1 = 4$. The strawberries are to be shared between 4 children. As $4 \times 3 = 12$, then $12 \div 4 = 3$. Frida will eat 3 strawberries.

6. $\frac{1}{4}$
2 out of 8 small rectangles are not shaded. This is the same as one quarter of the shape.

7. **$109.90**
You need to add $70 and $39.90. As $70 + $30 + $9.90 = $100 + $9.90 = $109.90, the total cost is $109.90.

8. **15**
The sequence is 3, 5, 7, 9, 11, 13, 15 … On Sunday Geoff completed 3, on Monday 5, and so on. He plans to complete 15 laps on Saturday.

9. **500 mm**
There is 1000 mm in 1 metre. As half of 10 is 5, so half of 1000 is 500. The town received 500 mm.

10. **7 L**
The watering can contains 9 L of water. As $9 - 2 = 7$, there is still 7 L in the watering can.

11. **260 g**
$28 - 2 = 26$. This means $280 - 20 = 260$. There is 260 g of honey remaining.

12. **2:50**
You need to find the time which is 20 minutes before 3:10. Ten minutes before 3:10 is 3:00. Ten minutes before 3:00 is 10 to 3, or 2:50.

13. **1, 1**
The new shapes are hemispheres. Each hemisphere has 1 curved surface and 1 flat surface.

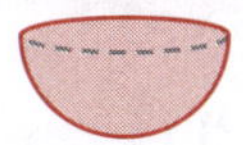

14. **4**
F7, G6, A4 and C3 need to be shaded. Kamari needs to shade 4 more squares.

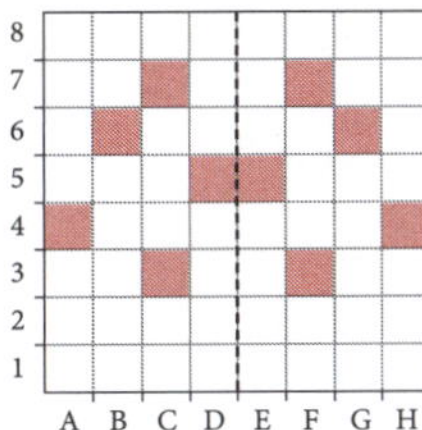

15. **quarter past 7 or 7:15**
The time will be quarter past 7, or 7:15.

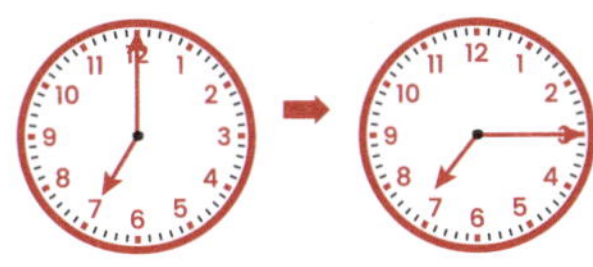

16. **E5**
Reverse the directions. From B7, move right 5, down 4, to the left 2 and up 2. The disc is at E5. You can check this answer by starting at E5, following the instructions in the question and finishing at B7.

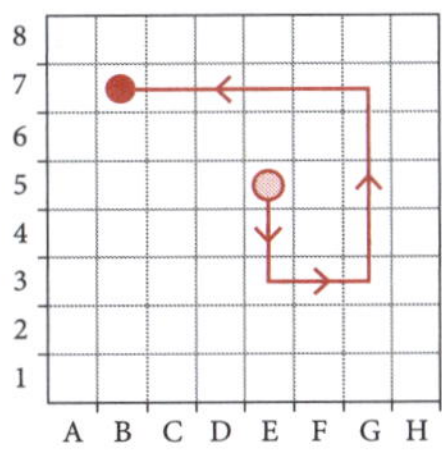

17. **blue**
There are 2 blue discs and 3 yellow discs. This means it is less likely Rosie will select a blue disc.

18. **6**
8 students have brown hair and 2 students have red hair. As $8 - 2 = 6$, there are 6 more students with brown hair.

Unit 24A PAGE 84

1. **2**
You need to work out the even numbers between 8 and 14. These numbers are 10 and 12. There are 2 houses.

2. **86**
$43 \times 2 = 43 + 43$. This is 86. Wesley has 86 toy soldiers.

3. **12**
As $30 - 20 = 10$, then $32 - 20 = 12$. There are 12 squares not shaded.

4. **8**
As $5 \times 8 = 40$, then $40 \div 5 = 8$. There are 8 columns on the grid.

5. **80**
$42 + 38 = 42 + 30 + 8$. This is $72 + 8 = 80$. The coin was tossed 80 times.

6. **3**
One-quarter of 12 is $12 \div 4$. As $4 \times 3 = 12$, then $12 \div 4 = 3$. Three fish were too small.

7. **$160**
As $8 \times 2 = 16$, then $8 \times 20 = 160$. Henry is paid $160.

8. **25**
Phoebe's numbers were 40, 35, 30, 25 … Her fourth number was 25.

9. **3 cm**
Most rulers are between 3 cm and 4 cm wide. Sawyer's ruler is likely to be about 3 cm wide.

10. **70 L**
There are 7 days in a week. As $10 \times 7 = 70$, Luke uses 70 L every week.

11. **9 kg**
$12 - 9 = 3$. Anabelle's mass had increased by 9 kg.

12. **20 minutes**
It takes 5 minutes for the minute hand to move from one number to the next. As $6 - 2 = 4$ and $4 \times 5 = 20$, it takes 20 minutes.

13. **hexagonal pyramid**
There is 1 hexagon and 6 triangles. This is the net of a hexagonal pyramid.

14.

15. **a right angle**
The angle is a right angle.

16.

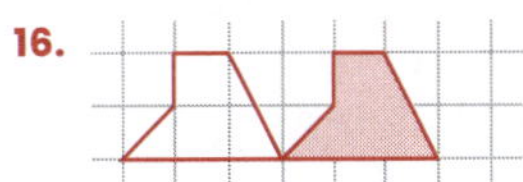

17. **win, loss, draw**
A draw is when both teams have scored the same number of goals. The outcomes are win, loss and draw. A draw can be called a tie.

18. **Gabby**
Cam scored 10 goals and Gabby scored 9 goals. This means Gabby scored the second highest number of goals.

Unit 24B PAGE 85

1. **11**
   The odd numbers between 3 and 27 are 5, 7, 9, 11, 13, 15, 17, 19, 21, 23 and 25. This means 11 houses are built.
2. **25**
   3 + 2 = 5. There are 5 balls in each bag. As 5 × 5 = 25, there is a total of 25 balls.
3. **24**
   42 – 18 = 42 – 10 – 8. This is 32 – 8 = 24. There are 24 peaches that are not ripe.
4. **12**
   You need to find 120 ÷ 10. As 10 × 12 = 120, then 120 ÷ 10 = 12. There are 12 groups of students.
5. **1170**
   500 + 670 = 500 + 500 + 170. This is 1000 + 170 = 1170. There are 1170 sheep.
6. $\frac{1}{4}$
   One row out of 4 rows is $\frac{1}{4}$. Addison has turned $\frac{1}{4}$ of the cards over.
7. **$1.05**
   61 + 43 = 61 + 40 + 3. This is 101 + 3 which is 104. The items cost 104 cents, or $1.04. This is rounded to $1.05.
8. **118**
   102, 106, 110, 114, 118 … Joseph's fifth number is 118.
9. **2040**
   There are 1000 mm in 1 m. This means there are 2000 mm in 2 m. Also there are 10 mm in 1 cm. This means there are 40 mm in 4 cm. As 2000 + 40 is 2040, there are 2040 mm in 2 m 4 cm.
10. **8 L**
    You need to work out 24 ÷ 3. As 3 × 8 = 24, then 24 ÷ 3 = 8. Peyton's shower uses 8 L every minute.
11. **27 kg**
    22 + 5 = 27. The total baggage allowance is 27 kg.
12. **50 minutes**
    When the minute hand is on 7 it is '25 to'. When the minute hand is on 5 it is '25 past'. As 25 + 25 = 50, it has taken 50 minutes.
13. **12**
    3 and 4 are on opposite faces. As 3 × 4 = 12, the numbers on opposite faces multiply to give 12. *X* and 1 are on opposite faces. As 1 × 12 = 12, then *X* represents 12.
14. 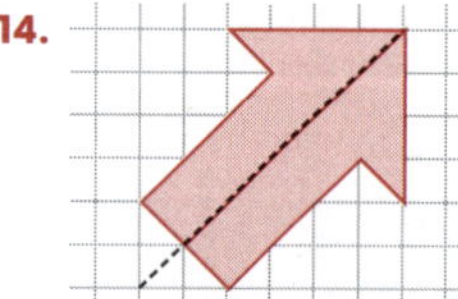
15. **3**
    Two angles are easily spotted but these angles form a third angle. All 3 angles are less than a right angle.
    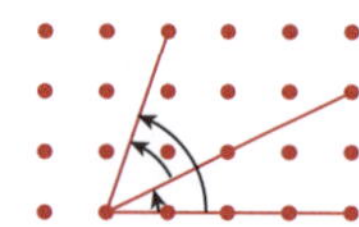
16.
17. **head + tail, tail + head, tail + tail**
    The 10-cent coin could land as a head and the 20-cent coin could land as a tail. This could be reversed to give a tail and a head. Finally both coins could land on tails. The three outcomes can be written as head + tail, tail + head, tail + tail.
18. **32**
    6 + 2 + 9 + 5 + 10 = 32. The total number of goals was 32.

Unit 25A PAGE 86

1. **209**
   Look at the hundreds digit. The smaller numbers start with 2. Now look at the tens digit. The smallest number is 209.
2. **6**
   As 3 × 6 = 18, then 18 ÷ 3 = 6. There are 6 books on each shelf.
3. **102**
   97 + 5 = 97 + 3 + 2. This is 100 + 2 = 102. Her grandmother will be 102.
4. **13**
   50 – 37 = 50 – 30 – 7. This is 20 – 7 = 13. Kate did not answer 13 questions correctly.
5. **18**
   6 × 3 = 18. The florist used 18 roses.
6. 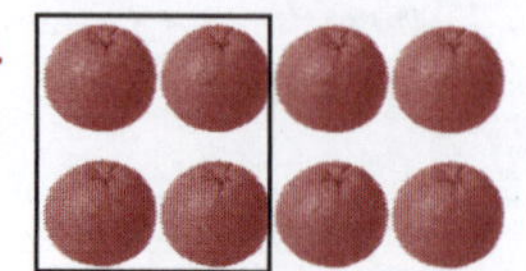
   As 2 × 4 = 8, half of 8 is 4. There will be 4 oranges in the box.
7. **$1.40**
   From $18.60 to $19 is 40c and then another $1 makes $20. The change was $1.40.
8. **41**
   The sequence is 20, 27, 34, 41 … The fourth number is 41.
9. **8 m**
   80 × 10 = 800. Otis has walked 800 cm. There is 100 cm in 1 m. As 800 cm = 8 m, Otis has walked 8 m.
10. **800 mL**
    As 4 × 2 = 8, then 4 × 200 = 800. The total amount was 800 mL.
11. **80 g**
    As 4 + 4 = 8, then 40 + 40 = 80. The mass is 80 g.
12. **6:02**
    The time is 8 minutes to 6. As 10 – 8 = 2, the time will be 2 minutes past 6. This is written as 6:02.
13. **true**
    The net has 1 square and 4 triangles and folds to a square pyramid.
14. 
    There is only 1 line of symmetry.
15. -
    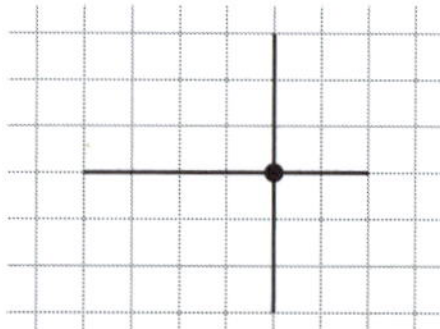
16. **7**
    There are 7 lines on the map. This means there are 7 roads.
17. **green**
    There are more green counters than any other colour. The most likely colour is green.
18. **9**
    The middle of 8 and 10 is 9. There were 9 students who said they showered for 4 minutes.

Unit 25B PAGE 87

1. **Mia**
   Compare 2671, 2983 and 2967. Each number has 2 thousands. Looking at the hundreds digit, 9 is larger than 6. In the tens place, 8 is larger than 6.

The largest number is 2983. Mia has the most stamps.

2. **9**

As $100 \times 9 = 900$, then $900 \div 100 = 9$. This means 9 stacks are needed.

3. **99**

$32 + 32 + 35 = 64 + 35$. This is 99. Kyle completed 99 push-ups.

4. **34**

$80 - 46 = 80 - 40 - 6$. This is $40 - 6 = 34$. The other number is 34.

5. **18**

$3 \times 4 = 12$. Also, $2 \times 3 = 6$. As $12 + 6 = 18$, the team scored 18 goals.

6. $\frac{4}{5}$

The pattern is going up by fifths. As $1 = \frac{5}{5}$, the missing number is $\frac{4}{5}$.

7. **6**

$2 + $2 + $1 + 50c + 20c + 10c = $5.80. He can use 6 coins.

8. **26**

The tenth number will be 71 minus 9 lots of 5. As $9 \times 5 = 45$, you need to find $71 - 45$. As $71 - 41 - 4 = 30 - 4$, which is 26, the tenth number in the sequence is 26.

9. **11 cm**

You need to find $33 \div 3$. As $3 \times 11 = 33$, then $33 \div 3 = 11$. The length of each glue stick is 11 cm.

10. **490 mL**

$500 - 10 = 490$. There is 490 mL remaining in the sauce bottle.

11. **5 kg**

As $2 \times 10 = 20$, the mass of 2 blocks is 20 kg. This means the mass of 4 balls is also 20 kg. As $4 \times 5 = 20$, then $20 \div 4 = 5$. The mass of each ball is 5 kg.

12. **12:53**

The time is 18 minutes past 1. As $25 - 18 = 7$, the time will be 7 minutes to 1. This is written as 12:53.

13. ***Y***

Mabel should draw a square in the *Y* position.

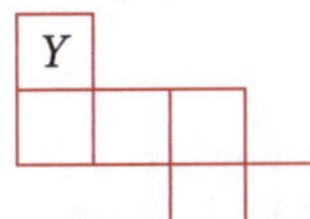

14. **4**

The shape is a square. A square has 4 lines of symmetry.

15. 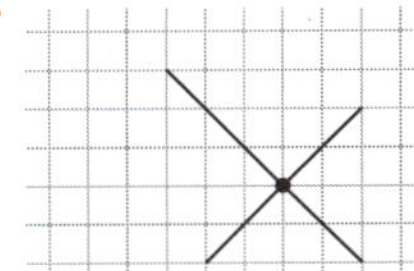

16. **5**

Ravi drives from *F* to *G*, from *G* to *H*, from *H* to *E*, from *E* to *B* and then from *B* to *C*. Ravi drives 5 roads.

17. **2**

There are more 2s on the dice than any other number. This means the most likely number will be 2.

18. **9**

More than 4 minutes is 5 minutes or 6 minutes. 6 students showered for 5 minutes and 3 students showered for 6 minutes. As $6 + 3 = 9$, there were 9 students who showered for more than 4 minutes.

Unit 26A PAGE 88

1. **Jeremy**

Comparing the three numbers 1957, 1983 and 1964, the highest number is 1983. As Jeremy was born last, he is the youngest.

2. **21**

$6 + 5 + 4 + 3 + 2 + 1 = 21$. The total is 21.

3. **3**

As $6 \times 3 = 18$, then $18 \div 6 = 3$. Lucy cooked 3 pizzas.

4. **21**

$7 \times 3 = 21$. There were 21 students.

5. **23**

$64 - 41 = 64 - 40 - 1$. This is $24 - 1 = 23$. He scored 23 when he batted second.

6. 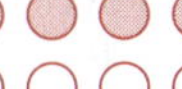

There are other correct answers.

7. **$100**

As $40 + 20 = 60$, Alexander has $60. As $6 + 4 = 10$, then $60 + 40 = 100$. Altogether the boys have $100.

8. **200**

Each number ends in 0. Look at the pattern of the other numbers: 8, 11, 14, 17 … These numbers are adding 3. The next number would be $17 + 3 = 20$. This means the missing number in the sequence will be 200.

9. **2 m**

$160 + 40 = 200$. Rylee's line was 200 cm long, which is 2 m.

10. **250 mL**

As $30 - 5 = 25$, then $300 - 50 = 250$. There is 250 mL of milk remaining in the jug.

11. **58 g**

$64 - 6 = 64 - 4 - 2$. This is $60 - 2 = 58$. The mass of the mandarin is 58 g.

12. **10:30 (or 22:30)**

Imagine the numbers around the outside of the clock. The time is half past 10, which is 10:30. This is 10:30 in the morning, or 22:30 at night.

13. **octagonal pyramid**

A cube has 6 faces, a hexagonal prism has 8 faces and an octagonal pyramid has 9 faces.

14. **3 cm**

A rhombus has 4 equal sides. You need to find $12 \div 4$. As $3 \times 4 = 12$, then $12 \div 4 = 3$. The length of each side is 3 cm.

15. **6**

Here are the 6 right angles inside the shape:

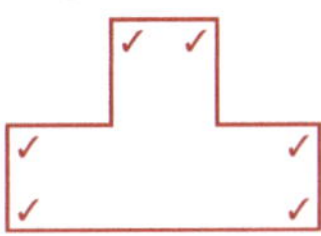

16. **3**

Students *C*, *D* and *E* live on Straight Street. This means 3 students.

17. **unlikely**

There are 30 days in June. It is unlikely that Nathan's birthday is on 17 June.

18. **9**

Halfway between 8 and 10 is 9. This means 9 students said their favourite pet was a dog.

Unit 26B PAGE 89

1. **794**

Compare the digits in the hundreds place, then the digits in the tens place. The order is 489, 748, 794, 824, 842. The middle number is 794.

2. **16**

$6 + 4 = 10$. This means Holly read 10 books. $10 + 6 = 16$. The girls read 16 books in total.

3. **20**

You need to work out $60 \div 3$. As $6 \div 3 = 2$, then $60 \div 3 = 20$. Lani has drawn 20 triangles.

4. **6000 L**

As $3 \times 2 = 6$, then $3000 \times 2 = 6000$. Joshua has a total of 6000 L of water.

5. **113**

$180 - 67 = 180 - 60 - 7$. This is $120 - 7 = 113$. There are 113 vacant seats.

6. 

There are other correct answers.

7. **$88**

As $20 + 16 = 36$, Callum has $36. As $36 - 4 = 32$, Beau has $32. $36 + 32 + 20 = 68 + 20$. As this is 88, the boys have $88 altogether.

8. **10**

Bob's list is 2, 6, 10, 14 … Jack's list is 4, 6, 8, 10 … The smallest 2-digit number on both lists is 10.

9. **8 mm**

There is 10 mm in 1 cm. This means there is 40 mm in 4 cm. $40 - 32 = 8$. One eraser is 8 mm longer than the other.

10. **36 cm³**

There are 12 blocks on each of the 3 layers. As $12 \times 3 = 36$, the volume is 36 cm³.

11. **900 g**

There is 1000 g in 1 kg. You need to subtract 100 g from 1000 g. As $10 - 1 = 9$, then $1000 - 100 = 900$. The mass of flour remaining is 900 g.

12. **4:47 (or 16:47)**

Imagine the numbers around the outside of the clock. The time is 13 minutes to 5. This is 4:47 written in 12-h time or possible 16:47 in 24-h time.

13. **hexagonal pyramid, cube**

A hexagonal pyramid has 12 edges, a pentagonal prism has 15 edges and a cube has 12 edges.

14. **26 cm**

$8 - 3 = 5$. The sides of the parallelogram are 8 cm, 8 cm, 5 cm and 5 cm. As $8 + 8 + 5 + 5 = 26$, the total is 26 cm.

15. **2**

Here are the two right angles outside the shape.

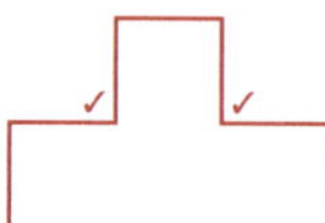

16. ***C* and *D***

Students *C* and *D* both live near each other on Straight Street.

17. 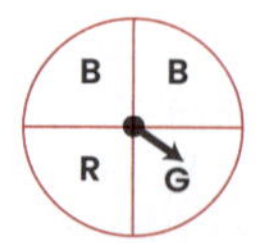

The fact that it is equally likely to stop in red and green means place a R and G in one section each. The other 2 sections should be labelled B as it is more likely to stop in blue.

18. **2**

There were 8 votes for a bird and 9 votes for a dog. This means 2 pets gained more than 5 votes.

Unit 27A PAGE 90

1. **73**

Henry counts 43, 53, 63, 73 … The fourth number is 73.

2. **21**

$7 \times 3 = 21$. Lewis scored 21.

3. **87 cm**

$55 + 32 = 55 + 30 + 2$. This is $85 + 2 = 87$. Trent has 87 cm of string.

4. **7**

As $3 \times 7 = 21$, then $21 \div 3 = 7$. Lachlan will take the tablets for 7 days.

5. **89**

The largest 2-digit number is 99. As $99 - 10 = 89$, the number is 89.

6. **2**

To find one-quarter you divide the number by 4. As $4 \times 2 = 8$, then $8 \div 4 = 2$. Lucy is 2 years old.

7. **$8**

You need to add $4.80 and $3.20. $4 + $3 = $7 and 80c and 20c is $1. As $7 + 1 = 8$, the total cost is $8.

8. **even**

When Pedro adds an odd number to 11, he will get an even number. Subtracting an even number gives another even number.

9. **11 cm²**

There are 2 rows of 3 squares and a row of 5 squares. 2×3 is 6 and then adding 5 is 11. The area is 11 cm².

10. **50 L**

As $2 + 3 = 5$, then $20 + 30 = 50$. There is 50 L of petrol in the car.

11. **8 kg**

$3 + 3 + 2 = 8$. The total mass is 8 kg.

12. **2 hours**

The minute hand takes 1 hour to move through one revolution. $2 \times 1 = 2$. It will take 2 hours.

13. **triangular prism**

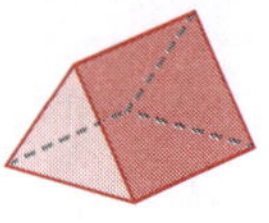

14. **rectangle, parallelogram**

The shapes are rectangle and parallelogram.

15. 

16. 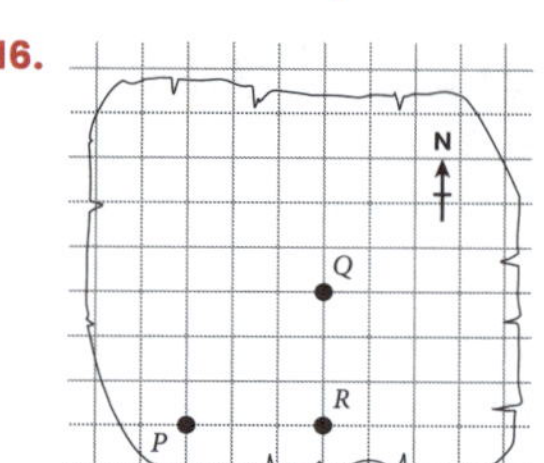

17. **apple**

As 4 is the largest number, the most likely fruit is an apple.

18. **Jack**

The longest bar is for Jack. This means Jack has the most after-school activities.

Unit 27B PAGE 91

1. **407**

The digit in the tens place is increasing by 1. The missing number will be 407.

2. **15**

$4 - 1 = 3$. There are now 3 chocolates in each bag. As $5 \times 3 = 15$, there is a total of 15 chocolates in the bags.

3. **31**

$19 + 12 = 19 + 10 + 2$. This is $29 + 2 = 31$. There are 31 cousins.

4. **6**
As $3 \times 10 = 30$, there is a total of 30 students. You need to find $30 \div 5$. As $5 \times 6 = 30$, then $30 \div 5 = 6$. There will be 6 students in each group.

5. **50**
The largest number is 63 and the smallest is 13. $63 - 13 = 63 - 10 - 3$. This is $53 - 3 = 50$. The difference between the two numbers is 50.

6. **15**
Suppose the squares are arranged in 4 rows of 5 squares. A quarter of the squares is one row. There are 3 rows that are not shaded. As $5 \times 3 = 15$, Tate has not shaded 15 squares.

7. **$6.50**
Sloan should buy a 1-L container and a 2-L container. $4 + $2.50 is $6.50. (This is cheaper than buying 3 1-L containers.)

8. **47**
The rule is to add 7. As $40 + 7 = 47$, the missing number is 47.

9. **1020**
There is 100 cm in 1 m. As $10 \times 100 = 1000$, there is 1000 cm in 10 m. As $1000 + 20 = 1020$, Mitchell threw 1020 cm.

10. **8**
There are 24 blocks in the prism which has the same number of blocks in each layer. You need to find $24 \div 3$. As $3 \times 8 = 24$, then $24 \div 3 = 8$. There are 8 blocks in each row.

11. **9 kg**
As $6 \times 3 = 18$, the total mass of the balls is 18 kg. This means the total mass of the 2 blocks is 18 kg. As $18 \div 2 = 9$, each block has a mass of 9 kg.

12. **10:35 or 25 to 11**
It takes 1 minute for the second hand to go around the clock once. This means it takes 5 minutes to go around 5 times. The time will be 25 to 11, or 10:35.

13.
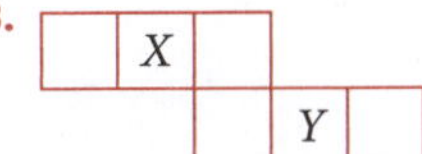

14. **18**
There are 6 sides, 6 angles and 6 lines of symmetry. As $6 + 6 + 6 = 18$, the total is 18.

15. **24**
There are 4 right angles on each face. There are 6 faces. As $6 \times 4 = 24$, the total is 24.

16.
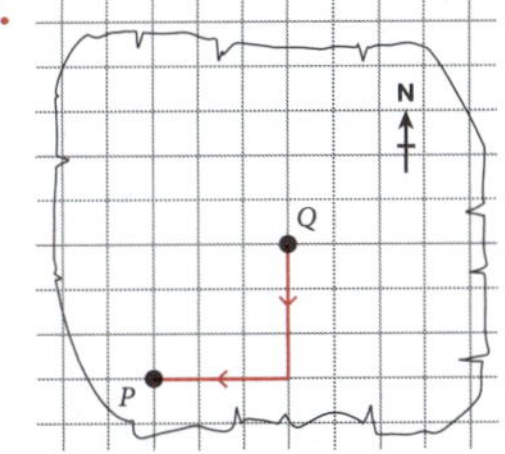

17. **banana**
There are now 2 apples, 2 oranges and 3 bananas in the bowl. As 3 is the largest number, the most likely fruit is a banana.

18. **11**
$2 + 3 + 1 + 5 = 11$. The total is 11 activities.

Unit 28A PAGE 92

1. **97 412**
The digit in the ones place is the smaller even number. The rest of the numbers are written in descending order. This means the number is 97 412.

2. **5**
As $8 \times 5 = 40$, then $40 \div 8 = 5$. Ms Jackson needs to buy 5 packets.

3. **96**
$136 - 40 = 136 - 36 - 4$. This is $100 - 4 = 96$. There are 96 women in the park run.

4. **26**
Reorder the numbers.
$12 + 8 + 6 = 20 + 6$. This is 26. There are 26 farm animals.

5. **30**
$10 \times 3 = 30$. This means 30 balloons are needed.

6. $\mathbf{\frac{6}{10}}$ **or** $\mathbf{\frac{3}{5}}$
There are 5 columns of squares. 3 out of 5 columns are shaded. This means $\frac{3}{5}$ of the squares are shaded. ($\frac{6}{10}$ of the squares are shaded.)

7. **$12.80**
You need to multiply $3.20 by 4. $4 \times 3 = 12$, and $20 \times 4 = 80$. This means the total cost was $12.80.

8. **18, 30**
The sequence is 10, 14, 18, 22, 26, 30 … The numbers to be circled are 18 and 30.

9. **64 cm**
As $32 + 32 = 64$, the combined length is 64 cm.

10. **300 mL**
As $5 - 2 = 3$, then $500 - 200 = 300$. There is 200 mL of sauce remaining.

11. **360 g**
$200 + 100 = 300$. Also $50 + 10 = 60$. As $300 + 60 = 360$, the total mass is 360 g.

12. **90**
There are 60 seconds in 1 minute and 30 seconds in half a minute. As $6 + 3 = 9$, then $60 + 30 = 90$. Liam was 90 seconds late.

13. **triangular pyramid**
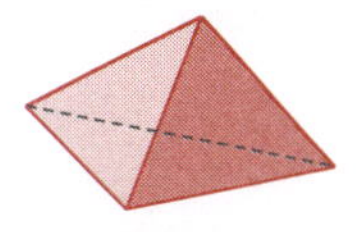

14.
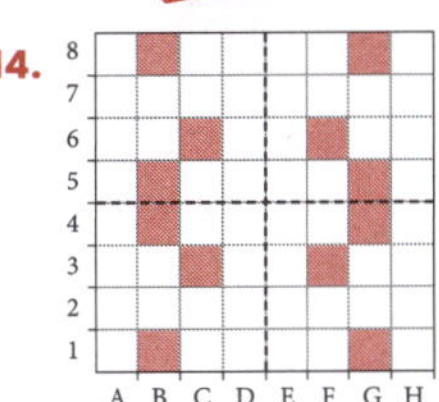

G8 and C3 need to be shaded.

15. **yes**
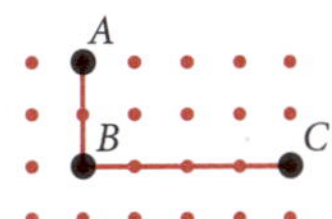

The angle is a right angle.

16. **4S**
Zayden walks through the door close to the canteen. He passes the 3K classroom and the second classroom on his left is 4S.

17.
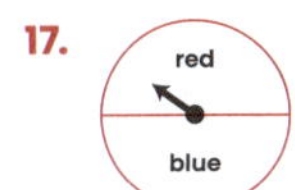

Look for the spinner with a larger red area.

18. **34**
You need to find the difference between 37 and 3. As $37 - 3 = 34$, Daniel was 34 when Logan was born.

Unit 28B PAGE 93

1. **537**
For the smallest number larger than 400, the hundreds digit is a 5. The other two digits are written in ascending order. The number is 537.

2. **6**
Each person has 2 legs. As $2 \times 12 = 24$, then $24 \div 2 = 12$. There are 12 people competing. As

12 ÷ 2 = 6, there are 6 people on each team.

3. **80 m**
50 – 20 = 30. 50 + 30 = 80. Michael swam 80 m.

4. **50**
15 + 15 + 12 + 8 = 30 + 20. This is 50. There is a total of 50 books.

5. **14**
4 × 3 = 12. The team earned 12 points from the wins. As 2 × 1 = 2, the team earned 2 points from the draws. As 12 + 2 = 14, the team has a total of 14 points.

6. **6**
There are three thirds, or $\frac{3}{3}$, in 1. As 2 × 3 = 6, there are six thirds in 2.

7. **$56**
As half of 8 is 4, then half of 80 is 40. The T-shirt cost $40. As 40 + 16 = 50 + 6 = 56, Nicole spent $56.

8. **32**
The numbers shown on the calculator are 17, 22, 27, 32. The final number is 32.

9. **1 m**
Use 1 cm = 10 mm and 1 m = 1000 mm. Change each length to mm. As 102 × 10 = 1020, the three lengths are 1001 mm, 1000 mm and 1020 mm. As 1000 is the smallest number, the shortest length is 1 m.

10. **36 cm³**
By counting, the volume of the layer shown is 12 cm³.
As 12 + 12 + 12 = 36, the volume of the prism is 36 cm³.

11. **$14**
As 3 × 2 = 6, Ben buys 2 bags of dog food. As 7 × 2 = 14, the cost will be $14.

12. **10 past 6**
You use 20 + 10 = 30.
From 20 to 6 until 6 o'clock is 20 minutes. Another 10 minutes is 10 past 6.

13. **60 cm²**
There are 6 identical faces on a cube. As 10 × 6 = 60, the total area is 60 cm².

14. 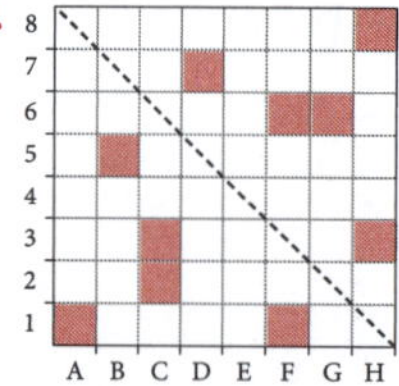

C3, G6 and H3 need to be shaded.

15. 

16. **3P**
Peyton leaves her classroom and walks towards the library. The first door on her right is the door for the 3P classroom.

17. 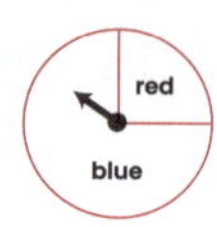

Look for the spinner with a smallest red area.

18. **43**
As 11 – 1 = 10, Owen will be 11 in 10 years. As 33 + 10 = 43, Kate will be 43 when Owen is 11.

Unit 29A PAGE 94

1. **3210**
The digits are 3, 2, 1 and 0. Bohdi's PIN is 3210.

2. **120**
5 + 4 + 3 = 12. This means 30 + 40 + 50 = 120. The total is 120.

3 **40**
76 – 36 = 76 – 6 – 30. This is 70 – 30 = 40. The rest of the team scored 40 points.

4. **11**
As 3 × 11 = 33, then 33 ÷ 3 = 11. There are 11 3s in 33.

5. **35**
5 × 7 = 35. Farmer Bob has 35 eggs.

6. **4**
If one row is removed, one row remains. This means 4 tomatoes remain.

7. **$11.49**
$9.99 is only 1c less than $10. The new price is $10 + $1.50 – 1c. This is $11.50 minus 1c, which is $11.49.

8. **35, 26**
The rule is to subtract 9. 44 – 9 is 35 and 35 – 9 = 26. The two missing numbers are 35 and 26.

9. **305 cm**
There is 100 cm in 1 m. This means there is 300 cm in 3 m. As 300 + 5 = 305, the height is 305 cm.

10. **30 L**
15 × 2 = 30. He uses 30 L.

11. **80 kg**
As 2 × 4 = 8, then 20 × 4 = 80. The total mass is 80 kg.

12. **8:35**
10 + 25 = 35. The time is 8:35.

13. **sphere**
Amarli sketched a sphere.

14. **octagon**
Harvey drew an octagon.

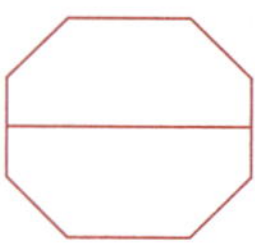

15. **quarter to 7**
A right angle is quarter of an hour. The time will be quarter to 7.

16. **shop A**
Thomas passes shops *D*, *C*, *B* and *A*. This means shop *A* is the fourth shop.

17. **brown**
The smallest number is 3. This is the number of brown balls. This means the colour which is least likely to be chosen is brown.

18.

Season of birth	
Season	**Number**
summer	5
autumn	7
winter	6
spring	8

Unit 29B PAGE 95

1. **7829**
Benji's original PIN is 5607. Adding 2 to each of the digits means his new PIN is 7829.

2. **877**
768 + 109 = 768 + 100 + 9. This is 868 + 9 = 877. Congewai house had scored 877 points.

3. **16**
30 – 8 – 6 = 22 – 6. This is 16. Myles keeps 16 golf balls.

4. 10

As $5 \times 4 = 20$, Michaela baked a total of 20 cakes. To find the number of containers you need to work out $20 \div 2$. As $2 \times 10 = 20$, then $20 \div 2 = 10$. There were 10 cakes in each container.

5. 36

12×3 is $12 + 12 + 12$. This is $10 + 10 + 10 + 2 + 2 + 2$ which is 36. Mila bought 36 carrots.

6.

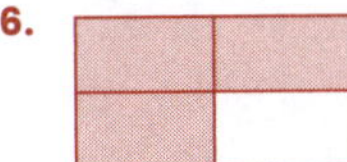

There are other correct answers.

7. $90

You need to work out $6 \div 2$ which is 3. As there are 3 2s in 6, the pizzas will cost 3 lots of $30. As 3×30 is 90, the pizzas cost $90.

8. 114

The pattern is formed by adding 9. This means X is $39 - 9 = 30$. Also $66 + 9 = 75$ and $Y = 75 + 9 = 84$. $X + Y$ is $30 + 84$ is 114.

9. 5 cm

The rectangle has 2 lengths and 2 widths. This means 1 length and 1 width add to 9 cm. As $9 - 4 = 5$, the length is 5 cm.

10. 30 cm³

The volume of Shape B will be half the volume of Shape A. As $6 \div 2 = 3$, then $60 \div 2 = 30$. The volume will be 30 cm³.

11. 2 kg

$16 - 7 = 9$. The rocks were 9 kg and 7 kg. As $9 - 7 = 2$, the difference was 2 kg.

12. 8:05 or 5 past 8

Quarter of an hour is 15 minutes. Three-quarters of an hour is 45 minutes. 20 past 7 can be written as 7:20. As $60 - 20 = 40$, it takes 40 minutes to reach 8:00. Another 5 minutes is 8:05.

13 30 cm

There are 12 edges on the cube. As $12 \times 10 = 120$, the total length of wire used was 120 cm. As $150 - 120 = 30$, there was 30 cm of wire remaining on the roll.

14. 6

A quadrilateral has 4 sides and an octagon has 8 sides. As $32 \div 2 = 16$, the quadrilaterals and the octagons each have a total of 16 sides. This means there are 4 quadrilaterals and 2 octagons. Kate has drawn a total of 6 shapes.

15. 5 past 3

A right angle is quarter of an hour, or 15 minutes. There are 10 minutes from 10 to 3 to 3 o'clock. Another 5 minutes is 3:05, or 5 past 3.

16. shop *L*

After Zeta St, he passes shops K and L on his right. This means the second shop is L.

17. green

There are now 3 red balls and 4 green balls in the bag. This means a green ball is more likely to be chosen.

18. 4

$7 + 4 + 5 = 16$. As $20 - 16 = 4$, there were 4 students born in autumn.

Season of birth	
Season	**Number**
summer	5
autumn	4
winter	4
spring	7

Unit 30A PAGE 96

1. 42 000

Taya's number written in digits is 42 397. There is a 3 in the hundreds place, which is less than 5. Her number rounds down to 42 000.

2. 10

A dog has 4 legs. As $4 \times 10 = 40$, then $40 \div 4 = 10$. There were 10 dogs in the park.

3. 60

$24 - 4 = 20$. There are 20 students present. As $3 \times 2 = 6$, then $3 \times 20 = 60$. The teacher handed out 60 shapes.

4. 17

$26 - 9 = 26 - 10 + 1$. This is $16 + 1 = 17$. There are 17 available players.

5. 37

$15 + 13 + 9 = 28 + 9$. This is 37. A total of 37 laps were completed.

6. 4

If two rows are removed, one row remains. This means 4 cakes remain.

7. $20

As $10 \times 5 = 50$, James has saved $50. As $70 - 50 = 20$, James needs another $20.

8. 15

The pattern is 3 matches, then 6, 9, 12, 15, and so on. He uses 15 matches to form 5 triangles.

9. 14 cm

The rectangle has 2 sides of length 4 cm and 2 sides of length 3 cm. $4 + 4 + 3 + 3 = 14$. The distance around the outside is 14 cm.

10. 12 L

As $2 + 2 = 4$, she brushes her teeth for 4 minutes each day. As $4 \times 3 = 12$, she uses 12 L of water.

11. 5

You need to work out how many 2s are in 10. As $2 \times 5 = 10$, then $10 \div 2 = 5$. Eden buys 5 bags of sugar.

12. 5:30 or half past 5

From 4 o'clock, adding an hour gives 5 o'clock. Another half an hour is half past 5.

13. *E*

The opposite faces are A and F, B and D, C and E. This means E will be on the opposite face.

14. 7

A square has 4 lines of symmetry and a regular triangle has 3. The total is 7.

15.

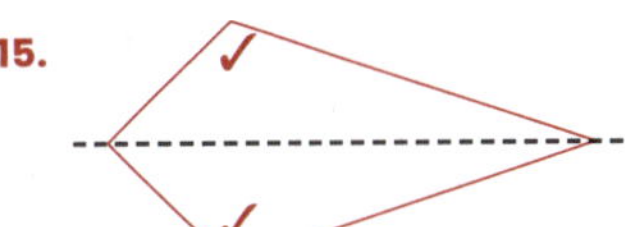

16. 7 units

Tahna walked 3 units to B2 and then 4 units to F2. As $3 + 4 = 7$, Tahna walked a total of 7 units.

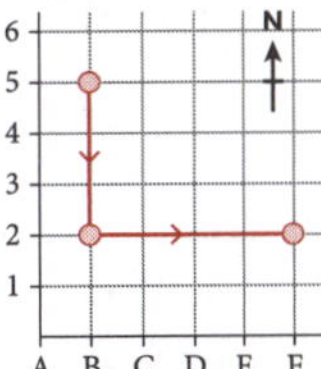

17.

red
blue
green

This spinner does not have a yellow section.

18. 14

Look at the sport columns. As $5 + 9 = 14$, a total of 14 students nominated sport.

Unit 30B PAGE 97

1. **5400**

Mariama originally wrote the number 5357. There is a 5 in the tens place. This means the number rounds up to 5400, to the nearest 100.

2. **5**

The answer to $20 \div 10$ is 2 because $10 \times 2 = 20$. This means the answer to $20 \div \boxed{?} \div 2$ is also 2. The missing number is 5 because $20 \div 5$ is 4 and $4 \div 2$ is 2.

3. **22**

As $4 \times 3 = 12$, there are 12 wheels on the tricycles. As $5 \times 2 = 10$, there are 10 wheels on the bicycles.
As $12 + 10 = 22$, there is a total of 22 wheels.

4. **27**

$1000 - 973 = 1000 - 900 - 73$. This is $100 - 73$. Now, $100 - 73 = 100 - 70 - 3$. This is $30 - 3 = 27$.
There are 27 students absent.

5. **100**

$68 + 23 + 11 = 88 + 3 + 11$. This is $91 + 11 = 102$. As 2 is less than 5, the number rounds down to 100. There are 100 vehicles, to the nearest ten.

6. **3**

6 is 4 more than 2. $\frac{6}{2}$ has a numerator of 6 and denominator 2. As $\frac{6}{2} = 3$, Olive's number is 3.

7. **10c**

$99 + 89 = 100 + 89 - 1$. This is $189 - 1 = 188$. The cost is \$1.88. This rounds to \$1.90 to the nearest 5c.
The change from \$2 is 10c.

8. **19**

Count the number of matches and form a pattern of numbers: 4, 7, 10, and so on. The rule is to add 3.
Continuing the pattern of numbers: 4, 7, 10, 13, 16, 19 … The sixth number is 19. Owen uses 19 matches to form 6 squares.

9. **no**

The 3 lengths are 6 cm, 7 cm and 15 cm. $6 + 7 = 13$, which is less than 15. The straws do not form a triangle.

10. **50**

You need to work out how many 10 mL are in 500 mL.
As $10 \times 50 = 500$, then $500 \div 10 = 50$.
The shampoo will last 50 washes.
The bottle will last 50 days.

11. **6 kg**

You need to imagine removing 1 cylinder from both sides of the pan balance. This means 1 cylinder has the same mass as 2 cubes. As the mass of 2 cubes is 12 kg, the mass of 1 cube is 6 kg.

12. **7:56**

$41 + 11 + 4 = 52 + 4 = 56$. The train arrived at 7:56.

13. **6 cm**

The other 2 rectangles measured 6 cm by 3 cm. The length was 6 cm.

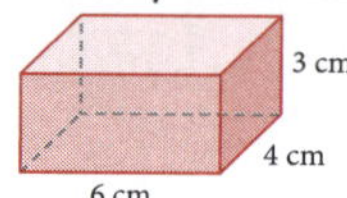

14. **360°**

Each angle in a square is a right angle which is 90°. As $4 \times 9 = 36$, then $4 \times 90 = 360$. The sum of the degrees is 360°.

15. **3**

The square has been cut in half. This means Lori drew a line of symmetry. There are 3 more angles that are the same size.

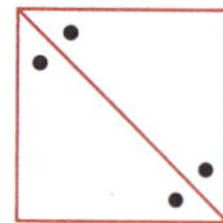

16. **D5**

Ritchie walked 4 units to B3.
Turning to the right, he is now facing north. He walks 2 units to B5.
Turning right again means Ritchie is facing east. He walks 2 units to D5.

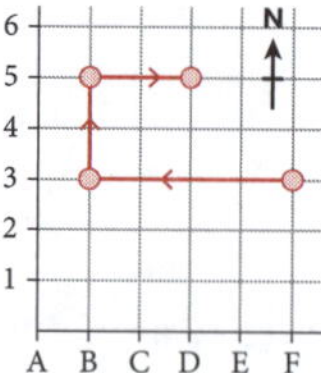

17.

It is the spinner that has the larger red area.

18. **23**

Look for the heights of the 3P columns. As $4 + 6 + 9 + 4 = 23$, there are 23 students in 3P.

NAPLAN-style Test 2 PAGES 98–99

1. **4**

You need to find $36 \div 9$.
As $9 \times 4 = 36$, then $36 \div 9 = 4$. There will be 4 rows of chairs.

2. **35**

$63 - 28 = 63 - 20 - 8$. This is $43 - 8$ which is $43 - 3 - 5 = 40 - 5 = 35$. The larger number was 35.

3. **B**

Start with 13 and use the inverse operations. 13 subtract 5 is 8. Now halving 8 gives 4. Sung Jae started with 4. Let's check: 4 times 2 is 8, then add 5 gives 13.

4. **D**

As $12 \times 2 = 24$, then $12 \times 20 = 240$.
The length of the line of pencils is 240 cm.

5. **258**

The last digit needs to be even. With the first digit 2, the last digit needs to be 8. The smallest 3-digit even number is 258.

6. **2.55**

For the dollars, $6 - 4 = 2$. For the cents, $75 - 20 = 55$. The cost of the drink was \$2.55.

7. **C**

There are 60 minutes in an hour. As $60 \times 2 = 120$, there are 120 minutes in 2 hours. The movie ran for 2 hours 15 minutes. From 7:30, add 2 hours to get 9:30 and then another 15 minutes is 9:45. The movie finished at 9:45 pm.

8. **B**

Student B lives at B5 which is on the corner of Ren Street and Mya Street.

9. **D**

Count the value of the coins.
\$2 + 50c + 10c + 10c + 5c + 5c is \$2.80. You need to work out how many 20s are in 280. This is $280 \div 20$, which is $28 \div 2 = 14$. There are 14 20c coins.

10. **A, C**

Count the squares in each shape.
Also 2 half-squares form a square.
The shapes have the areas 8 cm², 7 cm², 8 cm² and 9 cm². Here are the two shapes:

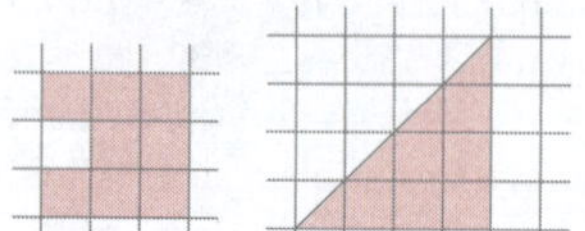

11. **6**

3 and 4 are on opposite faces.

As $3 \times 4 = 12$, opposite faces multiply to give 12. The * is opposite 2.

As $12 \div 2 = 6$, the missing number is 6.

12. **C**

Ignore any pattern of results. The coin is fair, which means a head or a tail is equally likely.

13. **C**

Count the numbers already in the table. $22 + 6 + 3 = 31$. As $36 - 31 = 5$, there were 5 trucks that passed the school.

14. **C**

Look at each of the 8 columns on the grid to see when the squares above and below the line of symmetry do not match. Another 6 squares should be shaded.

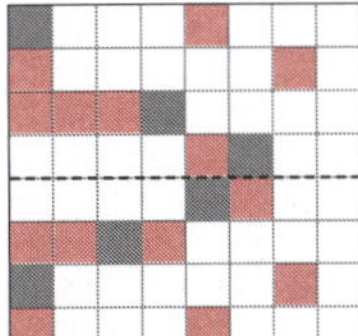

15. **E**

Count the cubes. A has 8 cubes, B has 9 cubes, C has 10 cubes, D has 10 cubes and E has 11 cubes.

This means E is made using the most cubes.

16. **D**

There are 4 columns of oranges. This means a quarter is 1 column of the oranges. This means there are 9 oranges remaining.

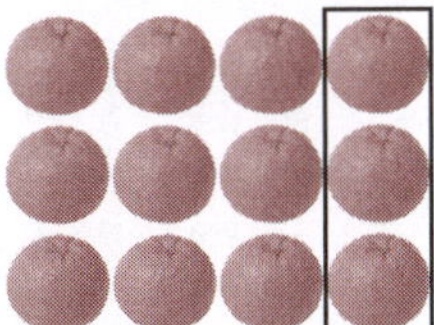

17. **A**

The rule for the pattern of numbers is adding 2. After 11, the numbers are 13, 15, 17, 19.

Adding the last two numbers is $17 + 19 = 17 + 20 - 1 = 36$.

The total is 36.

18. **B**

A quadrilateral has four sides. If it has one pair of parallel sides, it must be a trapezium.

19. **200**

$8 \times 10 = 80$. As $6 \times 2 = 12$, then $6 \times 20 = 120$. Adding 120 and 80 is 200. There are 200 potatoes.

20. **500**

You need to add 250, 350 and 400. As $25 + 35 = 60$, then $250 + 350 = 600$. Also $600 + 400 = 1000$. The total mass of 2 oranges, 2 bananas and 2 mangoes is 1000 g. This means the total mass of 1 orange, 1 banana and 1 mango is 500 g.

NOTES